Cooking *with* Spices

Cooking
with *Spices*

100 RECIPES
for Blends, Marinades, and Sauces
from Around the World

MARK C. STEVENS
Foreword by Martha Hall Foose

ROCKRIDGE
PRESS

Photography © Hélène Dujardin/Prop styling by Angela Hall, cover, back cover & pp. ii, v, vi, viii, xii, 20, 46, 68, 92, 112, 138, 162, 184, 206, 230 & 252. Shutterstock.com: Swapan Photography, pp. 25 & 31; India Picture, p. 27; Mahathir Mohd Yasin, p. 29; Bozhena Melnyk, p. 33; Wentus, p. 35; GooDween123, p. 37; Nito, p. 39; Nedim Bajramovic, pp. 41 & 217; Sommai, p. 43; Sea Wave, pp. 45, 85 & 219; Geshas, p. 73; Michelle Lee Photography, pp. 75, 81, 117, 127, 135 & 223; HandmadePictures, p. 77; Pilipphoto, p. 79; Matin, p. 83; Dziewul p. 87; Quanthem, pp. 89 & 225; Tods, p. 91; Alexander Ruiz Acevedo, p. 119; Kiattipong, p. 121; Brent Hofacker, pp. 123 & 179; Thanatip S., p. 125; Phil Reid, p. 129; Joshua Resnick, p. 131; Oksana Mizina, p. 133; Africa Studio, p. 137; Mahathir Mohd Yasin, p. 167; Images and Videos, p. 169; Abc1234, pp. 171 & 213; Lewal1988, p. 173; Alp Aksoy, pp. 175 & 229; Andris Tkacenko, p. 177; Furtseff, p. 181; Dipali S., p. 183; Alexandra_F, p. 211; Frank60, p. 215; Unpict, p. 221; Glevalek, p. 227. Author photo © Bron Moyi

ISBN: Print 978-1-62315-975-7 | eBook 978-1-62315-976-4

For Samantha and Amelia,
may you inherit the curiosity
required to take you as far and
wide as you want to go.

CONTENTS

Foreword ix
Introduction x

CHAPTER 1: THE POWER OF SPICES 1

CHAPTER 2: INDIA 21
AJOWAN ~ AMCHUR ~ ANARDANA ~ ASOFOETIDA ~ BLACK PEPPER
CARDAMOM ~ CEYLON CINNAMON ~ GREEN AND PINK PEPPER
NIGELLA ~ TURMERIC ~ WHITE PEPPER

CHAPTER 3: ASIA AND THE SOUTH PACIFIC 69
CASSIA CINNAMON ~ CLOVES ~ GALANGAL ~ GINGER ~ LEMON PEEL ~ MACE
NUTMEG ~ STAR ANISE ~ SZECHUAN, SANSHO, AND OTHER PEPPERS ~ WASABI

CHAPTER 4: THE AMERICAS 113
ALLSPICE ~ ANNATTO ~ CHILES ~ ANCHO (POBLANO) ~ CAYENNE
CHIPOLTE (JALAPEÑO) ~ GUAJILLO (MIRASOL) ~ HABENERO AND SCOTCH BONNET
PUMPKIN SEEDS ~ SASSAFRAS ~ VANILLA

CHAPTER 5: EASTERN MEDITERRANEAN,
MIDDLE EAST, AND AFRICA 163
ANISE ~ CORIANDER ~ CUMIN ~ GRAINS OF PARADISE ~ LICORICE ROOT
POPPY SEEDS ~ SAFFRON ~ SESAME SEEDS ~ TAMARIND

CHAPTER 6: EUROPE AND THE MEDITERRANEAN 207
CARAWAY ~ CELERY SEEDS ~ DILL SEEDS ~ FENNEL SEEDS ~ FENUGREEK
HORSERADISH ~ JUNIPER BERRIES ~ MUSTARD SEEDS ~ PAPRIKA ~ SUMAC

References 253
Resources 255
Recipe Index 256
Index 258

FOREWORD

I FIRST MET MARK STEVENS when he tooled up to my home in the rural Mississippi Delta on a European motorbike. He was on a cross-country journey with a dear old friend of mine. I had made a big pot of chicken and dumplings to feed the famished riders, and he found a way to circle back to the kitchen for a third helping. We fell into the easy banter food enthusiasts tend to, once they recognize they speak the same language. Soon we were frying squash blossoms and sharing tales.

Mark has a remarkable gift for storytelling. Through his visual art, acting, and music he has shared many of his travels, and has a profound understanding that by cooking and eating with folks, you participate in their world on an intimate level. This awareness of people and what they need makes him well-suited to write cookbooks. His travels seem to be fueled not so much by wanderlust as they are by his curious streak. It's that facet of his nature that leads him to kitchen backdoors, back-alley barrooms, remote campfires, and open-market stalls.

Learning to season foods with spices is much akin to learning a new language. With a new language, one first begins with the simple phrases and common words, and then idioms find their way into the mix. Slowly, fluency builds and one becomes more confident in conversation. With spices, the more one knows about the histories and lore of seasonings, the more a deeper appreciation for the subtleties of flavors builds. The nuance of a Cajun patois can be tasted in an étouffée. Many a traveler returns home having picked up on local vernacular and colloquialisms, the same way spices find their way into the kitchen back home.

Recipes can often be souvenirs from trips abroad or keepsakes from visits around the corner. Mark has dishes to share, because when words fail us there is always flavor to get the point across. This book is wonderful reading for cooks who dream of travel and travelers who want to share the flavors of the world.

—Martha Hall Foose
James Beard Award–winning author
of *Screen Doors & Sweet Tea*

INTRODUCTION

AS AN ITALIAN, MY MOTHER CRISTINA adheres to her instincts of using what's available to her. She considers it more important to understand the spirit of a flavor and intended use, rather than strictly following a recipe. This tactic is a diversion from the tried-and-true recipes of her mother. Garlic, nutmeg, paprika, black and white pepper, cinnamon, poppy seeds, pepperoncino, and saffron are the flavors she cast on my well-fed upbringing.

My nonna Yvelise is famous for responding (in Italian) with, *"Oh, you know little Marco, when you have enough,"* when asked how much of a spice she's added to a dish. In an unspoken but sacred ritual, Italian grandmothers never quite reveal the quantities of spice measurements in their dishes. With the noble task of preserving her recipes for future generations, I went to Chiavari, along Italy's rocky Mediterranean coast, for two months, and stood side by side with my nonna in an attempt to learn all of hers. Out of that endeavor came handwritten recipe books detailing Nonna's cherished creations: *pesto alla Genovese, coniglio con pinoli e olive, lasagna alla besciamella,* and many more. The measurements and directions in those books occasionally read like a sorcerer's book of spells: a small pinch; a half-handful; sift some through your fingers and throw the rest on the floor.

Growing up with the pedigree of my mother's innovation and my grandmother's tradition, I was indoctrinated on how flavors are properly balanced. In college, I became the friend who'd be asked if something tasted right. I still pride myself on being able to create a tasty meal with the items present in the pantry and refrigerator. In those days, as a broke student, there usually wasn't much, though that education led me to enhance, experiment, and redefine what I'd known. I started a fledgling limoncello company, Yvelise Limoncello, in New Orleans, using Nonna's original recipe. Soon, however, I was using local Meyer lemons and adding basil, vanilla, and orange peel.

In my other life, I am also a filmmaker. I've worked as an assistant director on many award-winning and critically acclaimed films and television shows. One of the most rewarding aspects of this way of life is interacting with folks who have such a wide breadth of experience and culture. Some of the amazing artists I have worked with have lent recipes to this book. In between films, traveling is my passion. Tracking and finding the beauty of diverse locales has led me to fall in love, over and again, with food traditions and flavors. Several years ago, pals and I ended up in Bariloche, Argentina, known for a style of open wood-fire grilling made popular by chefs like Francis Mallmann and his son Agustin. Adopted by locals, I was given a bootcamp in how to properly season fresh meat, craft empanadas, and tend the *parrilla* flame. It's such a simple, beautiful process where overseasoning is akin to sacrilege.

Cooking with locals is the ultimate entry point into their culture and a short-cut to understanding different perspectives and worldviews. It is my intention in these pages to share some of those lessons and engage you in an exchange that inspires you to try unfamiliar flavors and create new memories with those you love. For perhaps the most wonderful gift provided to us by spices is the ability to retain an experience through aromatic remembrance.

This book is organized by region for home chefs interested in becoming more familiar with spices and their uses in everyday cooking. I hope to demonstrate that incorporating a greater variety of spices into your cooking is an approachable and rewarding practice, while also demystifying some of its more overwhelming aspects. Cooking with improvisation, experimentation, and casualness is such a satisfying way to integrate flavors into your own dishes, as well as impress guests.

Cooking with Spices profiles 50 accessible spices and over 100 blends, rubs, oils, marinades, and sauces that you can use to build a complete, satisfying, and diverse culinary repertoire.

The Power of Spices

Spices have shaped our civilization, transforming our cultural exchange of ideas and expressions. Spice trade routes guided the Age of Exploration and European discovery of the New World. These flavoring agents have a tumultuous and, at times, violent past. Wars have been fought, lives saved, and symptoms cured by the secrets contained within them. They have been used as medicine, currency, and they determined locations for roads, outposts, and cities. Saffron once paid for a hospital in Italy. This dynamic heritage exists in your kitchen. Every time you reach toward the spice rack; you're unlocking their magical world. Spice flavors transform food from simple sustenance to centerpieces of our daily social and cultural experience.

What Is a Spice?

The difference between spices, herbs, and salt is muddled because professional and amateur chefs alike tend to avoid differentiating flavor categories. Yet it's rather simple when defined. While both herbs and spices enhance or add to the flavor of food, herbs refer to the fresh or dried leaves of a plant. Salt, naturally, is a mineral. Spices are derived from the fruit, berries, seed, flower, stigma, root, bark, twig, bud, rhizome, kernel, stem, or pod of a plant. These aromatic parts are dried before using whole, crushed, grated, toasted, or ground into powder and paste. Spices are a colorful natural additive for bestowing piquancy and flavor to food and beverages. From some plants both an herb and a spice can be garnered, which is why in this book we will stick to our rigid definition. For example, the pleasant-smelling seeds of the coriander plant provide the base of its namesake powder, while also supplying the herb cilantro, its leafy counterpart. Oregano, anise, and dill also have distinct players in both the spice (seeds) and herb (leaves) categories, making them effective and versatile home gardening partners. Other organisms are so charismatic that they give us two distinct spices. I'll introduce you to *Myristica fragrans Houttuyn,* the seed and rhizome of which are responsible for nutmeg and mace. Though spice characteristics are at least as numerous as the variety of spices themselves, they all carry the properties of transformation, preservation, and enhancement that have justified their popularity over the course of human history.

A Brief History of Spices

It's difficult to imagine now, but five hundred years ago several handfuls of pepper-corns could be worth a small fortune, such was the rarity of quality spices in Europe. Many exotic spices were originally cultivated in India, Indonesia, and Southeast Asia more than two thousand years ago. They were almost universally revered by the great civilizations of history. Spices were essential to the Egyptians' ceremonies and mummification practices. For the Romans, the luxury of spices fueled banquets, funerals, and even wars. As Christopher Columbus sailed west in search of new routes to India, Vasco de Gama sailed east. Upon his return voyage to Portugal, his supply of spices brought from India paid for his trip 60 times over. Land routes from Western Europe to the Middle East and India were vigorously defended. Water trade routes cruelly advanced the colonization of Africa, Asia, and expanded to the accidental European discovery of the Americas. At one time, the value of a sheep was equivalent to a pound of ginger, a cow as much as two pounds of mace.

This demand meant the powerful nations of the day—Spain, Portugal, France, the Netherlands, and Great Britain—engaged each other for control of trade. The geopolitical consequences of these battles should not be underestimated. Spices were used for taste, trade, perfumes, medicine, and as preservatives. In the days before refrigeration, it was necessary for food to be palatable long after tainting. Despite today's luxury of refrigeration and access to flavoring agents of all kinds, the ramifications of economic decisions made hundreds of years ago still permeate our relationship with food flavoring. Consider that some folks regard nutmeg to be a European spice. The Dutch two-hundred-year monopolization of the Spice Islands in Southeast Asia—where the nutmeg tree was originally cultivated—may have influenced the concept; however, both Europeans and Americans have made the spice their own.

How to Buy Spices

Thankfully, spices are more accessible now than at nearly any point in human history. Many generic varieties can be found at your nearest supermarket. However, if you are looking for something incredibly specific, say Madagascar Bourbon vanilla or New Mexico chile peppers, you may have to utilize online specialty stores that are geared toward those harder-to-find flavors, or try your luck at your local international markets. Most cities have stores specializing in foods

FOR YOUR HEALTH

Spices are known for the abundance of powerful antioxidants and antimicrobial elements they possess. Spices without a tested health benefit are few. Gastro-intestinal issues? Try ajowan, aniseed, black pepper, caraway, or cardamom. For heartburn, look to ginger or turmeric. There's an arsenal of spices poised to slay your heart disease. For erectile dysfunction, type 2 diabetes, or certain cancers try anardana and pomegranate juice. The list goes on. The Indian practice of Ayurvedic (holistic) medicine continues, as it has for thousands of years, the practice of natural health and healing by using spices to help balance the body's *doshas*, elements that control physical, emotional, and mental functions. Foods that best accomplish this task have a designed combination of all tastes: sweet, sour, bitter, strong, salty, and spicy. Chinese medicine focuses on *chi*, but still favors a balance of the tastes.

Since spices have become more available and prevalent, scientists and researchers are continually discovering new and sensational remedies for modern ailments. Asafoetida, due to its horrid stench, helped suppress the desire for cigarettes among long-term smokers. Saffron was used in ancient Persia to treat depression. Modern Iranian researchers found that saffron worked similarly to antidepressants in certain patients, without the side effects of manufactured drugs. The recipes that follow offer a few remedies that could help with one or more ailments. But before attempting to self-medicate or heal using spices, always consult your physician first. These teas and recipes are intended to soothe and revive and shouldn't replace prescribed medication.

DRAGON FYRE CIDER Makes 4 cups

Drink 1 teaspoon daily to ward off colds.

1 white onion
½ pound ginger
½ pound turmeric
½ pound horseradish

½ pound burdock root
½ cup dried hibiscus
4 cups raw unfiltered apple
   cider vinegar

Chop the onion, ginger, turmeric, horseradish, burdock root, and hibiscus into small pieces and place in a glass jar. Top with the apple cider vinegar. Seal the jar with its lid. Store in a cool, dark spot for at least 2 weeks, giving it a shake every couple of days. Strain and discard the solids. Store in the pantry for 1 to 2 years.

ASTHMA TEA Makes 4 cups

Clears the respiratory system, helps reduce inflammation and mucus production, and suppresses cough.

10 to 12 green cardamom pods

1 teaspoon toasted ajowan seeds

1 (1-inch) piece fresh ginger, chopped

Mint leaves

Juice of 1 lemon

Honey

In a medium saucepan, bring 4 cups water to a boil. Just as it comes to the boil, turn off the heat and add the cardamom pods and ajowan. Let them steep for 20 minutes. Strain the pods and seeds from the liquid. Add the ginger and several mint leaves to the liquid and let it steep for an additional 5 minutes, reheating the liquid if necessary, so it remains hot. Strain the ginger and mint from the liquid and stir in the lemon juice and honey to taste. If storing on the counter, consume within 3 days. Alternatively, refrigerate for up to 1 week. If refrigerating, wait to stir in the lemon juice and honey until you reheat the tea to drink it.

OMAM WATER Makes 4 cups

Used as a substitute for aspirin in India. Medicinal compounds in ajowan relieve gastrointestinal issues, heartburn, allergies, diarrhea, flatulence, and possibly aid weight loss. For little ones, omam water in smaller doses is a popular folk remedy for tummy aches. Adults can drink 3 tablespoons after a meal, children 1 to 2 tablespoons. But always consult your doctor first.

4 tablespoons ajowan seeds
   (or 4 teaspoons for children age
   two and up)

4 cups distilled or spring water

Honey

Dry roast the ajowan seeds in a cast-iron skillet over medium heat until their aroma is released, about 2 minutes. Stir the seeds constantly while roasting to prevent them from burning. Place the water in a medium saucepan (if you want a weaker tea, use more water; for a stronger tea, use less water). Once toasted, add the seeds to the water and bring it to a boil. Once the water is brown and begins to reduce, turn off the heat, strain the seeds from the liquid, and let it cool. Pour the liquid into a glass jar and add in a bit of honey to sweeten. Seal the jar with its lid and refrigerate for no more than 2 days.

continued

CRYSTALIZED GINGER Makes 1 cup

Great for sore throats and stomachaches.

1¼ cups fresh ginger, sliced and peeled

3 cups water, divided

1½ cups sugar, divided

Place the ginger slices and 2¾ cups water in a saucepan. The water should just cover the ginger. Separate the slices as best you can so they don't stick together. Bring the water to a boil, then reduce the heat to low and simmer for 30 to 40 minutes, stirring occasionally, until the ginger is soft and flexible. Drain the ginger and return it to the saucepan. Add ¾ cup sugar and the remaining ¼ cup water. Heat, stirring frequently, until the sugar dissolves and the water dissipates. Line a baking sheet with parchment paper or waxed paper and spread the ginger in a single layer on the baking sheet. Let it sit for 1½ hours. Place the remaining ¾ cup sugar in a bowl, add the ginger, and toss it to coat. Store in an airtight jar for up to 1 month.

THROAT TEA Makes 4 cups

For suppressing coughs and soothing sore throats, and to combat oncoming seasonal shifts.

4 cups water

1 teaspoon dried sage

1 teaspoon dried thyme

5 to 7 juniper berries

1 (1-inch) piece horseradish root, grated or sliced

1 lemon, cut into thin slices

1 tablespoon honey

In a medium saucepan, heat the water until it's just about to boil, then turn off the heat. Place the sage, thyme, and juniper berries in a cheesecloth pouch or tea canister. Submerge in the hot water and let it sit for 3 to 5 minutes. Place the horseradish in a separate cheesecloth pouch and add it to the water. Steep for 2 to 3 minutes more. Remove and discard the pouches. If consuming right away, stir in the lemon slices and honey. Alternatively, refrigerate in an airtight jar for up to 1 week. Reheat when ready to drink and add the lemon and honey.

from Latin, Middle Eastern, Indian, and Asian cuisines. Some even have specialty spice shops like Rosalie Apothecary in New Orleans and Christina's in Boston. Here are a few recommendations when considering all the options:

- When buying spices from ethnic shops or specialty spice stores, ask the owner or manager what's fresh and when they get supplies. These markets typically have a higher turnover of products than supermarkets, resulting in fresher spices to buy. If your area does not contain such shops, there are trustworthy internet options (see Resources on page 255); be sure to read the reviews prior to buying.

- Supermarkets rarely stock fresh spices and what they do have generally has been sitting on the shelf for months. They also stock from the back (i.e., freshest behind the oldest) to try and sell the older spices first. With whole spices lasting one to two years and ground spices lasting six months, you could be selling yourself short before you even get to the checkout aisle.

- Buying in bulk can be extremely cost effective. This is especially the case when you expect to use larger amounts. Consider the spices you use the most and plan your meals accordingly. I use dangerous amounts of cayenne pepper but a fraction of that in mustard, which I buy in minute quotas. Tailor your buying habits to the flavors you work with the most.

- Containers matter. Maintaining freshness is the name of the game. Look for tin and glass. It's most common for spices in bulk to come in plastic. Quickly transfer them to smaller tin and glass units, which can be bought separately. Avoid cardboard packaging, which does not preserve spices well.

- To maximize freshness, buy whole spices and grind them yourself. Spices lose flavor quite rapidly after becoming powder. When buying spices coarsely or finely ground, check the date of processing to ensure quality. See the Storage and Shelf Life section for suggestions on how best to handle your spices once you get them home.

Storage and Shelf Life

How you store your spices is as important as using the spices themselves. The following pointers can help you preserve the flavors and maximize the enjoyment and use of spices.

Store all spices in a cool place. Heat causes loss of flavor, so don't keep your spice rack above the stove. I banished my plates and bowls to the pantry to give my spices a starring placement at head height in the temperate cabinet next to the refrigerator.

Store in a dry environment. Wetness and moisture causes spices to clump and lose their richness. I live in New Orleans where humidity meters rarely drop below 90 percent. Half the battle is accomplished by tightly sealed, dehumidified storage. Consider storing a bag of rice with your spices or adding a dried bean or two to the spice jar and see if that helps prevent clumping.

Avoid adding spices from their container when cooking. I used to simply open the spice shaker and pour the contents into the hot skillet or saucepan. But that exposed my spice container to the steam coming off boiling water or heat coming off the range. Now I add the spice to a small bowl on the counter and add it to the dish from there, saving what's left in the container to season another day.

Store in a dark place. Direct sunlight causes the breakdown of flavors and freshness. What you gain in compliments for your publicly displayed showcase of spice jars, you lose little by little in the preservation of your flavors.

Freeze whole spices high in volatile oils. This slows down any degradation. Seeds, especially those of coriander, poppy, and sesame, are good examples of whole spices that can become tainted over time.

Replace older spices. Older spices not only lose their flavor but any healing benefits can also be diluted as oils and proteins break down. Use the old-fashioned smell test to identify if spices still carry their weight in flavor. Simply rub a spice between your two fingers and take a big ol' whiff. If the aroma is faint and weak, it's probably time to replace. Spices when ground will keep for six months to a year. When whole, shelf life doubles to two years.

Working with Spices

Given that spices have such a range of benefits in flavor, aroma, and health, it's a shame they are often confined to the degree of heat we want when ordering food or relegated to the little flame symbol on menus. Spices are so much more dynamic than we allow. They are sweet, sour, bitter, astringent, tart, acidic,

SPICES IN THE OPEN MARKET

In India, Turkey, Morocco, or anywhere you may find yourself, the desire to buy spices from open markets is understandable. You're lured in by the aromas, the colors, and the romance. However, there are real concerns to buying spices this way. While you are perhaps closer to the source of an ingredient, it is reasonable to think that the quality will be of a higher grade. However, often the best quality spices are reserved for export since they will fetch the highest price.

One method employed by certain open-market vendors to maximize price is to add filler, which could be anything from dirt to human waste to dried, ground insects—not the source of protein you're likely looking for. Even when the product is completely legitimate, the processing and storing of it may have invited some unwanted guests such as beetle or moth larvae. Microwaving or freezing your spices is one method to kill off hidden pests, but it's better to buy from known traders.

There are various ways to protect yourself when buying in open markets. Always purchase sealed containers as opposed to open bags, although this is no guarantee. The best option is to go with a friend who knows the local scene. Though reputable spice sellers don't gouge customers on prices (because most of them rely on repeat or daily customers), don't skimp. After all, you get what you pay for. Fresher, higher quality spices will be more expensive, but they also last longer. Have fun out there and be safe!

zesty, tangy, hot, earthy, nutty, musky, stinky, gamy, fruity, floral, and any combination of the aforementioned. They punctuate. They neutralize. They come in textures: grated, ground, crushed, broken, powdered, loose, shaved, sliced, pressed, pinched, peeled, rolled, milled, or whole. Each of these preparations yields different tastes, colors, and aromas.

This section introduces us to the complexity of spices by dissecting general best practices on how to work with them. Individual spice profiles later in the book will cover each with increased specificity. However, the nature of this project is to encourage you to experiment. Several of the procedures in this chapter give you a background on the techniques and tools I will refer to later.

All spices do more than merely flavor a dish, yet this is their most utilized purpose. One goal of this book is to help you understand the nature of spices so you can improve, innovate, tailor, and create more of your own recipes. This is not the standard specific-to-the-milligram recipe book. I don't cook that way and

SALT

I have two salt elephant figurines in my house. According to a bookshop keeper in Cartagena, Colombia, possessing three elephant statuettes brings good luck to their owner. The caveat is that one elephant must have been given, one bought for yourself, and one stolen. My two salt guardians await their third musketeer to bring me fortune and luck, and remind me to salt boiling water before cooking rice or pasta.

While salt is quite certainly not a spice, it warrants mentioning in this book and is included in many of the recipes. Since time immemorial, salt has played an instrumental role in food seasoning, preservation, trade, and health. Salt is one of the five basic tastes and is associated with the recently noted fifth flavor, umami. Monosodium glutamate, one of the sources of umami, is the sodium salt of glutamic acid.

Sodium chloride, salt's chemical name, is a naturally occurring mineral harvested from land-based deposits or from the sea. Sea salt generally has a greater content of other beneficial minerals. Rock salt, as land salt is sometimes known—not to be confused with the inedible mineral used to make ice cream—can be easier to find. Except for kosher salt, rock salt is less coarse than sea salts. In cooking, the range of salt quality and taste varies greatly. Fine, iodized rock salt is what your standard table salt amounts to. It is considered on the low end of the range among chefs and cooks—I use it only for salting pasta water. Himalayan pink (land) or Hawaiian sea salt are two of the higher-regarded varieties. Smoked salts have become one of my favorite methods to add a dynamic, smoky taste to any dish. Though if going this route, make sure you buy salt that was actually smoked and not treated with liquid smoke or artificial flavorings.

I'd bet a kilo of juniper berries you don't either. I prefer to think of the relationship between spices and food as like a painting. When I begin to understand the flavor profile of what I'm making, I can then support it with complementary layers. A balanced dish has a distinctive flavor, and the other tastes, smells, and textures support or intentionally oppose that flavor. My mom makes an otherworldly apple pie using cinnamon as the main spice to enhance the apples and buttery crust. Though her recipe does not call for any enhancers, she uses allspice and nutmeg in marginal quantities because she understands that those spices complement and support the main ingredient. Knowing that nutmeg, allspice, and cinnamon, for example, or cardamom, cumin, and tamarind, are natural combinations allows experimentation any time a recipe contains even just one of the components.

This organic dance of spice addition and substitution can help make a recipe more subtle and satisfying. It also avoids cluttering a recipe with competing or mutually neutralizing flavors. Layering spices or blends during cooking is an integral part of the process. My grandmother starts her famous ragù by browning the meat with a secret *soffrito* (sauce) and garlic, cloves, parsley, paprika, bay leaves, salt, and pepper before tomatoes even enter the picture. The tomatoes are peeled, salted, and simmered separately before being crushed and added to the mixture. During the course of an hour, spices are added to taste, resulting in one of the most satisfying culinary experiences of my childhood. Several years ago, I made a batch of her ragù for a large group during Mardi Gras, but I forgot to add the seasoning at the beginning of the process. Though I tried to make up for it at a later stage, the damage was done.

This book helps you navigate around those potential pitfalls by providing tried and true formulas, mixtures, pastes, blends, teas, sauces, marinades, rubs, and oils. These work perfectly without manipulation, but also give you the flexibility to improvise and experiment. Say, for instance, you want to add mustard into Queen's Carnitas Marinade (page 151) because you learned mustard pairs well with cumin. I would encourage you to try!

What follows is information on processing your spices to your particular tastes and preferences, as well as the tools and techniques generally recommended for each.

CRUSHING

Crushing a spice harkens back to images of ancient alchemists crumbling ingredients with their trusted mortar and pestle but—actually, no "but"—that's still how it's done. Specialty shops across the world still carry these tools, as their effectiveness has not waned since 35,000 BCE. Whether made from wood, stone, clay, glass, porcelain, metal, granite, or marble, the mortar-pestle combination is renowned for unlocking subtle flavors missed by modern mechanical crushing techniques. It also adds charm and allure—and time—to your cooking process. Yet slowing down is a way to cultivate a more intimate relationship with your food.

Using a mortar and pestle can be extremely versatile because the hand-worked nature of the process allows you to adjust the pressure and technique depending on the ingredient. You won't crush peppercorns or allspice in the same manner as you might cumin or nigella. You may only want to break apart star anise instead of powdering it. Mortars and pestles are also painlessly easy to clean, though perhaps wooden ones are not ideal as they can keep and transfer essential oil from one use to the next. Also, from an aesthetic perspective, the bigger 7- to 9-inch models add an analog and intimate flair to your kitchen that just isn't conveyed with an electric grinder. Not to mention opting for this prehistoric technology is well worth the results—as is the accompanying workout.

PULVERIZING

While the following methods do not have the scope of a pestle and mortar, there are certain advantages to using either a cast-iron frying pan or a heavy rolling pin to break apart your spices. This is also a useful alternative if you're cooking at a friend's place or visiting family. In an unfamiliar kitchen, it's best to be adaptable. Pour the whole spice onto a towel (so they don't scatter over a hard countertop) and pummel them until they break. Plus, by using a pan, you have it on hand to first toast the spices; just allow them to cool down before your thrashing begins. An alternative option is a hand chamber grinder, but this allows for only a very small amount of spice and is more of a single-service device best used when traveling.

GRINDING

The most efficient and quickest way to grind spices is with an electric spice grinder. This is especially useful when grinding large amounts, as it takes considerably less time than doing it by hand. It is often recommended to use a coffee grinder for grinding, and most modern coffee grinders double as spice grinders. It should go without saying that machines should not be used for both coffee and spices unless you're keen on curry-flavored cappuccinos.

Not all grinders are created equal; there are several varieties of electric devices that serve various purposes. I prefer a *burr* grinder for bulkier spices because the fineness of the grind can be controlled. However, burr grinders are more expensive and quite exhausting to clean, though one trick is to grind white rice in between spice grindings. Blade grinders are cheaper and usually have easy-to-clean, dishwasher-safe attachments. The danger of blade dulling, friction heat, and an inconsistent grind make it a slightly inferior practice. Additionally, if you have a small food processor, it probably has a handy, spice-friendly blade.

GRATING

Certain spices require grating and Microplanes and metal box graters work well. Good graters can last a lifetime. I grew up with a simple, four-walled, stainless steel cheese grater. Each side has a unique grating option. When I went away to college, my mom reluctantly parted with the indestructible grater to stock the sorely inadequate kitchen in my first apartment. Other graters have come and gone in the years since, yet that one remains.

If you aren't blessed with an instrument of such majesty, check out antique shops for vintage nutmeg graters. They come equipped with a storage box on the end to hold whole nutmeg and make for a rustic addition to your kitchen, especially if you hang it above your mortar and pestle. A Japanese grater called an *oroshigane* produces a much finer end product. There are no holes so the wasabi, ginger, or horseradish, among others, gets finely reduced. At one time, *oroshigane* were made out of sharkskin. These days, you can get them in stainless steel or aluminum. It, too, makes an interesting alternative if your traditional grater does not accommodate your grating specifications.

ROASTING AND TOASTING

While roasting and toasting are often used interchangeably, for the purposes of this section I'll refer to roasting as cooking a spice with oil or liquid in heat, like we might in an oven, and toasting (dry roasting) as lightly browning the outside of a spice in a pan. With either technique, it's recommended to heat whole spices as opposed to powder, which easily burns and may roast unevenly. It's best to roast or toast one spice at a time since different spices heat at different rates.

Toasting has the advantage of allowing you to smell the progress. Once your cast-iron pan has heated, add the spice and stir occasionally. Spices will first dry out and then release aromas and oils. You will be the judge of when to terminate the process based on smell. The whole affair should fall in the 1 to 10 minute range. If the spices start to burn, you have left them too long. When the spices smell appealing, transfer them to cool on a dish or on the towel you'll use to bust them apart. Dried chile peppers are a good example of a spice that benefits greatly from the flavor-releasing power of dry roasting.

CREATING PASTES

Pastes are spreads and sauces that are fun to make in advance and use as convenience allows. They can act as a rub, marinade, condiment, or alone as a filling or dipping sauce, like Black Tahini Paste (page 196) or Poppy Paste (page 200). If you're still trying to work out what a paste is, think of it like a dry rub or spice blend with at least one fresh ingredient or oil. Chile pepper–based pastes like Jerk-Style Pineapple Paste (page 148) and Harissa Paste (page 201) have increased in popularity. Since pastes generally contain one fresh ingredient, they are best kept refrigerated.

APPLYING DRY RUB

How are your massage skills? The best dry rubs are used to season food—usually meat, pork, or fish—before grilling, baking, or dry roasting. This "dry" method of cooking is particularly fun because your hands are the best instruments for coating your food with the rub. There are as many varieties of dry rub as there are people who have ever tried making one. The most important factor to consider is the subject of your rub and how the ingredients complement each other. Remember the painting analogy: certain spices will be too powerful for fish but not enough to season and tenderize red meat.

MARINATING

Marinating is the practice of soaking food in a substance to add flavor, pickle, soften, tenderize, and/or break down the food. While some marinades use acidic or enzymatic ingredients to achieve the intended effect, my focus is on adding flavor using spice marinades. Though you can marinate using a paste, a paste isn't necessarily always a marinade. Pastes can be used as a condiment, to eat with chips or pita for instance. Most marinating foods should be refrigerated to prevent bacterial growth and spoilage. You should never reuse an uncooked marinade after the marinating process because it has been in contact with raw meat, chicken, or fish, making it unsafe for consumption. Likewise, if you're basting with a marinade, you should stop during the second half of the cooking process to allow the marinade to cook thoroughly.

Marinating duration and potency depends squarely on the consistency and composition of the marinade itself. My dad marinates shrimp for half an hour or so, while a neighbor of mine once marinated a brisket for almost three days, which while delicious, may have a been a bit excessive. Marinades can also be used to mask the flavor of inferior meats, poultry, and seafood.

At the heart of any spice or blend is the knowledge that accentuating the natural flavors of a protein can be done subtly. It doesn't require overseasoning.

Spice & Herb Pairings

Spices and herbs dance together in such harmony that many books, blogs, and recipes do not differentiate between them. Yet, as in ballet, figure skating, or ballroom dancing, certain partners seem made for each other. I keep these pairings next to each other in the spice cabinet because I know they'll always get a standing ovation.

SPICE & HERB	FOOD PAIRING
CARAWAY and PARSLEY	baked goods, bread, cheese, fish, pork
CARDAMOM and MINT	beans, citrus, cocktails, lamb, mussels, potatoes, tea
CELERY SEEDS and MARJORAM	eggs, fish, tomato sauces
GINGER and LEMONGRASS STALKS	chicken, mushrooms, shellfish, shrimp, sushi, tea
JUNIPER and ROSEMARY	duck, game, pork, root vegetables
MUSTARD and DILL	cabbage, capers, cauliflower, vinegars, dressing, or with mayonnaise
NUTMEG and SAGE	butter and cream sauces, butternut squash, gravies, pumpkin
PAPRIKA and OREGANO	beef, chicken, mushrooms, pasta
SESAME SEEDS and SCALLIONS or CHIVES	chicken, eggplant, pasta, salads, salmon
SUMAC and THYME	chicken, fish, hummus, onion, quinoa
TURMERIC and CILANTRO	chicken, onions, rice, shrimp, stews
VANILLA and LAVENDER	berries, chocolate, custards, honey, rum and bourbon, yogurt

Fruit & Spice Pairings

The sweetness of fruit is a natural stage for the contrasting array of spice flavors. Fruit, often associated with dessert, salads, or baked items, can also enhance savory dishes when used in chutneys, al pastor, and Peach-Plum Sauce (page 106). The following list shows which spices enhance each fruit.

FRUIT	SPICE PAIRING
APPLES	ajowan, allspice, caraway, cinnamon, cloves, coriander, juniper, mace, nutmeg, star anise, vanilla
AVOCADOS	anardana, cumin, nutmeg
BANANAS	ginger, nutmeg, vanilla
BERRIES	black pepper, ginger, mace, vanilla
COCONUT	allspice, asafoetida, cardamom, cumin, curry leaves, galangal, ginger, turmeric
FIGS and DATES	cinnamon, cumin, ginger, star anise
LEMON/CITRUS	allspice, cayenne, coriander, cumin, ginger, pepper, poppy, sesame seeds, turmeric
MANGO	allspice, black cumin, cardamom, star anise
ORANGE	allspice, cloves, cinnamon, ginger, poppy
PEARS	caraway, cardamom, cinnamon, vanilla
PINEAPPLE	allspice, star anise, tamarind
PLUMS	chile peppers, coriander, ginger, star anise
POMEGRANATE	ajowan, cardamom, chile peppers, cumin, fennel, mustard, turmeric
TOMATO	aniseed, celery seeds, chile peppers, curry leaves, fennel seeds, tamarind

Vegetable & Spice Pairings

Learning how to season vegetables is akin to becoming the conductor of a deliciously edible orchestra. Veggies can be a side, a flavor addition, a filler, or be the central ingredient of the main course in lieu of proteins. The conductor must understand the intent of each instrumental part of the dish to make it all come together. These combinations help achieve that.

VEGETABLE	SPICE PAIRING
BEANS and LEGUMES	ajowan, amchur, asafoetida, cardamom, cayenne, coriander, cumin, kokum
BEETS	allspice, cloves, coriander, star anise
BRUSSELS SPROUTS	mustard seeds, poppy seeds, tamarind
CARROTS	cumin, mace, poppy seeds, saffron, turmeric
CAULIFLOWER	asafoetida, cumin, curry, mustard, poppy seeds, saffron, star anise, turmeric
CHICKPEAS	amchur, curry, fenugreek, sesame seeds, sumac, turmeric
EGGPLANT	cumin, curry, fenugreek, paprika, sesame seeds, sumac
LENTILS	asafoetida, coriander, curry, kokum, turmeric
MUSHROOMS	asafoetida, black cumin, cayenne, coriander, cumin, curry, fennel seeds, nutmeg, paprika, saffron
POTATOES and YAMS	allspice, cayenne, cloves, coriander, cumin, curry, fenugreek, ginger, kokum, mace, pepper, poppy seeds, saffron
PUMPKINS and SQUASH	allspice, cinnamon, cloves, fenugreek, ginger, mace, nutmeg, saffron, star anise, vanilla
SAUERKRAUT and CABBAGE	caraway, cloves, ginger, juniper, mustard
SPINACH	asafoetida, nutmeg, saffron, sesame seeds

Nut & Spice Pairings

The presence of spiced nuts is always a signal that winter is coming. Yet the holidays are hardly the only occasion when spices and nuts can perform together. Each of the following pairings can provide flavor and completeness to a meal.

NUT	SPICE PAIRING
ALMOND	allspice, cardamom, cayenne, cumin, nigella, poppy seeds, saffron, vanilla, wasabi
CASHEW	allspice, asafoetida, cardamom, cayenne, cumin, ginger, saffron
PEANUT	allspice, asafoetida, cardamom, cayenne, fennel seeds, mustard seeds, paprika, saffron
PECAN	allspice, asafoetida, cayenne pepper, cumin, horseradish, mustard seeds, paprika, saffron
PINE NUT	cardamom, cayenne, paprika, saffron
PISTACHIO	cardamom, saffron
WALNUT	allspice, cardamom, cumin, poppy seeds

Protein & Spice Pairings

This trusty cheat sheet should give you what you need to begin preparing a dish. Sometimes, just one of these spices is all you need to create a memorable dinner. Szechuan pepper and Himalayan sea salt can transform a steak by themselves. Here's a reference to some other helpful partnerships.

PROTEIN	SPICE PAIRING
CHEESE	aniseed, caraway, celery seeds, chile peppers, fennel seeds, nutmeg
EGGS	cayenne, cloves, horseradish, mustard seeds, paprika
FISH	celery seeds, fennel seeds, mustard seeds, saffron, sesame seeds, sumac, tamarind, turmeric, wasabi
LAMB	cardamom, cumin, juniper berries, nigella, sesame seeds, star anise
PORK	allspice, aniseed, caraway, celery seeds, cloves, fennel seeds, ginger, horseradish, juniper berries, mustard seeds, star anise
POULTRY	black pepper, cinnamon, cloves, coriander, cumin, fennel seeds, galangal, ginger, juniper, mace, nutmeg, paprika, saffron, sesame seeds, sumac
SHELLFISH	amchur, aniseed, ginger, horseradish, nigella, nutmeg, saffron, vanilla, wasabi
STEAK/BEEF	asafoetida, berbere, chile peppers, coriander, cumin, ginger, horseradish, mustard seeds, paprika, Szechuan pepper
TOFU	black pepper, chile peppers, cinnamon, cumin, ginger, paprika, tamarind, turmeric
VEAL	black pepper, cinnamon, coriander, cloves, cumin, ginger, mace, nutmeg, paprika, star anise

India

SPICES 23 **RECIPES** 47

Indian cuisine is legendary not only as the source of many fabled spices that shaped the modern world, but also for the almost mythical blends of those spices. Curry, in all its various forms, is ubiquitous in conversations about Indian cuisine. Each region has its own variation of curry—and they extend beyond the subcontinent, too. Menu items like curry, chutney, and masala have become recognizable and commonplace from South East Asia to the Caribbean to the Americas. There is so much diversity and range in Indian cuisine that adequately covering it all easily could be a book for each region.

Northern and Southern Indian cuisine is one way to understand the divide. For those less familiar, you're likely more acquainted with the food of Northern India. This includes garam masala, roti breads—naan, paratha, and chapatti—and tandoori-style cooking in clay ovens. Goat, chicken, and lamb are popular proteins. Cows are sacred to the majority Hindu population and, as such, beef is less common in what is otherwise a meat-heavy culinary tradition. Southern Indian cuisine favors vegetarian dishes using lentils, legumes, and grains. There are noteworthy exceptions. Goa, colonized by the Portuguese, is known for a blend of northern-style use of meat, southern flavor mixes, Indian spices, and European influences. The dish that most exemplifies this is Vindaloo Curry (see Vindaloo Curry Paste on page 59).

This culinary tradition has nurtured the exchange of ingredients since the earliest explorers crossed paths in search of valuable trade articles. India's origin spices include some most revered by chefs and natural healers. This list, in which Ceylon cinnamon, turmeric, and cardamom are stars, boasts black pepper at the top of the playbill. Less common forms like green and white pepper provide a different dynamic. It's difficult to imagine Indian food without these alluring flavors.

SPICES

Ajowan 24   Amchur 26

Anardana 28   Asafoetida 30

Black Pepper 32   Cardamom 34

Ceylon Cinnamon 36

Green and Pink Pepper 38

Nigella 40   Turmeric 42

White Pepper 44

Ajowan

ajwain, bishop's weed, carom, omam

I was a late bloomer to Indian cuisine, but any culinary reluctance was washed away the moment I tried *parathas*, those sultry flatbreads from India, for the first time. My favorite paratha is seasoned with toasted ajowan seeds.

Ajowan is a natural cure-all that comes in the form of an annual herbaceous plant. Though native to India and the eastern Mediterranean, it's grown and harvested in Iran, Afghanistan, Pakistan, and Egypt. Related and similar to parsley in appearance, its tiny seeds are harvested when ripe, and then dried. They are used whole or crushed.

Disciples of ajowan use it in fritters called pakoras and samosas. Others use it to judiciously season root vegetable dishes and starchy foods such as lentils and legumes, or add it to curry, berbere, or chaat masala. The potency of the seeds is enough that they can overpower other flavors if used in even slight excess.

Boiled seeds were once believed to cleanse the eyes of the blind and cure deafness. An ancient belief in India's Gujarat region was that ajowan, when mixed with tamarind and then fried, increases the male sperm count.

Ajowan is a trusted dual ingredient. It provides enticing flavor and has a number of known health benefits. Adding to its multifunction status, ajowan's thymol compound is used in toothpaste, perfume, mouthwash, and as a food preservative. Try making the Asthma Tea (page 5) to help with your breathing and digestion.

CULTIVATION CENTER

India

AROMA & FLAVOR

Ajowan's potent flavor is reminiscent of cumin, anise, and thyme due to the concentration of thymol oil. The flavor of the seeds becomes subtler as they are cooked. For people with a dramatic tendency, try chewing on the seeds raw, which will briefly numb the tongue with a bitterness.

MEDICINAL USES

helps, treats, prevents, or aids pain (see Omam Water, page 5), flatulence, digestion, diarrhea, high blood pressure, asthma, and is also used as an antibacterial.

COMMON FORMS

dried seeds, whole and ground

COMPLEMENTS

breads, legumes, lentils, pancakes, pickles, root vegetables

PAIRS WELL WITH

coriander, cumin, garlic, ginger, mustard seeds, turmeric

Amchur

amchoor, dried mango powder

Many Westerners look at a green mango like they would a green banana: unripe and not ready for consumption. For thousands of years in Northern India, they have dried unripe, green mangos in the sun to make amchur. The name literally means "mango powder" in Hindi. Once the peeled slices are dried, they are ground into a light brown powder. It is tart and tangy and is an ingredient in many chutneys. In India, it is used as a general souring agent in a manner similar to the way Americans use lemons and limes. Mangos share with papayas an enzyme that tenderizes meat and chicken, making it key to cuisine cooked in tandoori ovens. Though often used to sour curries and relishes, it is more notably a highly regarded and essential ingredient for Chaat Masala Blend (page 48).

The quality of Indian mangos, especially the Alphonso mango, are considered unrivaled. They are a symbol of love and supposedly bestow wisdom. There exists a Hindu tale in which Ganesh outsmarts his brother Kartikeya to win a contest for the prize of a mango. A mischievous sage called Narada proposes the mango as a prize to the brother who can most swiftly travel around the world three times. Kartikeya, who travels on a peacock, sets off with confidence. Ganesh, who travels on a mouse, circles his parents three times and, as they are his world, wins the mango.

CULTIVATION CENTER

India

AROMA & FLAVOR

Amchur is warm and fruity to the nose and tart on the tongue. It is acidic and tangy enough to be used as a souring agent. Powdered green mango turns gray, but turmeric is often added before it hits the market, turning it yellowish or tan.

MEDICINAL USES

helps, treats, prevents, or aids heart disease, blood sugar levels, gum disease, enlarged prostates; contains antioxidants; contains lupeol, an anti-inflammatory chemical compound that can reduce cancer risk

COMMON FORMS

dried, whole slices, or ground

COMPLEMENTS

cauliflower, chickpeas, chutney, curry, eggplant, legumes, marinades, pastry filling, pickles, red meat, seafood, soups

PAIRS WELL WITH

ajowan, black pepper, chile peppers, cloves, coriander, cumin, ginger, star anise, tamarind, turmeric

Anardana

dried pomegranate seeds

The first time I was shown how to expertly dissect and dismember a pomegranate, I ended up with five hundred or so perfect jewels of fruit. Had I gone one step further, drying the seeds for 10 to 15 days and grinding them into a powder, I'd have ended up with sweet, sour anardana.

Fruity, tangy, dry, tart, sweet, and sour are all descriptors associated with the dried pomegranate seed spice. It is as comfortable in chutneys, relishes, and curries as it is as fillings in pastries, baked in breads, and sprinkled on salads. The best seeds come from daru pomegranates, the wild variety from the area around the Himalayas.

Anardana's health benefits section could perhaps be significantly shorter if we listed what pomegranate cannot heal. It is a staple in Ayurvedic medicine, used for a wide range of health benefits.

To explain barren winter seasons, one looks to Greece's tale of Persephone who, after being kidnapped, is tricked by the god Hades to eat six pomegranate seeds. In doing so she breaks a law of the underworld and must join her husband for six months of the year in his lair beyond the river Styx. During these months, her mother Demeter, goddess of the harvest, mourns, causing the plants of the Earth to cease growing.

Buy anardana online or in an Indian spice store. Whole seeds range from soft to hard. Soak the harder ones to make them pliable and slightly juicier.

CULTIVATION CENTER

India

AROMA & FLAVOR

Anardana is aromatically fruity with a touch of sourness and tastes sweet with a hint of that same sourness. It's not forceful, though it can be tart. Toasting whole seeds is recommended.

MEDICINAL USES

helps, treats, prevents, or aids blood vessels; heart damage; chest pain; cholesterol; diabetes; pancreatic cancer risk and mitigates the risk of breast, colon, lung, skin cancers, and leukemia; gum disease; plaque buildup in the mouth; erectile dysfunction; aging and development of wrinkles; athletic recovery; arthritis; may prevent the growth of a protein linked to Alzheimer's disease; obesity; male infertility; colon inflammation; contains many antioxidants and vitamin C

COMMON FORMS

seeds, whole and ground

COMPLEMENTS

bland vegetables, breads, chicken, chutneys, meat, pastries, relishes, rubs, salads, seafood, sweets

PAIRS WELL WITH

ajowan, allspice, chile peppers, cilantro, cinnamon, cumin, fennel seeds, garlic, mint, onion, turmeric

Asafoetida

asafetida, devil's dung, stinking gum

What does a poor spice need to do to inherit a name that in Latin means foul-smelling? Perhaps assault the nostrils to such a degree that it also earns the brutal moniker "devil's dung." Thankfully, asafoetida loses its pungent, sulfurous aroma when cooked. Still, only a pinch should be used so as to not overpower other ingredients. (When I mentioned asafoetida to the award-winning actor Alfre Woodard, with whom I had worked with, she texted back: "My gawd. My Big Mama Ada used to say 'keep some Ass-fizidee soaking in some bourbon and drop a lil' in the baby's bottle if they get fussy!'")

Asafoetida is used abundantly in the vegetarian cuisines of India and Iran, where chefs first fry it before adding it to other ingredients. Curries, brined and pickled fish, beans, and sambar podi are some of the dishes enhanced by asafoetida. It is one of the noticeable ingredients in Chaat Masala (see Chaat Masala Blend on page 48). It is common practice to add asafoetida to lentils, beans, and legumes, because it helps prevent flatulence and aids digestion.

Certain religious groups, like the Jains and Brahmins, do not eat garlic, and flavor their food with asafoetida instead. Known as an aphrodisiac (if definitely not a perfume) to the Romans, it was a popular condiment and known as the "food of the gods." Legend has it, if one's desire is to curse a witch, there's a potion designed for such purposes that incorporates asafoetida.

CULTIVATION CENTERS

India, Iran, Afghanistan, Pakistan, China, Russia

AROMA & FLAVOR

Asafoetida smells appalling. Thankfully, the acerbic scent vanishes during the cooking process, revealing more pleasant aromas similar to garlic and onion. The sulfuric component can come across as a mildly garlic taste when used in small quantities.

MEDICINAL USES

helps, treats, prevents, or aids digestion, flatulence, certain cancers; has antimicrobial, antibiotic, anticoagulant, antispasmodic, and sedative properties; is possibly an aphrodisiac

COMMON FORMS AND VARIETIES

solidified granules of resin, in chunks or ground; varieties include water-soluble (hing) and oil-soluble (hingra)

COMPLEMENTS

chickpeas, fish, grains, legumes, nuts, potatoes, spiced seafood

PAIRS WELL WITH

ajowan, black pepper, cardamom, chile peppers, cumin, curry leaves, garlic, ginger, mustard seeds, tamarind, turmeric

Black Pepper

pepper, peppercorn

We feel like we know the "king of the spices" so well, but in reality our experience is perhaps limited to the shaker ubiquitous on dinner tables. Yet black pepper has an illustrious, complex history.

Pepper dictated trade and commerce for centuries. The value of pepper approached gold, and in some cases was worth as much. It was used to pay rent, salaries, taxes, dowries, and it funded exploration of trade routes over both land and sea. The Roman Empire funded generations of Arab traders, who kept the source of their fortune secret to keep prices high. Roman merchants cut their supply with juniper berries to increase profits. This was a true black (pepper) market. The fifteenth- and seventeenth-century conflicts between the Dutch and Portuguese, called the Spice Wars, were for the control of the pepper and spice trade.

Black pepper grows on vines that can stretch to 30 feet. After the berries turn green, they are picked and dried. The berries do not all ripen at the same rate, requiring a laborious harvesting process. Once the dark green peppers are picked, they are dried until the outer layer turns black, oily, and coarse. When the process is complete, you have black pepper.

Pepper is notorious for losing flavor once ground. Peppermills, regardless of price, deliver a noticeably superior taste and aroma in contrast to preground pepper, even with simmered and marinated dishes. Favor whole peppercorns when possible and use ground toward the second half of the cooking process.

CULTIVATION CENTERS

India, Malaysia, Indonesia, Brazil

AROMA & FLAVOR

Black pepper is spicy, pungent, and biting on the palate. It has a botanical and woody aroma. You will smell a mixture of spices depending on your olfactory sense, but some common aromas are lemon, clove, and nutmeg.

MEDICINAL USES

helps, treats, prevents, or aids Alzheimer's disease; arthritis; constipation; depression; digestive problems including diarrhea and indigestion; memory loss; heart disease and high blood pressure; cancers such as colon, breast, and lung; promotes brain function.

COMMON FORMS AND VARIETIES

peppercorns (dried berries): whole, cracked, and ground; varieties include Malabar and Tellicherry pepper (from Malabar in India), Sarawak pepper, Lampong pepper, Penja pepper (West Africa), Wynad pepper

COMPLEMENTS

everything, but especially meat, chicken, soups and stews, adobo, barbecue, berbere, cheese plates, curries, dry rubs, eggs, fruit masalas, and grilled or fresh vegetables, lemon dishes, marinades, pickling spices, vinegars, and dressings

PAIRS WELL WITH

almost everything

Cardamom

green cardamom, cardamum, cardamon

Cardamom, "queen of spices," has been long venerated for its piquancy, aroma, shelf life, and versatility. One of the earliest commodities, it spread east and west from India and became a staple in Arabian, Turkish, and Persian cooking. Traders passing through Constantinople introduced it to the Vikings, who brought it to Scandinavia.

Cardamom is still one of the more expensive spices. Its growing territory is marginal and harvesting is labor intensive. Cardamom grows in pods on a stem from the bush's roots. Laborers pluck the pods before they ripen or lose the seeds once the pod cracks. Seeds ripen at different rates, so attention to detail is key. Special furnaces dry the pods.

Uncracked pods can remain unspoiled for several years. Once loose or powdered, the seeds lose flavor. For this reason, it's best to avoid buying preground cardamom. Discard the green pods before grinding to maximize flavor and aroma. Store-bought powders give no guarantee of quality and may have ground pods in with the seeds.

My tip when cooking with whole cardamom is to crack and "bruise" the pod by gently thumping it with the flat end of a knife or blunt object. This releases the oils of the seeds and allows them to blend with whatever you're cooking.

Chinese black cardamom, Thai green cardamom, and Nepal large cardamom are all varieties of "false" cardamom. Brown cardamom has culinary value, and with its earthy flavor evocative of camphor is used in rustic meat and vegetable dishes.

CULTIVATION CENTER

India

AROMA & FLAVOR

Cardamom's sweet and delicate flavor is punctuated by a citrusy hint of lemon. The aroma is warm, sweet, and described as floral and piquant. Look for green pods, not white. The seeds inside will be brown (not to be confused with brown cardamom).

MEDICINAL USES

helps, treats, prevents, or aids blood clotting and high blood pressure, asthma and sinus infections, heart disease, colon cancer, ulcers, and even kills bacteria responsible for bad breath. Cardamom is a celebrated anti-indigestion agent and is used to soothe stomachaches and aid digestion.

COMMON FORMS AND VARIETIES

seeds, ground or loose; whole pods; varieties include Kerala and Bengali cardamom, Sri Lankan cardamom, Mexican cardamom, Guatemalan cardamom

COMPLEMENTS

cakes, chicken, cookies (especially in Scandinavia), curries, custards and puddings, desserts, lamb, nuts, rice, rice and vegetable dishes; stews, tropical and citrus fruits, Turkish coffee

PAIRS WELL WITH

allspice, cinnamon, clove, coriander, nutmeg, star anise, turmeric

Ceylon Cinnamon

cinnamon, canela, true cinnamon, Sri Lankan cinnamon

Though cinnamon originated in Sri Lanka and Southwest India, in some ways it's as American as apple pie, essential to our Thanksgiving. But perhaps you've never even tasted cinnamon. In the United States, most packaged cinnamon is actually a similar spice called cassia cinnamon (page 72). On most palates, true cinnamon is less sweet and more delicate than its cassia relative.

Ceylon cinnamon enjoys a status as one of the most decorated spices in historical records of civilizations. First mentioned in Chinese texts, it makes an appearance in the Bible, the Torah, and ancient Sanskrit manuscripts. The Egyptians used it in procedures for embalming pharaohs. Romans and Greeks valued it for perfume, incense, and medicine.

Harvested from the bark of the tree, cinnamon generally comes in the form of rolled, cigar-like quills. These are the interior bark of the tree, which has been stripped of the rough outer layer and dried. Pieces broken off from the quills and bark from branches are ground into powder. Quills are slim and smooth and are of a higher quality; they can last two to three years if stored correctly. So pull out those old sticks and smell them; they still may have usefulness.

It seems every culture has cultivated a use for cinnamon because it pairs with so many different flavors. Just be aware that overcooking can make cinnamon bitter, and using too much can overpower a dish.

CULTIVATION CENTERS

India, Sri Lanka, Mexico, South America, Seychelles, Madagascar

AROMA & FLAVOR

Cinnamon imparts a clove-like, warm, sweet aroma with a hint of citrus. It is gentler than cassia, and the color echoes that aspect by being fairer and paler.

MEDICINAL USES

helps, treats, prevents, or aids gastric upsets, cancer, circulatory disorders, depression, diarrhea, nausea, tooth decay; used as a cold remedy; lowers blood sugar and cholesterol; preserves food; is antibacterial/microbial.

COMMON FORMS AND VARIETIES

quills (rolled sticks), quillings (broken pieces), ground; varieties include Ceylon cinnamon, Seychelles cinnamon, Madagascar cinnamon

COMPLEMENTS

beef soups, chicken, chocolate, confections, curries, fruits (apples, bananas, cantaloupe, citrus, grapes), pastries, pork, sauces, vegetables (corn, cauliflower, onions)

PAIRS WELL WITH

allspice, caraway, cardamom, coriander, cumin, ginger, nutmeg, star anise, tamarind, turmeric

Green and Pink Pepper

peppercorn

Green pepper is fascinating because of the procedures required to produce a yield. It can be picked several weeks prior to the harvesting time for black pepper. Once collected, the enzymes responsible for turning the outer layer black are deactivated by flashing the peppercorns in boiling water, pickling them in brine or wine vinegar, or freeze-drying them. Pickled green pepper should be rinsed prior to use but are excellent in pâtés, sauces, flavored oils and butter, and with soft cheeses and steak. Freeze-dried and dried green pepper can be reconstituted by soaking them in water or broth. The green of this peppercorn adds a burst of color to many dishes.

Pink pepper isn't even a pepper at all, nor is it pink. The black and green peppers turn red if left on the vine, and sometimes are harvested in-country for culinary purposes. However, the red peppercorns you see as pink peppercorns are the berries of a tree of South American origin, *Schinus terebinthifolius,* or the Brazilian peppertree or Christmasberry. This is the same plant family as cashews and pistachios. Like green pepper, pink pepper is sold dried, freeze-dried, and pickled. The flavor is more delicate, as is the consistency of the outer layer, which is prone to crumbling off. Pink pepper has a higher toxicity so should be used parsimoniously.

CULTIVATION CENTERS

India, Malaysia, Indonesia, Brazil, Peru

AROMA & FLAVOR

Green pepper is aromatic and fresh with a crisp bite. It's understated and smoother than its white and black counterparts. Pink pepper has a mild, peppery aroma but is fragrant as well. It is often masked by other types of pepper in a mix. Visually, pink pepper adds color and a subtle flavor.

MEDICINAL USES

See Black Pepper (page 32)

COMMON FORMS AND VARIETIES

peppercorns, whole or cracked; if whole, dried, freeze dried, or pickled; varieties are similar to black pepper, although fresh green pepper will likely only be found in country of origin; pink pepper will be Brazilian or Peruvian peppertree or from Réunion, a French island in the Indian Ocean.

COMPLEMENTS

Green pepper is especially sought after on charcuterie plates and cheese boards, duck, fish, flavored butters, pâtés, salads, seafood, soups, terrines. Pink pepper as a garnish or with delicate game, fish, and seafood.

PAIRS WELL WITH

black and white pepper, chile peppers, salt; and any spice that pairs well with black pepper but when you require less astringent and forceful pepper

Nigella

black seed, black caraway, kalonji, black onion, fennel flower

Nigella, the lovely, peppery black seeds, are sometimes called black cumin. Having no botanical relation to cumin, and the existence of an actual black cumin spice makes it even more confusing. Because of its plump seed pod that's enveloped by delicate, thorny greenery, nigella in wildflower form is blessed with a host of magical names by which to be identified, such as "Devil in a bush" and "Love in a mist."

Nigella is a resilient annual, indigenous to western Asia and the Middle East but grown today mostly in India. The seedpods must be collected before the pods ripen, or risk them popping and scattering the tiny, triangular seeds. The pods are dried and crushed. Nigella features prominently in cuisines stretching from Asia to southern Europe and Africa. Because of the name confusion, look for its botanical name *Nigella sativa* to ensure you're receiving the correct spice. You can also look for its triangular shape.

Nigella can be a playful spice. It imitates pepper for use in a pepper mill. The impersonation is spicier, more bitter, but effective and distinct. Nigella is one of those fun ones to toast before using—emboldening the nutty flavor—which also makes them brittle, thus easier to grind. You can also roast them in oil to start a dish with more intensity. When baking, try first toasting them for the tops of your bread dough or naan. If you enjoy Greek yogurt, keep some toasted nigella seeds on hand to sprinkle in to complement strawberries or mangos.

CULTIVATION CENTERS

Northern India, western Asia, northern Africa, Middle East, central Europe

AROMA & FLAVOR

Nigella's fragrance is aromatic and recalls pepper, while the taste is nutty, acute, and slightly bitter.

MEDICINAL USES

helps, treats, prevents, or aids heart disease and high blood pressure, cancer development, asthma and allergies, ulcers, pain, multiple sclerosis, skin conditions, and epilepsy. It boosts immunity. In India, it's used for flatulence reduction, to treat nervous disorders, induce sweating as well as inducing lactation.

COMMON FORMS

seeds, whole or ground

COMPLEMENTS

breads, flatbreads, and naan; cabbage; chutneys, and pickles; eggplant; legumes, lentils, and dal; lamb; poultry; salads; string, hard, and soft cheeses; vegetables; yogurts

PAIRS WELL WITH

ajowan, black pepper, cardamom, chile peppers, cinnamon, cloves, cumin, ginger, kokum, mustard seeds, nutmeg, turmeric, vanilla

Turmeric

yellow ginger, Indian saffron

Turmeric, a cousin of ginger, has renowned medicinal properties. It is also extremely easy and fun to cook with. Turmeric is referred to in sacred Hindu texts as far back as 1500 BCE.

Like ginger, turmeric is the rhizome (the underground stem of the bush). The plant, a perennial that thrives in tropical climates, is cultivated extensively outside its native India and Southeast Asia. Marco Polo compared it to saffron for the vivid yellow hue it donates to a dish, though the two spices share only that trait in common. Turmeric is a colorant in mustard and is a mainstay in deviled eggs, sausages, Worcestershire sauce, and, of course, curry powders.

Curry powder is not a spice, but rather a blend invented by the English two centuries ago. Eastern cultures mix their own proprietary curry blends, and they nearly all have turmeric in common. Turmeric contributes to an impressive set of spice mixes, too. Curcumin, a chemical compound found in the spice, is its secret weapon: an antioxidant, antimicrobial, and anti-inflammatory powerhouse.

Nonculinary uses include turmeric soap, lotion, and creams. Buddhist monks use it to dye their robes. Indonesians use turmeric to ward off evil spirits and paint their bodies.

Preground turmeric can keep comparatively well as long as it's kept out of direct sunlight. It mellows once it's cooked, so if the powder is a little intense, throw a bit of oil in a pan and stir in some turmeric until the aroma fills the room (not too long).

CULTIVATION CENTERS

India, Sri Lanka, Indonesia, Asia, South America, Peru, Caribbean, Jamaica

AROMA & FLAVOR

Turmeric is musky, woody, and can lean into undertones of ginger and pepper. All turmeric has a bit of bitterness. Zedoary, a relative known as white turmeric, is sometime used.

MEDICINAL USES

helps, treats, prevents, or aids gastrointestinal problems, heart disease and stroke, eye infections, pain, obesity, gum disease, acne, eczema, bruises, sores and rashes, liver problems, high cholesterol, depression, gout, flatulence; digestion; blood flow and clotting; prevents cancer cells from forming and combats breast, colon, cervical, lung, pancreatic, prostate, and skin cancers as well as Alzheimer's and Parkinson's; alleviates arthritis pain

COMMON FORMS AND VARIETIES

fresh, whole; dried, whole and ground; varieties include Madras turmeric (common in the United States), Alleppey turmeric (more fragrant, higher concentration of curcumin)

COMPLEMENTS

bread, chicken, chutneys, curry, desserts, deviled eggs, fish, legumes, lentils, noodles, pilafs, rice, shellfish, soups, tomato sauces, vegetables (cauliflower, onions, potatoes)

PAIRS WELL WITH

allspice, bay leaf, black pepper, caraway, cilantro, coconut, coriander, cumin, dill, fennel seeds, galangal, garlic, ginger, lemongrass, mustard, nutmeg

White Pepper

To achieve white pepper, the berry is left on the vine longer, until the pepper is red or yellowish. When picked, the seeds are soaked to loosen the outer pericarp, which is rubbed off, leaving the "heart" of the pepper. There is a mechanized version of this, but the most distinct white peppers—those of Muntok, Sarawak, and Brazil—are usually done in the old-fashioned way. Because this process can be laborious, white pepper is considered decadent and gourmet.

White peppers are produced from Livorno, Italy to India to Cameroon, each with their own production style. In England, several layers of the berry are removed resulting in decertified white pepper, which has an exceptionally polished taste. While black pepper is prevalent in the cuisine of Europe, Southeast Asia, India, and North America, white pepper is widespread in Thai, Japanese, Chinese, and certain European fare.

It's hard to go wrong with any pepper when seasoning your food, and pepper complements and goes well with almost any other flavoring agent. It neither overpowers nor underwhelms its associate spices. Colored peppers pair well together and make an aesthetically pleasing mixture called mignonette pepper.

CULTIVATION CENTERS

India, Indonesia, Italy, England, West Africa

AROMA & FLAVOR

White pepper is sharper, winey, and more acute than black pepper. Some would say white pepper is slightly bolder, but a bolder flavor may be varietal or imagined due to its rarer, costlier nature.

MEDICINAL USES

Similar to Black Pepper (page 32); however, because it lacks the pericarp it does not contain chavicin and some of the essential oil found in the oily outer layer. That could affect some of its medicinal uses; however, all of the piperine, the compound that gives pepper its pepperiness, is there. This is the chemical that has been researched to help, treat, or prevent cancers, hearing loss, brain function, Alzheimer's, heart disease, and blood pressure.

COMMON FORMS AND VARIETIES

peppercorns, whole and ground; varieties include Sarawak pepper (from Malaysia; popular for both black and white pepper), Muntok (Indonesian), Penja (West Africa)

COMPLEMENTS

Same as Black Pepper (page 32); where white pepper is desired but the black is not: béarnaise; Boursin; curries and soups; dishes with egg, custards, mayonnaise; especially an ingredient in quatre épices, berbere, ras el hanout, baharat, jerk seasoning; stir fries; used especially in French and Thai cuisines; white or cream sauces such as Alfredo

PAIRS WELL WITH

ajowan, allspice, cardamom, chile peppers, cinnamon, coriander, ginger

RECIPES

Chaat Masala Blend 48

Garam Masala Blend 49

Panch Phoron Blend 50

Sambaar Masala Blend 51

Tandoori Chicken Blend 52

Cinnamon-Turmeric Rub 53

Sri Lankan Curry Rub 54

Madras Curry Rub 55

Peppercorn Paste 56

Dhana Jeera Vegetable Paste 57

Kashmiri Masala Paste 58

Vindaloo Curry Paste 59

Mango Chutney Marinade 60

Garam Masala Yogurt Marinade 61

Yogurt Marinade 62

Vadouvan-Lassi Poultry Marinade 63

Nigella Seeds Meat Marinade 64

Indian Carrot Sauce 65

Mustard Seeds Curry Sauce 66

Curry Seafood Sauce 67

Left: Garam Masala Blend (page 49)

Chaat Masala Blend

fruit, grilled meats, salads, soups

Chaat masala is the signature ingredient of many Indian street foods. It incorporates unique flavors by accentuating the distinct Indian black salt and tart, tangy amchur. The heat of cayenne and sweetness of the dried pomegranate play nicely with the mint and ginger, giving this blend a multifaceted flavor.

MAKES ½ CUP

1 tablespoon cumin

1 tablespoon
coriander seeds

1 teaspoon fennel seeds

1 teaspoon ajowan seeds

1 teaspoon dried mint

Black peppercorns (optional)

¼ teaspoon ground
asafoetida

2 tablespoons
ground amchur

2 tablespoons black salt

2 teaspoons ground
cayenne pepper or freshly
ground black pepper

2 teaspoons ground
anardana

1 teaspoon ground ginger

1 teaspoon sea salt

1. In a small skillet over medium heat, toast the cumin, coriander, fennel seeds, and ajowan seeds for about 1 minute until fragrant. Transfer to a dish and let cool.

2. Combine the toasted spices, mint, and black peppercorns (if using) to a spice grinder and pulverize. Transfer to a small bowl.

3. In the same skillet, toast the asafoetida powder until the aroma turns from stinky to floral. Add it to the bowl.

4. In the bowl, mix in the amchur, black salt, cayenne, anardana, ginger, and salt. Store in an airtight jar for 1 to 3 months.

Recipe Tip: Adjust the heat levels by substituting black pepper for the cayenne pepper. Anise seeds can substitute for fennel if needed.

Garam Masala Blend

chicken, meat, rice and pilafs, salads

Garam masala is a versatile, slightly sweet Northern Indian spice blend that has as many variations as there are chefs. It features heavily in Moghul cooking and is used across India. Add right before serving or as a seasoning similar to the use of salt and pepper. **MAKES ⅔ CUP**

4 tablespoons coriander seeds

2 to 3 tablespoons cumin seeds

1 tablespoon black or green cardamom seeds, or a combination, hulled

1 tablespoon black peppercorns

2 bay leaves

2 cinnamon or cassia sticks

1 teaspoon whole cloves

1 teaspoon mace

1 teaspoon grated nutmeg

1. In a small skillet over medium heat, toast the coriander, cumin, cardamom, peppercorns, and bay leaves, stirring often, to release their flavors, 1 to 2 minutes. Transfer to a dish and let cool.

2. In a spice grinder, grind the cinnamon, cloves, mace, and nutmeg. Add the toasted, cooled mixture and grind to a fine powder.

3. Store in an airtight jar for 6 to 9 months.

Recipe Tip: If you dare, add half or whole of a habanero chile to the blend—seed it first to mitigate the heat. It gives a nice kick and brings out the sweetness of the cinnamon.

Panch Phoron Blend

legumes, beans, lentils, potatoes, and starchy foods

Panch phoron is a whole-seed blend of five spices and features prominently in Bengali cuisine. It is one of the niftier platforms for nigella seeds. Panch phoron is best utilized for flavoring the oil used to roast starchy foods. It can be ground for sprinkling on yogurts or chutneys. MAKES ABOUT 1 CUP

¼ cup nigella seeds

¼ cup yellow mustard seeds

¼ cup cumin seeds

¼ cup fennel seeds

2 tablespoons fenugreek seeds

½ teaspoon vegetable oil or ghee (optional)

1. In a bowl, mix together the nigella, mustard, cumin, fennel, and fenugreek.

2. Place a medium skillet over medium heat and add the oil or ghee (if using). When hot, drop in a handful of the spice mixture and stir it constantly until aromatic, 1 to 2 minutes. Immediately add the rest of the spice mix and stir constantly for 3 minutes.

3. Store in an airtight jar for 8 to 9 months.

Recipe Tip: Many panch phoron formulas call for an equal share of each spice. The fenugreek seeds can be tough and bitter so I use a little less. Modify your levels as you see fit.

Sambaar Masala Blend

lentils, soups, vegetarian dishes

Sambaar masala is a traditional blend that flavors the vegetarian dishes of India's southern regions. Sambaar incorporates dals, or toasted lentils and legumes. It's used sparingly as a thickener in soups, stews, and the occasional chutney. This one is spicy, so use fewer chile peppers if you want something milder. **MAKES ½ CUP**

1 tablespoon dried
lentils (urad dal)

1 tablespoon dried yellow
peas (chana dal)

5 dried chiles, such as
cayenne or Kashmiri,
seeded, or 2 teaspoons
chili powder

1½ tablespoons
coriander seeds

1½ tablespoons cumin seeds

1 tablespoon black
peppercorns

2 teaspoons ground
cinnamon

2 teaspoons turmeric

½ teaspoon salt

1. In a small skillet over medium heat, toast the lentils, yellow peas, and chiles for 2 to 3 minutes, stirring often. Transfer to a dish and let cool.

2. Toast the coriander, cumin, and peppercorns in the same skillet, stirring often, 1 to 2 minutes. Add to the dish and let cool.

3. In a spice grinder, grind together the toasted spices with the cinnamon and turmeric. Add the salt.

4. Store in an airtight jar for 6 months to 1 year.

Recipe Tip: Sambaar masala gets its flavor from the lentils and yellow peas. It is typically used for flavoring but also as a thickening agent. I much prefer sambaar to be on the sweet side, hence the addition of cinnamon. Fenugreek, asafoetida, and mustard are alternative spices to include in this blend.

Tandoori Chicken Blend

chicken, lamb, poultry

Tandoori-style cooking is named for the high-temperature clay oven—tandoor—used in the northern state of Punjab. Tandoori chicken is the region's most familiar dish, recognizable for its bright red color. This blend uses paprika, cayenne, Kashmiri chiles, and saffron to embolden the red as naturally as possible. **MAKES ¼ CUP**

2 Kashmiri chiles, stemmed and seeded

1 tablespoon Garam Masala Blend (page 49)

1 tablespoon Hungarian or Indian paprika

1 teaspoon turmeric

1 teaspoon ground cayenne pepper

1 teaspoon ground ginger

1 teaspoon Himalayan pink salt or Indian black salt

⅛ teaspoon saffron (several threads)

1. In a small skillet over medium heat, toast the chiles for 3 to 4 minutes. Their aroma should be released but they should not burn. Transfer to a dish and let cool. Grind in a spice grinder. (If making the Garam Masala Blend at the same time, grind the chiles with that mix.)

2. Mix with the garam masala, paprika, turmeric, cayenne, ginger, salt, and saffron. Store in an airtight jar for up to 6 months.

Recipe Tip: To make Tandoori chicken, crosshatch the skin on 2 chicken pieces (legs or thighs are best). Make a paste using all the spice blend and a few teaspoons water. Rub the chicken with the paste and refrigerate overnight. Preheat the oven to 375°F. Bring the chicken to room temperature for 20 to 30 minutes. Skewer the chicken and place it in a baking dish so you can easily turn the pieces while they're in the oven. Bake for 40 minutes to 1 hour, turning the chicken every 10 minutes or so, basting with ghee each time and use a pan to catch the drippings. If in doubt, cut one chicken piece open to make sure it is cooked through.

Cinnamon-Turmeric Rub

goat or lamb, poultry, soups

This rub is a basic, approachable seasoning featuring the vibrant combination of cinnamon and turmeric. It's a simple, flavorful mix that was my introduction to Indian flavors. I haven't looked back since and neither will you. **MAKES ¾ CUP**

2 tablespoons cumin seeds

½ teaspoon white peppercorns

½ teaspoon black peppercorns

¼ cup ground cinnamon or cassia

¼ cup turmeric

1 teaspoon celery salt

1. In a small skillet over medium heat, lightly toast the cumin, white peppercorns, and black peppercorns, stirring often, for 1 to 2 minutes. Transfer to a dish and let cool.

2. Grind the toasted spices in a spice grinder. Transfer to a jar and mix in the cinnamon, turmeric, and celery salt.

3. Seal the jar and store for as long as the cinnamon stays potent, 3 to 6 months.

Recipe Tip: Use this blend to season meat and flavor soups.

Sri Lankan Curry Rub

Beef, especially hearty brisket, meat, pork shoulder

Sri Lankan brown curry is noted for its dark, rich color. The fullness of flavor comes from dry roasting each spice to its toasty limit, turning each one several shades darker. Black pepper is the primary heat source, resulting in a smoky, mild curry perfect for red meats. MAKES ¾ TO 1 CUP

3 tablespoons coriander seeds

2 tablespoons cumin seeds

2 tablespoons black Malabar peppercorns

1 tablespoon black mustard seeds

2 teaspoons brown cardamom seeds

1 teaspoon fennel seeds

1 teaspoon basmati rice

1 teaspoon fenugreek seeds

4 dried curry leaves, stemmed

2 pandan leaves (optional)

1 Ceylon cinnamon stick

Smoked black salt

1. Because each spice has a different ideal toasting level, toast the spices separately. In a small skillet over medium heat, add the coriander and toast, stirring constantly, for 2 to 5 minutes until the seeds turn several shades darker and their aroma is at their height. Transfer to a small bowl and let cool.

2. Repeat step 1 for the cumin, peppercorns, mustard, cardamom, fennel, rice, fenugreek, curry leaves, pandan leaves (if using), cinnamon stick, and black salt, transferring each to the bowl to cool.

3. In a spice grinder, grind all the ingredients into a powder. Store in an airtight jar for up to 6 months.

Recipe Tip: If heat isn't your thing, this is the curry for you. Simply use fewer peppercorns. This rub lends itself better to meats than seafood, although thicker cuts of swordfish and fish can handle it. Rub on both sides of the protein and let it sit for 30 minutes to 1 hour before frying in oil.

Madras Curry Rub

chicken, fish, rabbit, scallops, shrimp, and as salad dressing

Store-bought curry powders are generally a stale replica of a Madras curry. It's a straightforward blend, not too spicy, hot, sour, or tart. MAKES ½ TO ¾ CUP

4 tablespoons coriander seeds

2 tablespoons cumin seeds

1 tablespoon white peppercorns

1 teaspoon green cardamom seeds

1 teaspoon whole cloves

1 tablespoon ground cinnamon

1 teaspoon ground cayenne pepper

In a small skillet over medium heat, toast the coriander, cumin, peppercorns, cardamom, and cloves for 1 to 2 minutes. Transfer to a dish and let cool. Then grind the toasted spices in a spice grinder and mix them with the cinnamon and cayenne pepper. Store in an airtight jar for up to 6 months.

Recipe Tip: To use as a paste, combine the spice blend with about 2 teaspoons white vinegar. Then baste your protein and pan-fry it in ghee or clarified butter.

Peppercorn Paste

marinade for steaks, serve atop any proteins or your favorite tartine

This is spicy! I love this chunky, crunchy paste because a few hours later a pepper-corn may come out of your teeth, reminding you how delicious your meal was. This recipe is courtesy of Angela Zingale, a New York City–based private chef who is currently training in Paris. MAKES ½ TO ¾ CUP

1 cup canola or peanut oil

¼ long or cubeb pepper

¼ cup black Tellicherry peppercorns

¼ cup pink peppercorns

2 tablespoons coriander seeds, dry roasted

1 tablespoon coarse salt

1. In a medium skillet over medium heat, heat the oil for 10 minutes. Carefully add the long pepper, black peppercorns, pink peppercorns, and coriander seeds. Turn off the heat and cover the pan. Let it sit for 30 minutes to 1 hour.

2. Strain and reserve the oil. Place the spices in a mortar and pestle and add the salt. Crush until a paste has formed, adding some of the reserved oil to reach your desired consistency.

3. Refrigerate in an airtight container for up to 1 month. Serve at room temperature.

Recipe Tip: Use whatever peppercorns you have on hand. This is a great one to experiment with to find your ideal combination.

Dhana Jeera Vegetable Paste

baked fish, eggs, poultry (especially fried chicken), pork

Dhana jeera is used frequently on India's west coast. The all-star pairing of ajowan and apples makes a great baking addition for proteins and vegetables. **MAKES 1¾ TO 2 CUPS**

½ apple, sliced

½ red bell pepper, diced

½ green bell pepper, diced

1 Roma tomato, diced

½ small onion, diced

½ carrot, diced

2 tablespoons sea salt

6 tablespoons coriander seeds

3 tablespoons cumin seeds

1 teaspoon ground cinnamon

2 teaspoons ajowan seeds

3 teaspoons coconut oil, divided

2 tablespoons apple cider vinegar

1. Put the apple, red and green bell peppers, tomato, onion, and carrot in a strainer and toss them with the salt. Let them stand for 1 to 2 hours to drain off their natural liquids.

2. In a small skillet over medium heat, toast the coriander and cumin, stirring frequently, for 1 to 2 minutes. Transfer to a dish and let the mixture cool. In a spice grinder, grind the toasted seeds with the cinnamon.

3. In the same skillet over medium heat, toast the ajowan seeds. Transfer to a dish and set aside.

4. Place the vegetables and apples in a food processor with 1 teaspoon of coconut oil. Process until a mash is formed.

5. Add the remaining 2 teaspoons of coconut oil to the skillet and place over medium heat. Transfer the mash to the skillet and sauté, stirring occasionally, for 3 to 5 minutes or until golden brown. Stir in the toasted spices in the last minute of cooking.

6. In a small saucepan, boil the vinegar until the volume decreases by half. Slowly stir this into the vegetables in the skillet until it achieves a paste consistency. Remove the skillet from the heat and let cool.

7. This is best used quickly, but will keep in an airtight container in the refrigerator for up to 1 week.

Kashmiri Masala Paste

beef, goat, lamb, steak, veal cubes or shanks

Kashmiri masala is a blend of spices from Northern India and is most commonly used in rhogan josh lamb curry. This is a yogurt-free variation of that sauce, although you can use yogurt in place of the vinegar if you prefer. **MAKES ⅓ CUP**

1 tablespoon cumin seeds

1 tablespoon black or green cardamom seeds

1 teaspoon coriander seeds

1 teaspoon white Wynad, Malabar, or Tellicherry peppercorns

½ teaspoon ajowan seeds

½ teaspoon fennel seeds

1 tablespoon ground cinnamon

1 teaspoon ground turmeric

1 teaspoon ground mace

1 teaspoon ground ginger

½ teaspoon ground paprika

3 Kashmiri chiles, stemmed and seeded, or use chipotle or peppers of choice

1 tablespoon ghee

¼ cup vegetable oil

¼ cup red wine vinegar

1. In a small skillet over medium heat, toast the cumin, cardamom, coriander, peppercorns, ajowan, and fennel seeds, stirring often, for 1 to 2 minutes. Transfer to a dish and let the mixture cool. In a spice grinder, grind the toasted spices with the cinnamon, turmeric, mace, ginger, paprika, and chiles. This is your Kashmiri masala blend, which can be stored in an airtight jar for 4 to 6 months.

2. To make the paste, add the ghee, oil, and some of the vinegar until you achieve your preferred consistency. Use immediately.

Recipe Tip: Pair this recipe with Mango Chutney Marinade (page 60) or cucumber raita. To make raita, dice 1 cucumber and season with salt. Add 1 cup Greek yogurt and ½ tablespoon Panch Phoron Blend (page 50).

Vindaloo Curry Paste

chicken, game, lamb, pork, shrimp

Vindaloo curry is a popular hot paste from sunny Goa. Portuguese colonization influenced this cuisine, which incorporates elements of heat and vinegar. Originally called carne vinha d'alhos—*"meat of wined garlic"—vindaloo curry paste marries two traditions. It is best made a few days ahead of time.* MAKES ¾ CUP

2 tablespoons
coriander seeds

1 tablespoon cumin seeds

1 tablespoon black
peppercorns

4 whole cloves

1 cinnamon stick

5 to 10 dried chiles or
2 to 5 teaspoons
dried chili powder

1 tablespoon ground
turmeric

2 teaspoons salt

1 (1-inch) piece fresh ginger,
minced, or 2 tablespoons
ground ginger

1 teaspoon ground nutmeg

¼ cup white vinegar

3 tablespoons
vegetable oil, divided

2 garlic cloves, minced

1. In a small skillet over medium heat, toast the coriander, cumin, peppercorns, and cloves for 1 to 2 minutes. Transfer to a dish and let cool.

2. In a spice grinder, grind the toasted spices with the cinnamon and chiles. Transfer to a medium bowl and mix in the turmeric, salt, ginger, and nutmeg.

3. Whisk in the vinegar to make a thick paste, using as much vinegar as you need to achieve your preferred consistency.

4. Heat 1 tablespoon of oil in the skillet over medium heat. Add the garlic and sauté until fragrant, about 1 minute. Add the remaining 2 tablespoons of oil to the skillet. When it is hot, add the paste, stirring constantly to keep it from sticking to the pan, for 5 to 10 minutes until well blended and smooth. The aroma will mellow out.

5. Refrigerate in an airtight jar for up to 2 weeks.

Recipe Tip: Add a protein to the skillet after you've completed step 4. Sear your choice of meat over high heat until golden on each side, then finish cooking it in the paste. Reduce the heat to low and add ¼ cup water and ¼ cup stock. Simmer for 45 minutes to 1 hour. If cooking a thick chicken breast or pork chop, shred the meat with a fork and mix it into the sauce. Serve with rice.

Mango Chutney Marinade

chicken, duck, and other fowl, flatbreads and naan, pork and barbecued meats

Mango chutney is a popular condiment that enhances meat, poultry, and pork dishes. Its tanginess offsets salty and gamey proteins. Its sweetness can mask deficiencies if something is overcooked or overseasoned. It also doubles as a marinade and is an outstanding basting ingredient for foods cooked on the grill.

MAKES 3 TO 4 CUPS

2 tablespoons coconut oil

1 (1-inch) piece fresh ginger, grated

1 medium carrot, grated

¼ onion, grated

1 tablespoon Panch Phoron Blend (page 50)

1 tablespoon Chaat Masala Blend (page 48)

1 teaspoon ground anardana

1 cup white wine vinegar

½ cup white sugar

3 ripe mangos, peeled and diced

1 teaspoon freshly ground green or black peppercorns

1. In a large saucepan over medium heat, heat the coconut oil. When hot, add the ginger, carrot, and onion and cook, stirring constantly, until golden brown, 4 to 5 minutes. Add the panch phoron, chaat masala, and anardana and continue stirring for 1 to 2 minutes. Add the vinegar and sugar, stirring until the sugar dissolves.

2. Turn the heat to high, bring the mixture to a boil, and stir in the mangos. Reduce the heat to medium-low and let simmer 30 to 45 minutes, or until the chutney starts to thicken.

3. Stir in the pepper. Turn off the heat and let the chutney cool. Refrigerate in an airtight container for up to 2 weeks.

Recipe Tip: Try adding a handful of fresh pomegranate seeds just as the chutney finishes cooking. They'll end up as little bursts of flavor. Use this chutney as a marinade by taking the mixture off the heat before it becomes thick. Put your protein in a zip-top bag and add the chutney, shake, and refrigerate for 2 to 3 hours. Then grill on open heat, basting with additional chutney as needed.

Garam Masala Yogurt Marinade

fowl, game, rabbit, poultry

Yogurt is a versatile cooking ally. It is used as a thickening agent if your sauce is too thin or a diluting agent if you overdo it on flavor. With practice, you'll get a feel for how the ingredients work together. Combining garam masala with yogurt is just one method. MAKES ABOUT 2 CUPS

2 cups Greek yogurt

1 tablespoon Garam
Masala Blend (page 49)

2 teaspoons freshly
squeezed lemon juice

1 teaspoon sea salt

1 teaspoon ground turmeric

1 tablespoon ground
cayenne pepper (optional)

In a medium bowl, mix all the ingredients together until well combined. Refrigerate in an airtight container and use within 5 days.

Recipe Tip: Place 1 cup marinade in a zip-top bag with the protein you are cooking. Marinate in the refrigerator for 12 to 24 hours. Discard the marinade in the bag. Grill or cook the protein over medium heat, covered. Baste the protein during the cooking process with the remaining ½ cup marinade.

Yogurt Marinade

chicken

This simple tandoori-style chicken marinade is great for barbecues or even just oven roasting. It's so easy, and you can substitute powders for the whole dry spices to make it even easier. This recipe is courtesy of Salmaan Mirza, PhD candidate at Harvard University and a modern-day Indiana Jones. MAKES 2 TO 2½ CUPS

1 tablespoon
coriander seeds

1 tablespoon cumin seeds

¼ cinnamon stick or
½ teaspoon ground
cinnamon

2 bay leaves

2 or 3 cardamom pods

1 teaspoon nigella seeds

1 teaspoon mustard
seeds, a mix of black
and brown if possible

1 teaspoon black
peppercorns

1 fresh Thai chile, seeded
and chopped, or to taste

1 (1-inch) piece fresh
ginger, minced

3 garlic cloves, minced

Vegetable oil

2 cups plain yogurt

1 teaspoon ground turmeric

1 teaspoon ground
cayenne pepper

Salt

1. In a skillet over low heat, toast the coriander, cumin, cinnamon stick (if using ground cinnamon, add it in step 3), bay leaves, cardamom, nigella seeds, mustard, and peppercorns until the aroma is released, 1 to 2 minutes. Transfer to a dish and let cool.

2. Grind the toasted spices in a spice grinder to a powder. Transfer to a medium bowl.

3. Add the fresh chile, ginger, and garlic to the bowl with a generous drizzle of oil, and combine to make a paste. If the paste is too thick, stir in a little water. Add the yogurt, turmeric, and cayenne. Season with salt and add another drizzle of oil. Mix until well combined.

4. Use immediately or refrigerate in an airtight container for 3 to 4 days.

Recipe Tip: For the best flavor, marinate chicken in this mixture in the fridge overnight or longer.

Vadouvan-Lassi Poultry Marinade

bean soups, chicken, lentils, seafood

Vadouvan curry is French-influenced and uses garlic, onion, and sometimes shallots. Traditionally, the ingredients are sun-dried, but oven-drying is your best bet for expediency. Combined with lassi, an Indian yogurt drink that comes in several flavors, this "French"-style curry makes a phenomenal marinade for poultry. **MAKES ABOUT 2 CUPS**

1 tablespoon cumin seeds

1 teaspoon mustard seeds

1 teaspoon green cardamom seeds

½ teaspoon coriander seeds

½ teaspoon black peppercorns

1 teaspoon fenugreek seeds

1 tablespoon ground turmeric

1 teaspoon ground cayenne pepper

3 curry leaves, stemmed

1 tablespoon coconut oil, plus additional if needed

1 large onion, minced

4 garlic cloves

1 teaspoon dried rosemary

1 pint lassi yogurt, such as mango lassi with honey or flavor of choice

1. Preheat the oven to 325°F. Line a baking sheet with parchment or waxed paper.

2. In a small skillet over medium heat, toast the cumin, mustard, cardamom, coriander, and black peppercorns until the aromas are released, 1 to 2 minutes. Transfer to a dish and let cool.

3. In the same skillet, toast the fenugreek until fragrant. Transfer to the dish and let cool.

4. In a spice grinder, grind together the toasted spices, turmeric, cayenne pepper, and curry leaves.

5. Heat the oil in the skillet over medium-high heat. Add the onion and garlic and sauté until golden brown, 4 to 5 minutes. Mix in the spice blend, adding a little more oil if necessary to help everything blend together.

6. Spread the mixture in an even layer on the baking sheet. Bake for about 1 hour or until the mixture is dry. Stir in the rosemary and let cool.

7. Refrigerate in an airtight jar for up to 1 month. When ready to marinate your protein, whisk the blend into the yogurt and use immediately.

Recipe Tip: Smother chicken, game hen, or turkey with 1 cup Vadouvan-Lassi Poultry Marinade and refrigerate for 12 hours.

Nigella Seeds Meat Marinade

lamb with spiced yogurt or labneh

My friend Angela Zingale uncovered nigella seeds' fine pairing with lamb and came up with this marinade. Toasting the seeds first is optional, but they are often very hard if not ground. Angela recommends 2 pounds of top round lamb as the perfect protein. MAKES ABOUT 1 CUP

1 tablespoon black Sarawak peppercorns

1 bunch scallions

3 tablespoons dried oregano

2 tablespoons sesame oil

2 tablespoons coconut oil

2 tablespoons Dijon mustard

1 tablespoon coarse sea salt

1 (2-inch) piece fresh ginger, grated

½ cup nigella seeds

1. In a small skillet over low heat, lightly toast the peppercorns for 1 to 2 minutes. Transfer to a dish and let cool, then grind in a spice grinder.

2. Combine the scallions, oregano, sesame oil, coconut oil, mustard, salt, ginger, and pepper in a food processor and pulse to combine. Transfer to a small bowl and stir in the nigella seeds. Use immediately.

Recipe Tip: To marinate your protein of choice, cover it with the marinade and refrigerate for at least 2 hours. Pull it out about 30 minutes prior to cooking to let it come to room temperature. If preparing lamb, cook it in ½ cup water with 3 halved shallots in a preheated 380°F oven. After 30 minutes, increase the temperature to 450°F and roast for 15 minutes more. Let the lamb rest for 15 minutes before serving.

Indian Carrot Sauce

chicken, fish, risotto, and as a salad dressing or on grilled vegetables

This sauce is a versatile component to finish any light protein or tofu. Cooking down the carrots allows the flavors to develop and heightens the flavors in soups, rice, and on winter veggies like squash and pumpkin. Beeta Mohajeri, a classically trained chef and veteran of New Orleans's famous Commander's Palace restaurant, provided this recipe. MAKES 2 TO 3 CUPS

8 large carrots

2 onions

5 garlic cloves

1 teaspoon ground Ceylon cinnamon

½ teaspoon ground turmeric

½ teaspoon cardamom pods, toasted and ground

½ cup extra-virgin olive oil

2 tablespoons white wine vinegar

Coarse sea salt

Freshly ground black pepper

1. Juice the carrots, onion, and garlic.

2. Pour the juices into a medium saucepan and cook over medium-low heat until the sauce is reduced and the flavors develop, about 10 to 15 minutes.

3. Transfer the reduction to a blender and add the cinnamon, turmeric, cardamom, olive oil, and vinegar. Blend until well combined. Season to taste with salt and pepper. Use immediately.

Recipe Tip: Use as a garnish on other recipes or to take the edge off hot dishes that are too spicy for your tolerance.

Mustard Seeds Curry Sauce

potato curry

This recipe makes use of mustard seeds and curry leaves. Luckily for mustard lovers, it's one of Salmaan Mirza's favorites. His knowledge of spices is as great as anyone I know, and this recipe is his. **MAKES ABOUT ⅓ CUP**

1 teaspoon mustard seeds, mix of black and brown, if possible

1 teaspoon black peppercorns

1 teaspoon coriander seeds

½ teaspoon cumin seeds

¼ teaspoon fenugreek seeds

2 tablespoons vegetable oil

1 tablespoon ghee

1 (1-inch) piece fresh ginger, minced

2 garlic cloves, minced

1 fresh Thai chile, seeded and finely chopped, or to taste

12 fresh curry leaves

2 bay leaves

½ teaspoon ground turmeric

½ teaspoon ground cayenne pepper

1. In a medium skillet over low heat, toast the mustard, peppercorns, coriander, cumin, and fenugreek. Leave whole for a nice crunch in this sauce. Pour into a bowl and set aside.

2. In the skillet over low heat, warm the oil and ghee. Add the ginger, garlic, and chile, and cook for about 3 minutes.

3. Add the toasted spices, stirring frequently to make sure the garlic does not burn, for 2 to 3 minutes. Stir in the curry leaves and bay leaves. Remove the skillet from the heat and stir in the turmeric and cayenne. Use immediately.

Recipe Tip: To cook with potatoes, add 4 potatoes, peeled and cubed, to the warm sauce. Cook over medium heat until the potatoes start to stick to the bottom of the pan, about 2 minutes. Add 1 cup water (or more, as needed) and simmer until the potatoes are cooked through. Season with coarse sea salt and stir in 1 cup of chopped fresh cilantro.

Curry Seafood Sauce

fish, mollusks, shellfish

Coconut and curry are two of my favorite flavors. This recipe accentuates them with cardamom and turmeric, giving a gentle backing to the rich and succulent proteins. This recipe works best with mussels and clams, but scallops, white fish, and shrimp fit the bill, too. MAKES 1 TO 2 CUPS

1½ teaspoons cumin seeds

1 teaspoon coriander seeds

4 green cardamom pods

½ teaspoon ground turmeric

Salt

1 tablespoon coconut oil

1 cup chopped onion

2 garlic cloves, minced

1 (1-inch) piece fresh ginger, grated

1 cup yogurt or sour cream

½ cup coconut milk

Freshly squeezed lemon juice

1. In a medium skillet over medium heat, toast the cumin, coriander, and cardamom, stirring frequently, for about 2 minutes. Transfer to a dish and let cool.

2. Add the toasted spices to a spice grinder and grind. Transfer to a small bowl and mix in the turmeric and salt. This blend will keep in an airtight jar for 2 to 3 months.

3. Heat the oil in the skillet over medium heat. Add the onion, garlic, and ginger and sauté until golden and soft, 4 to 5 minutes. Stir in the spice mixture and cook for 30 seconds. Stir in the yogurt, coconut milk, and a squeeze of lemon juice when ready to make the dish, and cook over low heat for 5 to 10 minutes. Use immediately.

Recipe Tip: For mussels and clams, steam them in oil and ¼ cup chicken or vegetable stock until they open, about 10 minutes. Drain the liquid and return the mollusks to the pan. Add the yogurt and coconut milk at this point. Increase the heat until the liquid comes to a boil, then reduce the heat to a simmer, stir in the spices (mixed with ¼ cup of coconut milk before adding), and cook, covered, for 5 to 10 minutes, stirring occasionally. Add more stock or oil as needed to prevent drying out.

Asia and the South Pacific

SPICES 71 RECIPES 93

Though Westernized versions of Asian cuisines permeate the American and European food landscapes, the authentic flavors that come from Asia, particularly nutmeg, mace and cloves, were sought long before the discovery of a sea route between Europe and South East Asia.

Early traders exchanged so often with India and Sri Lanka that it can be mystifying to know where one spice blend regionally begins and another ends. However, each territory has developed distinct culinary styles based on shared ingredients. The dissemination of these flavors across the continent was spurred on by vast ruling dynasties, religions, agricultural practices, and advances in medicine. Genghis Khan and the thirteenth-century Mongol Empire violently brought much of the continent under one sociopolitical umbrella and protected large swaths of the Silk Road. This enabled cultural and gastronomic currents to flow unencumbered through an immense stretch of territory from the Pacific to Eastern Europe.

China has its fingerprints on the roots of many of the flavors and cooking styles of Asia and the south Pacific. Japanese cuisine is deliberate, clean, and attends closely to detail. Wasabi is the spice that most lingers on the tongue when discussing Japanese cuisine, though in its pure form it's not easy to find unless within proximity of the mountain streams of Japan. From Thai food you'll recognize the taste of galangal, even if you may not be familiar with the spice. Other flavors are not so uniquely nationalistic. Star anise, ginger, cloves, nutmeg, mace, and cassia cinnamon are prevalent in all manner of cuisines.

All five basic flavors—salty, sour, sweet, bitter, umami—are celebrated in Asian cuisine. Each of the spices in this chapter represents that phenomenon, from sweet star anise and cinnamon, to sour lemon peel and black lime. Once you become familiar with that harmony in your own cooking, you will use those instincts to make your food satisfying on a previously undiscovered level.

SPICES

Cassia Cinnamon 72   Cloves 74

Galangal 76   Ginger 78

Lemon Peel 80   Mace 82

Nutmeg 84   Star Anise 86

Szechuan, Sansho,
and Other Peppers 88

Wasabi 90

Cassia Cinnamon

cassia, Chinese cinnamon, cinnamon (in the United States)

In many ways superior, cassia cinnamon perhaps will never be as recognized as Ceylon cinnamon. Cassia is a close relative of the popular spice cinnamon. While the distinction is required on labels in some countries, in the United States there is no such labeling requirement: it is simply cinnamon.

The quills of cassia cinnamon, which are dried and rolled bark, are bigger and coarser than Ceylon cinnamon. The powder is exceedingly popular for use in sweets, cakes, pies, cookies, and breads. Sticks are used in tea, mulled wine and cider, hot chocolate, and hot toddies. The French use cassia in some versions of Quatre Épices Blend (page 233), a blend used on game, sausages, and charcuterie. On the other side of the world, it lends itself to savory dishes.

Cassia cinnamon was first cultivated between 4000 and 2500 BCE in the area now encompassing Indonesia, China, Myanmar, and Vietnam. In China, it was an essential element in the spice trade. It's one of the five in Chinese five-spice powder and is used also in soups and braised dishes. In the Middle East, it is one of the components of ras el hanout. In India, a common practice is to cook cassia sticks in oil and then judiciously add it to curries or rice.

Unfortunately for the United States, the cassia we import is on the lower end of the quality scale. Maximize your cassia cinnamon experience with a higher quality product from a specialty market. A common "cinnamon hack" is to do a 50/50 cassia-Ceylon blend, resulting in a stronger aroma and a sweeter taste.

CULTIVATION CENTERS

Indonesia, Malaysia, Vietnam, China, India

AROMA & FLAVOR

Cassia is spicy and warm on the nose, with a fainter aroma than true cinnamon. The taste, however, is sweeter but also more intense than its relative.

MEDICINAL USES

helps, treats, prevents, or aids cholesterol problems, food poisoning, heart disease, high blood pressure, stroke, ulcers, cancer; controls blood sugar; lowers risk of type 2 diabetes; has antibacterial and antifungal properties

COMMON FORMS

quills (rolled sticks), quillings (broken pieces), ground, whole buds (unripe fruit).

COMMON VARIETIES

Indonesian cassia, Chinese cassia, Vietnamese cassia, and Korintje, which is the closest to Ceylon cinnamon.

COMPLEMENTS

bananas and plantains, cakes, chicken, chocolate, citrus, corn, curries, fruit-based confections, pastries, pho bos, tea, soups, squash and pumpkin,

PAIRS WELL WITH

allspice, anardana, caraway, cardamom, cloves, coriander, cumin, ginger, nutmeg, star anise, tamarind, turmeric, true cinnamon

Cloves

Traditionally, in the Spice Islands where cloves are native, a clove tree was planted when a baby was born. If the tree grew strong and straight, so would the child. When the child was six, the tree would be ready for its first harvest. He or she might pick the first flower bud that would be dried and become a clove.

Clove buds are picked before the flower opens and then sun-dried. They turn reddish-brown and become hard. They look like rustic nails, which explains the French name *clou,* or nail. And they stick to almost anything. Studding a ham, roast, pineapple, or onion with cloves provides taste and aesthetic appeal. Each clove is packed with intense flavor so they are best used prudently. When you understand the nature of cloves, you can use them for a variety of purposes. They pair well with most spices and can be used in teas, pickling spices, mulled wine and cider, or ground over desserts. Cloves can be quite bitter, but cooking them tempers their flavor.

Cloves were among the hottest commodities in the fifteenth century. The Dutch and Portuguese traded control of the Spice Islands in their attempts to monopolize the clove trade. The Dutch employed a scorched clove policy when they torched all the clove trees save for those on Ambon island. Pirating a seedling was punishable by death. It wasn't until Pierre Poivre (yes, the Peter Pepper/Piper who picks pickled peppers) smuggled cloves out that the Dutch stranglehold was broken and cloves then thrived worldwide.

CULTIVATION CENTERS

Indonesia, Brazil, Madagascar, Zanzibar, Sumatra, Malaysia, Sri Lanka, Caribbean, Tanzania, Grenada

AROMA & FLAVOR

Cloves have an earthy, burning but sweet and musty aroma. They have a bitter taste, accompanied by a sharpness and numbing quality if chewed.

MEDICINAL USES

helps, treats, prevents, or aids circulatory disorders, digestion, blood clots, herpes, cancer, toothaches, hepatitis C, gum disease, and bad breath; clove oil repels mosquitos (fewer bites); antimicrobial and antifungal properties

COMMON FORMS

whole and ground

COMPLEMENTS

cakes like apple tarts, chocolate and sweets, coffee, fruit, ham, meat, roasts, sausage, stews, winter and root vegetables (pumpkins, squash, carrots, beets, cabbage)

PAIRS WELL WITH

allspice, amchur, cardamom, chiles, cinnamon, cocoa, coriander, cumin, nutmeg, star anise, tamarind, turmeric

Galangal

Laos root, Thai ginger, greater galangal

If you enjoy Thai food, you're already familiar with one of the signature flavors. In Thai, galangal is *kha,* recognizable to some from the chicken soup with coconut, *tom kha gai.* The warming, substantiating nature of this spice will have you wondering what else it can be used for.

Greater galangal is the mildest, most familiar to our palettes and used most often for cooking. Both lesser and kaempferia galangal are found in Indonesian, Thai, and Malaysian cuisine, and are used medicinally. They are harsher than greater galangal and have a hot, pungent taste—lesser galangal with a eucalyptus kick, and kaempferia with a camphor note.

Comparing greater galangal side-by-side with ginger leaves no doubt as to their relation. Galangal is the knobbier, bulkier sibling. There is some debate on the interchangeability of galangal and ginger in recipes. They have distinct flavors, but the suggestion to use double the amount of ginger for the quantity called for galangal is a good starting point.

You'll have to go to the specialty store or online for this gem, but it's worth giving it a try. Stored properly, ground galangal can last 6 months to 1 year and dried slices up to 3 years. Experiment first with its ground form as the slices require soaking before using. When using fresh galangal, store it wrapped in plastic in the refrigerator.

CULTIVATION CENTERS

China, Thailand, Malaysia, Indonesia

AROMA & FLAVOR

Galangal has a bit of pepper and ginger in its fragrance with a note of sourness. It tastes woody and bitter, even peppery-hot, on its own, but when added to other flavors it becomes calmer and augments its companions.

MEDICINAL USES

helps, treats, prevents, or aids allergies, cancer, type 2 diabetes, ulcers, indigestion, respiratory problems, digestive issues; eases arthritis

COMMON FORMS AND VARIETIES

rhizomes, dried and sliced, then ground: varieties include greater (used most), lesser, and kaempferia

COMPLEMENTS

chicken, coconut, curries, marinades, soups, stews, stir-fries, Thai food

PAIRS WELL WITH

allspice, cardamom, chiles, cinnamon, coriander, fenugreek, garlic, lemongrass, mustard seeds, tamarind, turmeric

Ginger

gingerroot, root ginger, green ginger, stem ginger, black ginger

Ginger is the heralded rhizome (underground root) of a flowering tropical plant native to Asia—China, India, or both. The name derives from the Sanskrit *shringabera,* which translates as "the shape of an antler." When fresh, the root evokes a blunt, knobby horn. Cutting into the fingers—the small branches—reveals a fibrous but succulent interior. When dried, it shrinks and from there can be ground into a fine powder.

Ginger features heavily not only in regional Chinese cuisines, but also in every region in this book. Arab traders introduced it to the Middle East and Europe. The Portuguese brought it to Africa. The Spanish realized early in the sixteenth century that it would grow well in the Caribbean, where it went on to thrive.

Using ginger in your cooking is enjoyable, healthy, and rewarding. Experimentation is boundless because of the various forms and methods by which ginger is processed. It can be chopped, julienned, diced, or shaved. Pickled, preserved, or Crystallized Ginger (page 6) is a delight. Dried and ground gingers are equally useful, if less intense and pungent than fresh. Try finely grating fresh ginger and adding the residue juice to embolden fish marinades and steak sauces.

Growing your own ginger is easy. Break off a fresh 2-inch long piece. Plant it with cactus soil, and water occasionally for a month. It will start to grow! Break off and plant additional pieces as needed.

CULTIVATION CENTERS

India (Cochin and Calicut ginger), Jamaica, Africa, China, Japan, Hawaii, northern Australia

AROMA & FLAVOR

Varies by variety and origin and type. Fresh ginger smells like spring. It is spicy, fresh, citrusy, and biting as well as quite fragrant. Dried ginger is less piquant and less aromatic but still warming.

MEDICINAL USES

helps, treats, prevents, or aids nausea, motion sickness, morning sickness, asthma, digestion, sore throat, pain stemming from arthritis, migraines, heartburn, stomachaches, cholesterol issues, blood clotting that leads to heart attacks and strokes

COMMON FORMS AND VARIETIES

fresh, whole rhizomes; dried, slices and ground; crystalized; varieties include Cochin ginger, Chinese ginger, Jamaican ginger, African ginger

COMPLEMENTS

baked goods, cakes, cheese plates/ dishes, chutneys, curries, fish, ginger beer or cider, honey or coconut, meats (particularly for tenderizing and preserving), mulled wine, pork, pumpkin and squash, pickles, poultry, puddings, shellfish, soups, stir-fries, sweet potatoes, sushi, tea, vegetables

PAIRS WELL WITH

allspice, anardana, chiles, cinnamon, cloves, coriander, cumin, fennel seeds, garlic, lemon peel, mustard seeds, parsley, scallions, sesame seeds, star anise, tamarind, turmeric, vanilla

Lemon Peel

Ever present on the counter of my nonna's kitchen in Italy is a large jar of lemon peels soaking in high-proof alcohol. They're on a journey to becoming bright and delicious limoncello.

Lemon and lime peel has been cherished since the first cultivation of citrus in Asia thousands of years ago. As they moved west, different cultures developed them to varying degrees of utility. Egyptians made lemons part of their embalming practices. Greeks and Romans valued the fruit for its medicinal attributes. The Spanish brought seeds of the fruit to the Americas. On the high seas, so effective was citrus at preventing scurvy, the British Navy mandated every seaman be given a ration.

Lemon zest, which can be used fresh or dried, can magnify a variety of dishes. In baking, especially with fruit, my mother's secret trick is to always add a dash of lemon zest in the crust *and* in the filling, especially for blueberry pie.

Both lemons and limes are used as a souring agent in cooking, and go well in chutneys. Working with them is satisfying because you can use the flesh, juice, and zest for different purposes, sometimes in the same recipe.

CULTIVATION CENTERS

Asia, India, southern and eastern Europe, South America, southern United States and California, Mexico, Caribbean

AROMA & FLAVOR

Citrus zest is aromatically piney, clean, and sweet. The taste is generally bitter and astringent, depending on the type.

MEDICINAL USES

helps, treats, prevents, or aids vitamin C deficiency and scurvy, builds immunity for colds and flu, kidney stones, sore throats

COMMON FORMS AND VARIETIES

Lemon: fresh peel, grated, peeled, or julienned; dried, grated; varieties include Lisboa and Meyer. Black Lime: dried, whole, broken, or ground; varieties include Persian, called omani

COMPLEMENTS

baked goods like crusts, pies, and breads; garnish for ice cream, cakes, custards, or tarts; jams, jellies, and pie filling, especially fruit; liqueurs, cocktails, and tinctures marinades for fish and shellfish; sauces for rice and pilafs; vinegars, pastes, and rubs

PAIRS WELL WITH

allspice, basil, black pepper, caraway, cardamom, chiles, cilantro, cloves, coriander, cumin, dill, fennel seeds, ginger, oregano, poppy seeds, rosemary, sesame seeds, turmeric

Mace

fleur de muscade (flower of nutmeg)

In West Africa, I once spotted a scorpion so large that I diverted my course by way of a leafy tree littered at the base with small, plum-like fruits. A few had halved, revealing a pliable, lacelike red aril enveloping a dark nut. I picked one up. My colleague, Anointed, explained that the tree and seed was nutmeg and the brain-like covering was also used as a spice. That spice is mace.

Mace is one of the native ingredients responsible for the mythical stature of the Moluccas in Indonesia, known as the Spice Islands. Much like cassia to cinnamon, mace gets cast as nutmeg's understudy. This charismatic and blossoming spice can be used for a variety of purposes. In the spice lexicon, the brainy aril is referred to as blades. The blades are removed from the nutmeg seed and sun-dried for several hours. From there it is packaged whole, ground, or processed into oil or butter.

Mace is nice to have on hand, especially for pairing with sweets and desserts—think cheesecake, ice cream, or custard. If nutmeg is the heavy-handed bass note to a dish, mace's understated charisma is an uplifting side riff. It is more useful to purchase ground mace because grinding whole ones can be an ordeal.

CULTIVATION CENTERS

Indonesia (Molucca and Banda Islands), India, Sri Lanka, Malaysia, Sumatra, Brazil, Caribbean, Granada

AROMA & FLAVOR

Mace has a spiced, clove-like and piney scent, if not somewhat bitter. It tastes of cinnamon, pepper, and a subtler, sweeter, more herbaceous version of nutmeg.

MEDICINAL USES

helps, treats, prevents, or aids stomach pains, dysentery, vomiting, bad breath, malarial symptoms

COMMON FORMS AND VARIETIES

whole, as dried blades or ground; varieties include Indonesian mace (red-orange) and Grenadian mace (yellow-orange/brown).

COMPLEMENTS

béchamel and cream sauces; broths and stocks; cakes, cookies, and pastries; chocolate; curries; custards; desserts; doughnuts; ice cream; icings; poultry, lamb, fish, and sausages; pumpkins, squash, and winter veggies; seafood; soups, stews,

PAIRS WELL WITH

amchur, black pepper, cardamom, cinnamon, cloves, coriander, galangal, ginger, lemon peel, nutmeg, sugar, turmeric

Nutmeg

Nutmeg is the dried seed kernel of the nutmeg tree, indigenous to the Spice Islands. It shares a history with mace, the lacy membrane that surrounds the seed inside the nutmeg fruit. Nutmeg made its way to Europe early, as Arab traders understood the demand for its medicinal and seasoning qualities. Those attributes would come to be central to the great warring nations of the day. As a symbol of wealth, when the English established nutmeg groves in Grenada the supply of the spice increased. In eighteenth-century Connecticut—the Nutmeg State—residents imitated their European forbearers who would carry around a silver grater with nutmeg so they could sprinkle fresh spice on their meals, and perhaps demonstrate they could afford to do so.

A steady supply of nutmeg lives in my kitchen. It is a multifaceted spice that carries its own weight, and more, in any dish. I find it an absolute necessity, along with smoked paprika and cinnamon, in half-Yukon, half–sweet potato shaved hash browns. My mother uses nutmeg in her dreamlike spinach lasagna. My nonna enhances her distinctive béchamel lasagna with it.

Nutmeg quickly fades once ground, so buy whole and grate it when needed. You only need a little because of its potency. If you find an antique nutmeg grater, it adds a nostalgic flair to your kitchen.

CULTIVATION CENTERS

Indonesia (Molucca and Banda Islands), India, Sri Lanka, Malaysia, Sumatra, Brazil, Caribbean, Granada

AROMA & FLAVOR

The aroma of nutmeg is earthy, peppery, and sort of sweetly clean in the way that menthol or eucalyptus smells fresh. The taste is woody and bitter but warm. It leaves a pungent, almost antiseptic or minty feeling on your tongue.

MEDICINAL USES

helps, treats, prevents, or aids anxiety, digestion, nausea, diarrhea, cholesterol, depression, suppressed libido, memory loss, epilepsy

COMMON FORMS AND VARIETIES

large seed, whole and ground; varieties include Indonesian nutmeg (higher volatile oil content) and Caribbean nutmeg

COMPLEMENTS

coconut, chocolate, and lemon cake; cooked fruit (like fried plantains); custards and rice pudding; eggnog, punches, mulled wine, cider; pasta and rice; pies, sweet rolls, banana and pumpkin breads; potatoes, vegetable soup, and stews; seafood, shellfish, and poultry

PAIRS WELL WITH

allspice, amchur, black pepper, cardamom, cinnamon, cloves, coriander, ginger, lemongrass, vanilla

Star Anise

Indian anise, Chinese anise, Badian anise

There are generally eight adjoining wing-like, seed-filled hulls that comprise each star anise. It's known for settling the tummy and is delightfully refreshing.

Star anise could be considered the national ingredient of China. It is a trademark flavor across the country and a signature component of Thousand-Year sauce, a master stock that traditional Chinese cooks "keep going" for months or even years. The tree from which star anise fruit are picked is native to, not coincidentally, China. The tree begins bearing fruit after six years and continues for the next hundred. Once the fruits are dried, they harden to deep, driftwood brown and keep for years. This spice has longevity at every life stage.

It made its way out of China on the usual spice routes. In Southeast Asia, it is a requisite for many soups and curries. In India, it features in the cuisines of Kashmir and Goa. Eventually, the Caribbean embraced it for masalas and various spice mixes.

I find delight in the aesthetic and rustic visage that star anise delivers. Immediately identifiable by its starry appearance, it especially draws the eye because cooking with it only requires one or two stars. Generally, toss the star anise after cooking. It is notoriously difficult to grind so it's better to buy preground if using in that capacity.

CULTIVATION CENTERS

China, Vietnam, India, Japan, Korea

AROMA & FLAVOR

The aroma of star anise is unmistakably licorice-like with sweet tones of fennel. The taste is warming, spicy-sweet, and, in my opinion, includes hints of woody mint.

MEDICINAL USES

helps, treats, prevents, or aids stomach pain and colic, HIV/AIDS, flu, cold sores, certain cancers, dementia, digestion, bad breath, tooth decay, cough.

COMMON FORMS

Eight-point fruit pods, whole, broken, or ground; whole seeds

COMPLEMENTS

Asian dishes (stir-fries); braised fish and shellfish; cordials, liqueurs, syrups, and sweets; curries and masalas; roasted or steamed meats, poultry, and fish; simmered veggies; soups and stews, especially pho

PAIRS WELL WITH

allspice, anise, black pepper, cardamom, chiles, cinnamon, cumin, curry leaves, fennel and fennel seeds, ginger, mint, nutmeg, rosehips, vanilla

Szechuan, Sansho, and Other Peppers

Szechuan pepper (fagara), sansho pepper, long pepper, cubeb pepper

Szechuan pepper comes from a small, prickly ash tree native to China. It's not related to black pepper but can be used in a similar manner and is a delightful substitute. Its husks are reddish-brown to earthy burnt sienna. They ripen on the vine prior to picking and subsequent sun-drying. The bitter black seeds are discarded. The thorns and short stems can stay attached until you're ready to use it. Toasting it is highly recommended to intensify the bouquet of the spice. Most notably it is used in Chinese Five-Spice Blend (page 94).

Japanese *sansho* pepper also comes from a prickly ash and is a close relative of Szechuan pepper. It is almost always sold preground. In Japan, it is used as a table spice to sprinkle on a dish before eating. Sansho pepper contributes to a host of dishes including Shichimi Togarashi Blend (page 95) and Japanese seven-spice blend and is used for noodles, tempura, fatty foods, and soups.

Two other peppers you might encounter are long pepper and cubeb peppers. They are available, though uncommon, in the West, but you may find them in India, China, or Southeast Asia. Long pepper made its way to Europe from India before black pepper and is responsible for the actual word pepper. They look like 1-inch-long mini-pinecones. Cubeb peppers are native to Indonesia and are similar to cassia berries with a little tail. It is popular in Indonesian and West Africa.

CULTIVATION CENTERS

China, Japan, India, Southeast Asia, West Africa

AROMA & FLAVOR

Szechuan pepper is slightly bitter, but earthy and piquant with a note of citrus. Sansho pepper is tangy and pungent yet fainter and citrusy. They both provide the same tingly numbness as black pepper.

MEDICINAL USES

Folklore suggests ancient Chinese civilizations used Szechuan pepper for dysentery. This theory is unfounded by modern scientific methods. Cubeb oil is used in throat lozenges.

COMMON FORMS

Szechuan pepper: whole, cracked dried berries or ground; Sansho pepper: ground

COMPLEMENTS

citrus, fish, legumes, meat, poultry, soy and plum sauce, vegetable dishes

PAIRS WELL WITH

black pepper, chiles, citrus peel, poppy seeds

Wasabi

Japanese horseradish

Anyone who frequents sushi and sashimi restaurants is surely familiar with wasabi—that sculpted, toothpaste-like clump of green supervising your raw fish. Oftentimes this version is not made with real wasabi but horseradish.

Real wasabi, commonly used in its native Japan, is less known in the West unless we know where to look. The leaves of the plant have a lily pad–esque look about them. It grows along the mountain streams in the cooler parts of Japan. The rhizome of the wasabi plant is harvested and used fresh, or dried and ground into powder. Wasabi delivers a fierce punch of sweet heat. If fresh, to retain the oils and for texture, Japanese chefs grate it from an oroshigane (page 13).

We do have access to the dried powder online, at your specialty spice store, or perhaps even at your supermarket. It comes in neat little tins. You'll want to scope out the listed ingredients. If it has additional ingredients like mustard or dye, move on. Though it can be real, beware of wasabi in a tube. It may actually be horseradish or if it is wasabi, it loses flavor quickly. Mix your own instead.

Wasabi paste is incredibly easy to make: equal parts powder and water and let it sit for at least 10 minutes to develop its flavor. It is tremendous for experimenting with pungency. Put a dab in your next barbecue sauce or seafood marinade and see if you like the effect.

CULTIVATION CENTERS

Japan, some in Korea, New Zealand, Taiwan, China, Oregon

AROMA & FLAVOR

Dried wasabi does not pack much punch, but when water is added it activates and is piquant, although less aromatic than fresh wasabi. It singes the nostrils with a biting heat that has an almost sanitizing quality. It tastes like a sharp horseradish but also has sweetly nutty undertones.

MEDICINAL USES

helps, treats, prevents, or aids various cancers (breast, metastasis, stomach cancer, colon cancer, leukemia), food poisoning, ulcers, issues stemming from cholesterol, tooth decay, osteoporosis (helps increase bone density), eczema, skin itching, inflammation

COMMON FORMS

rhizome, dried powder, paste

COMPLEMENTS

beef and pork rubs and marinades; chicken; cooked fish; creamy dressings for salad; nori (seaweed); omelets; pickled veggies; raw seafood, sushi, and sashimi; rice and tofu; soba and udon noodles; soy sauce dishes

PAIRS WELL WITH

bay leaf, coriander, garlic, ginger, mustard seeds, parsley, sesame seeds, sugar

RECITES

Chinese Five-Spice Blend 94

Shichimi Togarashi Blend 95

Vietnamese Lemongrass Dry Rub 96

Thai Red Curry Rub 97

Malaysian Coconut Curry Paste 98

Chinese Sweet Bean Paste 99

South Pacific Honey Paste 100

Gomasio Lemon Dressing Marinade 101

Kalba Korean Marinade 102

Thai Satay Marinade 103

Asian Cold Noodle Dressing 104

Miso Doko Marinade 105

Peach-Plum Sauce 106

Sweet Orange Chili Sauce 107

Wasabi Mayonnaise Sauce 108

Mustard Miso Sauce 109

Wasabi Steak Sauce 110

Teriyaki Wasabi Sauce 111

Left: Peach-Plum Sauce (page 106)

Chinese Five-Spice Blend

duck, pork, poultry, roasted vegetables, tofu

Chinese five-spice blend is a popular flavoring agent and condiment across southern China and Vietnam. It's handy to have in your toolbox to deliver regional specificity when cooking Chinese food. It can be used to make pastes, marinades, and sauces when combined with jams, vinegars, and soy sauce.

MAKES ABOUT ¼ CUP

2 tablespoons Szechuan peppercorns

4 star anise

1 cassia cinnamon stick, broken into small pieces, or 2 teaspoons ground cassia cinnamon

1 tablespoon fennel seeds

1 tablespoon whole cloves

1. In a small skillet over medium heat, toast all the ingredients for 1 to 2 minutes. Transfer to a dish and let cool.

2. Pulverize the toasted spices in a spice grinder into a fine powder. Store in an airtight jar for up to 6 months, but the blend is best used as soon as possible.

Recipe Tip: If Szechuan peppercorns are not available, use allspice instead. Worst case scenario, use black peppercorns, but that is not ideal as they combine for a different taste.

Shichimi Togarashi Blend

grilled pork and chicken, oily fish, tempura, udon and soba noodles, use as a table condiment

This blend is a popular Japanese mixture sometimes called seven-spice powder. The blend's uniqueness is that the ingredients provide a layer of flavors as opposed to heat being the primary protagonist. It's a fun mix because it isn't pulverized into a fine powder, giving a textural element. **MAKES ABOUT ¾ CUP**

2 tablespoons sansho peppercorns

1 tablespoon red pepper flakes or 2 dried japonés chiles, if available

1 tablespoon dried orange peel

1 teaspoon grated black lime (optional)

2 teaspoons black sesame seeds, divided

2 teaspoons white sesame seeds, divided

1½ teaspoons ground ginger

1 sheet nori seaweed, flaked or shredded

2 teaspoons hemp seeds or poppy seeds

1. Combine the peppercorns, red pepper flakes, orange peel, black lime (if using), 1½ teaspoons of black sesame seeds, 1½ teaspoons of white sesame seeds, and ginger in a spice grinder. Pulse until coarsely ground.

2. Transfer the spices to a small bowl and combine with the remaining ½ teaspoon of black sesame seeds, remaining ½ teaspoon of white sesame seeds, nori, and hemp seeds.

3. Refrigerate in an airtight jar for up to 1 month.

Recipe Tip: Check at your local Asian market for sansho peppercorns or order them online. Citrus peel can be made by cutting the peel into thin slices and leaving them out in a dry, dark place for several days or by baking on low heat (150°F to 200°F) for 30 minutes to 1 hour.

Vietnamese Lemongrass Dry Rub

chicken, duck, gamey meats, pork

We're fortunate in New Orleans to have all the gifts of a local Vietnamese popu-lation, and there is no better cure for sickness than a steaming bowl of pho. This dry rub will get you on your way to seasoning the meat portion of any soup or stew. MAKES ¼ CUP

1 tablespoon Chinese Five-Spice Blend (page 94)

1 teaspoon ground ginger

1 teaspoon ground lemongrass

1 teaspoon dried dill weed

1 teaspoon mace

1 teaspoon palm sugar or brown sugar

1 cilantro stalk, shredded

Combine the Chinese five-spice blend, ginger, lemongrass, dill weed, mace, sugar, and cilantro in a jar. Shake to combine. Seal the jar and refrigerate for up to 3 months.

Recipe Tip: If you have an aversion to cilantro, use a few mint leaves instead. It changes the flavor but works just as well. You can also garnish your finished dish with chives.

Thai Red Curry Rub

chicken, beef, ground meat

Red curry is Thailand's fiery, tangy curry known as kaeng pet kat. *This version harnesses the sour-spicy majesty typical of Thai cuisine with lemon peel, lime leaves, and lemongrass. If the chiles are too hot, use as few as two; for more heat, use as many as 10.* MAKES ABOUT 1 CUP

1 tablespoon coriander seeds

1 teaspoon cumin seeds

1 teaspoon black peppercorns

8 Thai chiles, stemmed and seeded

1 tablespoon ground galangal

2 shallots, chopped

1 teaspoon dried lemon peel

1 bunch fresh cilantro, leaves only

2 dried kaffir lime leaves

3 garlic cloves, chopped

2 lemongrass stalks, chopped

2 tablespoons shrimp paste

1. In a small skillet over medium heat, toast the coriander, cumin, and peppercorns for 1 to 2 minutes. Transfer to a dish and let cool.

2. In the same skillet, toast the chiles. Transfer to a separate dish and let cool.

3. Grind the toasted spices in a spice grinder. Transfer to a small bowl. Add the galangal to the bowl. Then pulse the chiles in the grinder so they have large chunks, and add them to the bowl.

4. Chop the lemongrass by shedding the outer layers, cutting off the top, and slicing the soft yellow inner stalk.

5. Add the lemongrass, shallots, lemon peel, cilantro, lime leaves, garlic, and shrimp paste to a food processor and process until grainy and coarse, like grits. Transfer to the bowl with the spices and chiles and mix together until well combined.

6. Refrigerate in an airtight container for no more than 2 days.

Recipe Tip: If you can't find shrimp paste, you can use fish or anchovy paste. The alternatives substitute nicely, but the curry won't be red.

Malaysian Coconut Curry Paste

chicken, fish, shrimp, vegetable curries

I have a crush on coconut milk, which is used often in Malay curries. This curry is fun because it is an opportunity to use your mortar and pestle, leaving chunky bits of nuts and texture in the final product. **MAKES ABOUT 1½ CUPS**

1 tablespoon
coriander seeds

1 tablespoon cumin seeds

1 teaspoon fennel seeds

1 teaspoon black
peppercorns, Sarawak
if available

1 dried bird's eye
chile (optional)

¼ cup cashews or peanuts

2 teaspoons ground
turmeric

1 teaspoon ground mace

½ teaspoon dried
lemon peel

½ teaspoon ground
cayenne pepper

½ teaspoon ground
cassia cinnamon

¼ teaspoon grated nutmeg

1 teaspoon coconut oil

6 lemongrass stalks

1 (1-inch) piece fresh
ginger, minced

1 cup coconut milk

¼ cup chicken or
vegetable stock

Salt to taste

1. In a small skillet over medium-low heat, toast the coriander, cumin, fennel, peppercorns and chile (if using) until their aromas are released, 1 to 2 minutes. Transfer to a dish and let cool.

2. Grind the toasted spices in a spice grinder. Transfer to a small bowl. Grind the cashews and add them to the bowl. Add the turmeric, mace, lemon peel, cayenne, cinnamon, and nutmeg to the bowl and mix until well combined. This blend can be stored in an airtight jar for up to 3 months.

3. Chop the lemongrass by shedding the outer layers, cutting off the top, and slicing the soft inner stalk.

4. In a small skillet over medium heat, heat the oil. Sauté the lemongrass and ginger for 2 to 3 minutes. Reduce the heat to low and slowly whisk in the coconut milk and stock. Stir in the spice blend and continue cooking until the sauce thickens, 10 to 20 minutes. If the sauce becomes too thick, thin it with additional coconut milk. Season with salt and use immediately.

Recipe Tip: This recipe is enough for about 20 large shrimp, my preferred protein for this sauce.

Chinese Sweet Bean Paste

chicken, curries, fried and roasted vegetables, pork, seafood, shrimp, stir-fries, and as a marinade or paste

Black bean paste is a prominent flavoring sauce across Asia but especially in China and Vietnam. Korea, Cambodia, Thailand, and Laos have their own versions as well. The star anise in this paste takes it to an extra spicy-sweet level.

MAKES 1 TO 1½ CUPS

4½ tablespoons fermented black soy beans

6 teaspoons peanut oil, divided

1 (1-inch) piece fresh ginger, minced

2 garlic cloves, minced

½ teaspoon sesame oil

1 tablespoon rice vinegar

1 tablespoon mirin or rice wine

1 tablespoon chili paste, 2 teaspoons red pepper flakes, or 1 Thai chile pepper and 1 teaspoon vinegar

1 tablespoon brown sugar

1 teaspoon black peppercorns, toasted and ground

½ teaspoon soy sauce

¼ cup water

2 star anise

Salt to taste

1. In a small bowl, cover the fermented black beans in cool or room temperature water and let them reconstitute for about 30 minutes. Drain and rinse them. Put them in a small bowl and mash with a fork or the back of a spoon.

2. Heat 1 teaspoon of peanut oil in a medium skillet over medium heat. Add the ginger and garlic and sauté until golden brown, 1 to 2 minutes. Add the bean mash, remaining 5 teaspoons of peanut oil, and the sesame oil, rice vinegar, mirin, chili paste, brown sugar, black pepper, soy sauce, water, and star anise. Reduce the heat to medium-low and cook, uncovered, for 20 minutes, stirring and mashing until a thick paste develops. Remove and discard the star anise. Season with salt.

3. Refrigerate in an airtight container for up to 1 week.

Recipe Tip: Add several spoonfuls of black bean paste to almost any Asian recipe to increase the fullness of the dish. Veggies, meat, and chicken curries are particularly suitable.

South Pacific Honey Paste

chicken, light game, fish, pork, seafood such as shrimp

This paste, inspired by the Thai Red Curry Rub (page 97), doubles as a marinade for lighter fare. The sharp, hot chiles and peppercorns are intended to cut the sweetness of the honey. Make extra and use it to baste grilled pineapple, stone fruits, or vegetables. The chiles can be seeded before toasting to decrease the heat level, if preferred. **MAKES ABOUT ⅓ CUP**

2 teaspoons black
peppercorns

2 dried Thai chiles

2 teaspoons whole cloves

1 dried kaffir lime leaf

2 tablespoons
ground galangal

2 tablespoons ground ginger

1 teaspoon ground
lemongrass

1 teaspoon dried mint

1 teaspoon salt

6 tablespoons honey

1. In a small skillet over medium-low heat, lightly toast the peppercorns, chiles, and cloves for 1 to 2 minutes. Transfer to a dish and let cool.

2. Grind the toasted spices with the lime leaf in a spice grinder. Transfer to a small bowl. Add the galangal, ginger, lemongrass, mint, and salt to the bowl and mix to combine.

3. Melt the honey in a small saucepan over low heat, 2 to 3 minutes. Add to the bowl of spices and stir to combine. Use immediately.

Recipe Tip: To use as a marinade, massage the paste into the protein with your hands and refrigerate it, covered, for 4 hours. Pan fry the protein in a skillet in a thin layer of oil.

Gomasio Lemon Dressing Marinade

asparagus, broccoli, green vegetables (such as green beans), rice vegetable dishes, snow and snap peas

Gomasio is a traditional table condiment made with toasted black sesame seeds and a coarse salt and used to season rice and raw vegetables. This vegetable marinade goes one step further, combining gomasio with lemon and ginger to enliven fresh veggies. MAKES ABOUT 1 CUP

3 tablespoons black or white sesame seeds

1 tablespoon sea salt

1 teaspoon toasted sesame oil

1 tablespoon dried lemon peel

1 (1-inch) piece fresh ginger, grated

2 tablespoons rice wine vinegar

1 lemon (1 teaspoon freshly grated lemon zest and freshly squeezed lemon juice)

1. To make the gomasio, toast the sesame seeds in a skillet over low heat for 1 to 2 minutes, or until fragrant. Transfer to a dish and let cool, then grind in a spice grinder. Transfer to a glass jar and add the salt. This can be stored in the airtight jar for 1 year.

2. To make the marinade, heat the sesame oil in a small skillet over medium-low heat. Add the lemon peel and ginger and sauté until lightly browned, 1 to 2 minutes. Transfer to a small bowl with the gomasio, vinegar, lemon zest, and a squeeze of lemon juice. Stir to combine.

3. Store the marinade in an airtight container for up to 1 week, but it's best if used immediately.

Recipe Tip: To marinate, add your preferred vegetables to a large bowl and coat with the marinade. Let it sit for 30 minutes. Bring ⅛ to ¼ inch water to a boil in a saucepan. Add the marinade and vegetables to the pan, reduce the heat to medium, cover the pan, and cook until the veggies start to brown. Remove the pan from the heat, drizzle a squeeze of lemon juice over the veggies, and serve. Garnish with toasted white and black sesame seeds for color and to increase the intensity of flavor.

Kalba Korean Marinade

duck, goose, lamb chops, red meat, short ribs

How enchanting are Korean short ribs? Based on this recipe from Beeta Moha-jeri, who sharpened her Asian cuisine teeth in the LA food truck scene, you will be as thoroughly enamored as I am. Beeta's kalba uses star anise, kaffir lime leaf, and a healthy dose of ginger and garlic. **MAKES ABOUT 3½ CUPS**

1 cup soy sauce

½ cup water

¼ cup mirin or rice wine

4 tablespoons minced garlic

2 tablespoons dark sesame oil

1 (1-inch) piece fresh ginger, grated, or 2 teaspoons ground ginger

3 dried kaffir lime leaves

2 star anise

2 scallions, thinly sliced

1 small onion, finely grated

1 Asian pear, sliced

In a food processor or blender, combine all the ingredients and blend until smooth. Refrigerate in an airtight jar for up to 1 week, but the marinade is best if used immediately.

Recipe Tip: Beeta's kalba short ribs are easy to make: Sprinkle 1 cup brown sugar over 5 pounds Korean-style beef short ribs. Massage the sugar into the meat and let them sit for 10 minutes in a bowl covered with a kitchen towel. Put the sugared meat in a zip-top bag and pour in the marinade. Shake well. Refrigerate for at least 4 hours or overnight. Grill the ribs for about 4 minutes on each side. Be sure to first spray the grill or the grill pan with nonstick cooking spray.

Thai Satay Marinade

chicken, grilled beef, pork, skewered meats

Satay, the traditional marinade in Thailand and Malaysia, has roots in Arabic kebabs. Satay is typically served with a peanut dipping sauce, but chicken and beef can be the stars without it. Keep some chili paste to the side and use it as a dip. MAKES ABOUT 2¼ CUPS

1 tablespoon coconut oil

½ small onion, minced

1 garlic clove, minced

½ cup roasted, unsalted peanuts

2 tablespoons brown sugar

1 tablespoon peanut oil

1 tablespoon soy sauce

1 tablespoon chili paste, 2 teaspoons red pepper flakes, or 1 Thai chile pepper and 1 teaspoon vinegar

1 teaspoon ground galangal

1 teaspoon ground cumin

1 teaspoon ground lemongrass

1 teaspoon freshly grated lemon zest

½ teaspoon ground turmeric

½ teaspoon ground mace

1 cup coconut milk

Freshly squeezed lemon juice

Salt

1. Heat the coconut oil in a medium skillet over medium heat. Add the onion and garlic and sauté until golden brown, 4 to 5 minutes.

2. Process the peanuts in a food processor by pulsing so they are mostly crushed with some bigger bits remaining. Add the peanut mash, brown sugar, peanut oil, soy sauce, chili paste, galangal, cumin, lemongrass, lemon zest, turmeric, and mace. Stir to combine. Reduce the heat to low and add the coconut milk and a squeeze of lemon juice. Simmer, stirring constantly, for 3 minutes. Season with salt.

3. The marinade is best if used right away, but it can be refrigerated in an airtight container for 2 to 4 days. Bring it to room temperature before spreading it over meat to marinate.

Recipe Tip: Marinate chicken, beef, or pork with the marinade in a zip-top bag in the refrigerator for at least 3 hours and up to 24 hours. Overnight works best.

Asian Cold Noodle Dressing

noodle dishes, rice, salads

This recipe is inspired by one taught to me by Charles and Miranda "Wink" Shackleton, whom I met on an expedition to Antarctica. They're relatives of polar explorer Ernest Shackleton. It is perfect for a quick dressing, marinade, or mixing sauce, especially if you have Chinese Five-Spice Blend already made. I use toasted nigella seeds for a nutty, warm flavor, and a nice crunch. **MAKES ABOUT 1 CUP**

4 tablespoons nigella seeds (or 5 tablespoons black sesame seeds)

8 tablespoons toasted sesame oil, divided

1 garlic clove, minced

1 (½-inch) piece fresh ginger, minced

6 tablespoons soy sauce or tamari

1 tablespoon Chinese Five-Spice Blend (page 94)

1. In a small skillet over low heat, lightly toast the nigella seeds until they are brittle, 1 to 2 minutes. Transfer to a dish and let cool.

2. Heat 1 tablespoon of sesame oil in the skillet over medium heat. Add the garlic and ginger and sauté until golden, 1 to 2 minutes. Transfer to a small bowl and add the remaining 7 tablespoons of oil, soy sauce, Chinese Five-Spice Blend, and the toasted nigella seeds. Mix to combine well.

3. Refrigerate in an airtight container for up to 1 week.

Recipe Tip: Break fettuccine, linguine, or vermicelli noodles into thirds and boil until al dente. You'll want to use 2 cups noodles for every 3 tablespoons dressing. Mix with sautéed julienned green and red bell peppers, scallions, and stemmed watercress. Season with salt. Drizzle with the dressing and garnish with chopped fresh parsley for a perfect summer salad.

Miso Doko Marinade

beef, chicken, fish, pork

I thought I knew something about sushi and accompanying sauces until one meal with Chef Kaz Ishikawa obliterated my brain. He precisely builds all of his sauces and marinades to achieve certain flavor reactions. Ginger and sake support the miso in this insanely appetizing marinade, courtesy of Kaz. **MAKES 1¼ CUPS**

1 cup white miso

3½ tablespoons sugar

2 tablespoons sake

2 tablespoons mirin

1 teaspoon soy sauce

½ teaspoon ground ginger

½ teaspoon ground garlic

In a medium bowl, whisk together the miso and sugar. Combine the sake and mirin and slowly mix it into the miso. You can adjust how sweet you want the marinade by adding slightly more mirin. Lastly, mix in the soy sauce, ginger, and garlic. Refrigerate in an airtight container for up to 2 weeks.

Recipe Tip: Marinate proteins in this for several hours, refrigerated, then grill or fry. Instead of ground ginger and ground garlic, you can use fresh ginger and fresh garlic for a more potent flavor.

Peach-Plum Sauce

duck, goose, pork, poultry, scallops, veal

This peach sauce is a riff on tangy-tart Chinese-style plum sauce. The combination is pure magic. Sweet and tart, this sauce doesn't overpower fatty proteins. I've seen people lick their plates after finishing their meal to savor every last bit of sauce. Enjoy on meats and even on desserts. MAKES ABOUT 2 CUPS

1 apple, peeled and
thinly sliced

8 tablespoons sugar, divided

¾ cup apple cider
vinegar, divided

½ pound yellow
peaches, chopped

½ pound plums, chopped

1 star anise

1 (1-inch) piece fresh
ginger, grated

1 teaspoon cassia cinnamon

4 or 5 whole cloves

1 teaspoon Chinese Five-
Spice Blend (spage 94)

Soy sauce

1. Bleed the apple by mixing the slices with 2 tablespoons of sugar in a medium bowl. Let it sit for 30 minutes then drain the excess water.

2. In a large saucepan over medium-low heat, combine the apple and ¼ cup of vinegar, and soften for about 10 minutes. Add the peaches, plums, remaining 6 tablespoons of sugar, star anise, ginger, cinnamon, cloves, and remaining ½ cup of vinegar to the pan. Reduce the heat to low and simmer for 15 minutes. Remove and discard the star anise. Stir in the Chinese Five-Spice Blend. Cover the saucepan and cook for 30 minutes more. Remove the cloves.

3. Transfer the mixture to a food processor and purée the sauce. If you want a very fine consistency, strain the sauce through cheesecloth. Stir in a splash of soy sauce.

4. Refrigerate in an airtight container for up to 1 week.

Recipe Tip: If cooking duck, goose, pork, or other hearty, fatty meat, use the cloves to stud the meat, allowing their flavor to penetrate the flesh. It's also visually appealing.

Sweet Orange Chili Sauce

bison, duck, lamb chops

This recipe is inspired by my friend Wink and Charlie's friend Janet, who makes stellar lamb chops. This sauce is boosted by a star anise or two and a little galangal and nigella. The nigella goes especially brilliantly with lamb.

MAKES ABOUT 1½ CUPS

½ teaspoon nigella seeds

3 tablespoons dark sesame oil

6 thick lamb chops

½ cup minced onion

3 garlic cloves, minced

1 star anise

3 tablespoons soy sauce

3 tablespoons chili paste, like sambal oelek

¼ teaspoon ground galangal (optional)

¾ cup tart orange marmalade

1½ tablespoons rice wine vinegar

1 tablespoon minced fresh ginger

1. In a small skillet over medium heat, toast the nigella seeds for about 2 minutes. Transfer to a dish and let cool.

2. Heat the sesame oil in a large skillet over medium heat. Add the lamb chops and lightly brown on both sides. Transfer the chops to a paper towel–lined plate to drain.

3. Reduce the heat to low and add the onion, garlic, and star anise to the skillet. Cook, covered, for about 5 to 10 minutes or until tender and lightly colored. Stir in the nigella, soy sauce, chili paste, galangal (if using), marmalade, vinegar, and ginger. Simmer, stirring constantly, for 2 minutes.

4. Return the lamb chops to the skillet over medium heat, cover, and cook, turning them once, until done, about 8 minutes in total. Serve immediately, spooning sauce over the chops.

Recipe Tip: Lamb is the recommended protein for this sauce but it can be made with duck or game. The sauce recipe can be varied to suit different proteins. Play with the amounts to season each dish and determine what works best for you.

Wasabi Mayonnaise Sauce

burgers, fatty fish, and pork, or as a dipping sauce for fries, chips, and wings

Wasabi is a piquant addition to sauces and marinades. This mayonnaise sauce, based on a tip from the incomparable actor Alfre Woodard, works as a fish marinade and adds a flavor punch to pork, steak, or tuna. Alfre's note: "Wasabi in mayo and a squeeze of lemon changes the life of the spread." MAKES ABOUT ½ CUP

1 tablespoon water

1 tablespoon wasabi powder

4 tablespoons mayonnaise

1 tablespoon soy sauce

1 teaspoon freshly grated lemon zest

1 teaspoon sugar

1 teaspoon Shichimi Togarashi Blend (page 95)

Freshly squeezed lemon juice

1. In a small bowl, make a wasabi paste by mixing the water into the wasabi powder, stirring until it's well combined and consistent in texture. Let it sit for 10 minutes.

2. Add the mayonnaise, soy sauce, lemon zest, sugar, and spice blend and stir to combine. Stir in a squeeze of lemon juice. Refrigerate in an airtight container for 1 to 3 days.

Recipe Tip: Swap out the mayonnaise for 2 tablespoons rice vinegar to make a saucy steak marinade. Wasabi paste doesn't keep very long before it starts to lose flavor, so don't hold on to it for too long. You can also add more wasabi paste for a stronger kick.

Mustard Miso Sauce

chicken teriyaki, mushrooms, potatoes, sautéed pork, taro, tempe, tofu, vegetables

Miso, a wonderful flavor made from fermented soy and rice, is optimal as a sauce, soup, or marinade. Adding mustard, as Kaz Ishikawa has done in this recipe, takes it to another level. Skewered meat, dengaku *in Japanese, is a favored preparation to coat in plain miso before grilling.* MAKES ABOUT 2¾ CUPS

7 tablespoons red miso

7 tablespoons white miso

2 tablespoons sugar

⅔ cup soy sauce

⅔ cup mirin

½ cup sake

1 tablespoon tamari

1 tablespoon mayonnaise

1 teaspoon yellow mustard

In a medium bowl, mix the red and white miso together. Stir in the sugar. Then mix in the soy sauce, mirin, sake, and tamari. Lastly, stir in the mayonnaise and mustard. The sauce is best used right away, but it can be refrigerated in an airtight container for up to 1 week.

Recipe Tip: Add each liquid slowly, taking care to mix them in little by little. This enhances the textural smoothness of the miso.

Wasabi Steak Sauce

beef steak, chicken teriyaki, grilled fish

As Chef Kaz Ishikawa told me about how he orders wasabi and horseradish from Japan, where it grows along the cold mountain streams, all I could think about was eating his food. My mouth watering, he went on to describe the wasabi steak sauce he was thinking about contributing to this book. I'm so glad he did! MAKES ½ CUP

2 tablespoons red wine

4 teaspoons soy sauce

1 consommé cube dissolved in 2 ounces water

2 tablespoons mirin

2 teaspoons Wasabi Mayonnaise Sauce (page 108)

1 teaspoon cornstarch

Whisk together the wine, soy sauce, consommé, mirin, and wasabi paste in a small saucepan. Place the saucepan over low heat and continue stirring while it heats. Right before the mixture boils, whisk in the cornstarch. You can adjust the sauce thickness according to your preference by continuing to cook the sauce until it reaches your desired consistency. The sauce is best used right away, but it can be refrigerated in an airtight container for up to 1 week.

Recipe Tip: I've wanted to learn how to better use wasabi and use it more often. As an experiential learner, sometimes it takes knowing a trusted ally to teach you a recipe. This is a good one to open that door.

Teriyaki Wasabi Sauce

chicken

Teriyaki is a familiar flavor for many of us. It's actually easy to make and fun to experiment with. Here's how to use wasabi powder to make a kicking teriyaki marinade. Adjust the wasabi level (page 90) how you see fit. MAKES ABOUT 1½ CUPS

1 cup mirin

1 cup chicken or
vegetable stock

1 cup soy sauce

1 tablespoon Shichimi
Togarashi Blend (page 95)

1 teaspoon Wasabi
Mayonnaise Sauce
(page 108)

In a saucepan, bring the mirin, stock, and soy sauce to a boil. Boil the liquid down for about 10 minutes. Whisk in the shichimi togarashi blend and wasabi mayonnaise. Boil down another 10 minutes. Remove from liquid and let cool. Use immediately as a marinade or sauce.

Recipe Tip: Use the sauce to baste your protein to prevent it from drying. Add sherry or port to thicken the sauce and give it some "drunken" flavor.

4

The Americas

SPICES 115   **RECIPES** 139

An irreversible link was forged with the European "discovery" of the New World. The ingredient exchange since contact was made in 1492 serves as an example of unbridled, if accidental, collaboration. Though the Vikings had previously made journeys, the sustained agricultural impact of European exploration of the Americas introduced tomatoes, corn, potatoes, avocados, beans, chocolate, vanilla, and chile peppers to the Old World.

In New Orleans, known colloquially as the northernmost city of the Caribbean, we lack neither flavorful nor colorful food. We enjoy the best aspects of French, Spanish, and Dutch Caribbean cuisine with influences from Latin and Native North America. The best of American cooking—North, South, and Central—is at the heart of this culinary infusion, and the soul of gastronomic blending. The development of that soul, however, was achieved under horrendous circumstances.

When the conquistadors exploited and desecrated the people, land, and resources of Latin America, they introduced new flavors and cooking practices to already robust traditions. Citrus was introduced, as were pork, cattle, milk, butter, cheese, wheat, and sugar. In the succeeding centuries, enslaved Africans brought flavors and cooking methods from that continent, redeveloping their own practices with the ingredients available to them.

The main contribution of our hemisphere to the culinary landscape was chile peppers. But chiles are not the only spice defining the Americas. Vanilla is and was incredibly scarce until cultivators figured out how to hand-pollinate the flowers, which previously had been performed by a specific type of Mexican bee. Allspice has had many lives, having been confused for black pepper or a blend of different spices. Annatto has traditionally been used to color Caribbean food like arroz con pollo.

The different cuisines of the Americas have been amalgamated so many times that there are endless permutations and arrangements.

SPICES

Allspice 116   Annatto 118

Chiles 120   Ancho (Poblano) 122

Cayenne 124   Chipotle (Jalapeño) 126

Guajillo (Mirasol) 128

Habanero and Scotch Bonnet 130

Pumpkin Seeds 132   Sassafras 134

Vanilla 136

Allspice

Jamaica pepper, myrtle pepper, pimento, clove pepper

Did you assume allspice is a spice blend? You're not alone. The first explorers to the New World confused the dried berries for pepper, naming it pimiento. When it arrived in England, it was renamed to reflect the complexity of its aroma and flavor, which evoked so many other spices. If cinnamon, black pepper, clove, and nutmeg had a love child, that'd be allspice.

Though it is a star of Jamaican jerk cooking, allspice is not just a clever name. A host of cultures and food traditions claim allspice. It makes flavorful contributions to baked goods, sweets, puddings, mincemeat, and sausages in England. In the United States, it's a component in chewing gum, sodas, barbecue sauce, canned meats, ketchup, ice cream, jams, and apple and pumpkin pies. Moroccan tagines and ras el hanout blends incorporate it, as does Ethiopian berbere and Mexican mole. Part of allspice's mystery is that it can replace other spices but no single spice can replace it. Perhaps this is why it makes an appearance in Spanish escabeche, Sweden's pickled herring, and France's quatre épices.

Both Mayans and Aztecs flavored early incarnations of chocolate with allspice. Because of its preservative qualities, both cultures used it in embalming procedures. It was also considered to be an aphrodisiac. That's quite the trifecta. Caribbean pirates used the entire plant to slow-roast meat and then preserve it. It was called boccan and, later, *boucane* by the French, who became known as *boucaniers*—or buccaneers. Ahoy!

CULTIVATION CENTERS

Jamaica, Brazil, Guatemala, Honduras, Mexico

AROMA & FLAVOR

The aroma reminds me of an old perfume bottle, one that has been empty for a year but retains a lingering bouquet. Its scent is faint, but there it is a definite collaboration of peppery and clove-like notes. The taste is undoubtedly warm and woody and carries that subtle pepper undertone.

MEDICINAL USES

helps, treats, prevents, or aids mild pain, menopausal symptoms, stomachaches, gastrointestinal issues; it also has anti-oxidants, antibacterial, antifungal, and preservative properties

COMMON FORMS AND VARIATIONS

dried berries, whole and ground; varieties include Jamaican allspice (considered the best), Mexican and Central American allspice (common in the United States)

COMPLEMENTS

all Caribbean cooking but especially fish, shellfish, and seafood; beef and pork; chocolate, coconut, and fruit; game, chicken, and poultry; pickled vegetables and fruits, potatoes and yams; rice and pilafs; sweets, cakes, pies, puddings, baked goods; vegetable stews and soups

PAIRS WELL WITH

black pepper, cardamom, cinnamon, cloves, cumin, garlic, ginger, mint, nutmeg, onion, oregano, tamarind, turmeric

Annatto

achiote, urucul, achuete, bija/bijol, hot dieu do

Perhaps you too have been put under the spell of *arroz con pollo*, one of Central America's signature meals. I had some in Costa Rica that had me dreaming in divine yellow for weeks. The goldenrod hue is thanks to an annatto-dyed cooking oil.

Annatto is the secret agent of food coloring, inserting itself without detection in a wide multitude of dishes. In the United States and Europe, annatto colors butter, margarine, and American, Velveeta, Gloucester, Muenster, and Leicester cheeses.

Fried annatto seeds enrich oil with extra flavor and a deep yellow-orange tint. Once the seeds are extracted, the oil is used to cook vegetables, fish, chicken, meat, and rice among other ingredients. In the Yucatán and Guatemala, whole seeds are ground into a paste and mixed with cumin, pepper, and other spices into a rub called *recado*. In Puerto Rico, it is one of the principals of *sofrito*, a Latin base sauce and sazón.

Ancient Central Americans used annatto to paint their faces red for ceremonies and war preparations. The Aztecs used it to flavor chocolate drinks. Native Americans and Mayans used the oil as sunscreen.

Annatto seeds should be a deep red; beware the brown seeds. Make annatto oil by combining 2 tablespoons of seeds with 1 cup of canola or peanut oil. Simmer over medium heat until their color is released and small bubbles form. Strain and let it cool.

CULTIVATION CENTERS

Caribbean, Mexico, Brazil, Peru, India, western Africa

AROMA & FLAVOR

The fragrance of annatto is earthy, faintly pepper-like, and its flavor is musky, fragrant, and slightly acrid.

MEDICINAL USES

helps, treats, prevents, or aids heartburn, stomach distress, cholesterol; improves liver function

COMMON FORMS

ground or whole, small seed in a prickly, dark-red or brown pod

COMPLEMENTS

beans and lentils; yucca and sweet potatoes; chicken, pork, lamb, and beef; fish (salt cod in particular); fruit like bananas and plantains; shellfish, shrimp, and fish stews; veggies such as green bell peppers, pumpkins, and squash

PAIRS WELL WITH

black pepper, chiles, coriander, cumin, garlic, oregano, vanilla

Chiles

chili pepper, chile pepper, chilli pepper

The chile pepper plant originated ten thousand years ago, likely in the Andean hillsides of Peru and Bolivia. Sacred to the Incas, chiles were among the offerings to the gods. Mayans and Aztecs so cultivated peppers that by the time Columbus landed in the West Indies, they were already widespread. Since the first plants, over three thousand varieties have been developed, and the count is growing as cultivators pursue unique flavor combinations and increasingly record-breaking heat platforms.

The Scoville scale is the standard for gauging the capsaicin concentration in a given chile pepper. The Scoville scale will be referred to in the individual chile entries in this chapter. For reference, a green bell pepper has a score of 0, jalepeños come in at 8,000, and the world record hottest chile, the Carolina Reaper, clocks in at 2.2 million with the Dragon's Breath pepper in position to take top billing.

Chile peppers have so reshaped our culinary universe that a library of books have been written on them. I asked Denver Nicks, author of *Hot Sauce Nation,* about how impactful chile peppers have been to the global palette. He said, "There's the sexier fact that you can cultivate chiles in a head-spinning variety of heat levels and tastes. There are more than two dozen compounds that lend chiles their burn and even more compounds that give them unique tastes, and growers select traits to highlight some over others."

Toasting dried chiles adds to their complexity of flavor. Simply add chiles to a hot or medium-hot skillet and press them down for a short minute. Turn them over and repeat. The chiles will soften; just be sure to remove them before their color changes.

One important note: When handling chiles, use rubber gloves, and be mindful that the capsaicin, a highly volatile oil, remains on whatever it touches. Handling chiles and then touching your eyes can be a painful, if not dangerous, experience.

CULTIVATION CENTERS

Mexico, Latin America and the Caribbean, India, Thailand, Southeast Asia, Africa, Japan, China, southwest United States (New Mexico)

AROMA & FLAVOR

Depending on the variety, chile peppers can be spicy, hot, sweet, musky, tangy, smoky, and definitely hot.

MEDICINAL USES

helps, treats, prevents, or aids sore throats and coughs, arthritis pain, nerve damage, shingles, headaches, obesity, increased metabolism, fat reduction, ulcer, mouth sores, infected wounds, blood clotting, heart attack recovery, heart disease, strokes, prostate and breast cancers; increases circulation; aids digestion; releases endorphins

COMMON FORMS AND VARIETIES

dried chiles: whole, flakes, ground; see individual chile pepper sections for varieties

COMPLEMENTS

beans, legumes, and lentils; bread, toast, and parathas; coconut and chocolate; fish and shellfish; grilled fruit and vegetables; hot sauce; meat, sausages, and poultry; pickled veggies and relishes; rubs, chutneys, marinades, pastes, and dipping sauces; sauces with tomato and salsas; soft cheeses like mozzarella, goat, and ricotta as well as Cheddar; soups and stews; use as a dusting on cakes and sweets

PAIRS WELL WITH

allspice, amchur, anardana, black pepper, cardamom, celery seeds, cilantro, cinnamon, cumin, fennel seeds, fenugreek, ginger, oregano, parsley, sumac, turmeric

Ancho (Poblano)

fresh poblano (meaning "people's chile pepper"), dried ancho (meaning "wide chile pepper"), and serrano (a close relative to both poblano and ancho)

Mexico's most popular dried chile is the ancho, the dried version of the poblano pepper, a common pepper named for and first cultivated in Puebla, Mexico. Poblanos are a rather large pepper at 3 to 6 inches long. Ancho chiles are flat, heart shaped, and slightly shorter than the fresh form. They become wrinkly and dark red, even brown-tinted to almost black when dried.

My friend Paul turned me on to ancho chiles and I am forever in his debt. Anchos are a wonderful gateway beyond the world of cayenne and paprika. They are a slightly spicy chile, 1000 to 2000 on the Scoville scale, but they can be sneaky-hot. They are still a little supple when dried, so working with them is forgiving if you're new to cooking with chiles. Anchos can be slightly sweet, floral, and fruity, though I love them because of their smokiness.

To get into the chile rhythm, try quickly charring an ancho and putting it in the center of a homemade pizza. If you like Hawaiian pizza, cut the ancho up into pieces with scissors and spread it near the pineapple for an explosive flavor skirmish where your mouth is the fortunate battlefield.

To char a chile pepper, use tongs to spin it over an open flame, such as a gas burner, until it is blackened, or scalded, all around. Take precautions: The burned capsaicin can irritate eyes, nose, and skin. Consider gloves and safety glasses.

CULTIVATION CENTER

Puebla, Mexico

AROMA & FLAVOR

Ancho peppers are floral and fragrant. The flavor ranges from mild to hot.

MEDICINAL USES

see Chiles (page 120)

COMMON FORMS AND VARIETIES

dried chiles: whole, flakes, and ground; they are closely related to mulato and pasilla peppers

COMPLEMENTS

see Chiles (page 120), but specifically beef, chicken, mole sauce, pork, poultry

PAIRS WELL WITH

see Chiles (page 120)

Cayenne

cayenne chile peppers (dried), cili kering or Ginnie/Guinea pepper

Cayenne peppers are likely from French Guiana on the northern crest of South America. They were known as milichilli in the sixteenth century, prior to taking the name of the Cayenne River that opens into the French Guianan coast. This is likely the etymology of the term "Guinea pepper," as cayenne is sometimes called.

Cayenne is, of course, hot. On the Scoville scale, it ranges from 30,000 to 50,000 Scoville heat units. It is red—all peppers start out green and ripen to a variety of yellow or red—and long with a slight bend, ending in a point. It is common to find it in powder or flakes at any store or supermarket. It's a mainstay in both Cajun and Creole cuisines. Any Louisianan has their hot sauce preference, Tabasco or Crystal, with the latter being the cayenne version.

Cayenne is one of the few chiles known by the same name both fresh and dried, unlike poblanos and jalepeños, which when dried are ancho and chipotle, respectively. Dried peppers are generally the focus in this book.

Experiment with cayenne on anything you'd like to embolden with a kick. When fire cooking on a parrilla (iron grill barbecue), we add cayenne to grilled fruit. Peaches, pears, pineapple, and papaya, all benefit from a moderate cayenne dusting before and during the cooking process. Try it with a dash of honey for an enchanting hot and sweet combination.

CULTIVATION CENTER

French Guiana

AROMA & FLAVOR

Cayenne is predominately hot. The aroma is sweeter and fainter than the taste.

MEDICINAL USES

see Chiles (page 120)

COMMON FORMS AND VARIETIES

dried chiles: whole, flakes, ground; varieties include Hot Portugal, Ring of Fire, Hades Hot, and Exotics; varietals include santaka, Hontaka, Thai chiles, and Chinese kwangsi

COMPLEMENTS

see Chiles (page 120), but in particular chocolate, coconut, and coffee; eggs, breakfast foods; fish, seafood, and shellfish; root vegetables and grilled fruit

PAIRS WELL WITH

see Chiles (page 120)

Chipotle (Jalapeño)

chipotle (dried) morita, huachinango (dried), jalapeño (fresh)

Mexico has arguably the most dynamic chile culture in the world, with more than 150 varieties. Dried chiles have more complexity and range of flavor than fresh, and so different names are given to the same pepper in its fresh and dried form. The chipotle is the dried version of a jalapeño.

Pickled jalapeños are those sour green slivers of heat ubiquitous at Mexican restaurants and barbecue joints. Jalapeños are green, an indication the pepper has been picked fresh. Jalapeños used for chipotles are left on the vine to ripen. They sweeten and become spicier as they mature and are then smoke-dried. When complete, chipotles are a deep, sultry burgundy-red.

At 5,000 to 10,000 on the Scoville scale, compared to the 2,500 to 5,000 of jalapeños, chipotles can deliver a right hook to your sensory receptors and are not to be underestimated. They are spicy step above anchos but still have a smaller furnace than cayenne peppers. That kick combines brightly with notes of chocolate and fruit.

Try puréeing chipotles and combining them with tomato or vodka sauce to make a barrel-chested sauce similar to an *arrabiata*. Soak whole, dried chiles in warm water for 30 minutes, or until they loosen up, if you're looking to purée them in a blender or use them where softness is needed. Use the soaking water to achieve your desired purée consistency. Very little will get you a paste. Add more for sauces and salsas.

CULTIVATION CENTER

Jalapa, Mexico

AROMA & FLAVOR

The fragrance of chipotles is spicy, floral, and hot. The flavor is full of chocolate and has a sweetness to its heat.

MEDICINAL USES

see Chiles (page 120)

COMMON FORMS AND VARIETIES

dried chiles: whole, flakes, ground; varieties include mecos (large, brown) and morita (smaller)

COMPLEMENTS

see Chiles (page 120), but in particular beef, chicken, mole sauce, poultry, pork

PAIRS WELL WITH

see Chiles (page 120)

Guajillo (Mirasol)

guajillo and dried chile travieso (meaning "naughty chile"),
and fresh mirasol

How can you not be intrigued by a pepper called "the naughty chile" in its native Mexico? While ancho may be the most popular chile, guajillo is perhaps the most common.

Sweet, musky, and jammy, guajillo chiles are a dried variety of the fresh mirasol pepper. When dried, they have a thin, tough skin; any paste or sauce you make with them should be strained. Soak the chiles before using, and if possible, choose guajillos that are already a bit soft as they retain their flavor better.

Chiles are more of a backdrop to illuminate other flavors in a dish, as opposed to being a spice on their own. Guajillo chiles are an excellent example of this because they are subtle enough in heat to not overpower other ingredients, and their flavors enhance and pair well with most ingredients. The Scoville heat scale has them at 2,500 to 5,000 units, on a par with a fresh jalepeño. They feature prominently in the vegetable-based sauces of Mexico, such as moles and *consomes*, as well as in meat dishes like, *carne adobada*.

Order whole guajillo chiles online. You'll know them by their reddish-purple or dark claret color and their length of 4 to 6 inches. Ground guajillo is hard to come by. When you're ready to graduate from ancho and chipotle chiles to something a little more "naughty," this is the chile.

CULTIVATION CENTER

Zacatecas, Mexico

AROMA & FLAVOR

Guajillo chiles are musky, earthy, warm with some smokiness. The taste is mild, distinct but fruity and tangy in the way wine can be.

MEDICINAL USES

see Chiles (page 120)

COMMON FORMS

whole dried peppers; ground is rare

COMPLEMENTS

see Chiles (page 120), but in particular beans, mole, *carne adobada*, chicken, *consomé*, *chilaquiles*, fish, legumes, *pombazos* (sandwiches), pork

PAIRS WELL WITH

see Chiles (page 120)

Habanero and Scotch Bonnet

If you think you can handle the heat, habaneros are your new best friend. Habanero and Scotch Bonnet chiles range from 100,000 to 500,000+ on the Scoville scale. They are your gateway chiles to the Trinidad Scorpion, the Ghost Chile, and the possibly soon-to-be-crowned hottest chile, the Dragon's Breath.

Capsaicin isn't the only compound in chiles that contributes heat. As Denver Nicks describes in *Hot Sauce Nation,* there are roughly 22 compounds, called capsaicinoids, that contribute to the "pepper's heat and the myriad of forms it takes." This is why some chiles come on strong but dissipate quickly or why others linger. Habeneros are slow to arrive but tend to linger. They are great in pastes, salsas, and rubs.

Scotch Bonnets are closely related to habaneros. They are extremely popular in the cuisines of Jamaica, the Caribbean, and North and West Africa. The name Scotch Bonnet derives from its shape, which is evocative of a Scottish tam o' shanter hat.

Use both chiles with caution.

Generally, small chiles are hotter than large ones. Whole dried chiles are best kept in a zip-top bag in a cool place or the refrigerator. Ground chiles are fine in a dark, dry, and cool spice cabinet.

Remember that most of the heat is contained in the ribs and seeds, which can be removed. It is generally easier to add heat than take it away, so start small and grow.

CULTIVATION CENTER

Cuba, possibly South America

AROMA & FLAVOR

Habaneros are famous for their heat. It's an inferno present in the aroma and very much so in the taste. Accompanied with the heat are notes of tropical fruit.

MEDICINAL USES

see Chiles (page 120)

COMMON FORMS AND VARIETIES

dried: whole, ground; varieties include red habanero and chocolate habanero

COMPLEMENTS

see Chiles (page 120), but in particular African sauces, beef, chicken, Jamaican jerk, pork

PAIRS WELL WITH

see Chiles (page 120)

Pumpkin Seeds

pepitas

Pumpkins are the crown jewel of the rather small contribution that the Americas north of the Caribbean made to the spice exchange between Old World and New. It's easy to think of pumpkin seeds as something other than a spice, but, as the dried seed of a plant, they are as much a spice as poppy seeds or sesame seeds.

Pumpkin seeds are delicious whole and toasted and are a splendid addition to salads, breads, soups, and hearty winter foods. They're also delicious to snack on with your favorite seasonings. They're used as spice in West Africa, Latin America, and Spain. In Mexico especially, *pepitas* are used in moles and to thicken soups. One of my go-to moves for fish is my Pumpkin Seeds Fish Marinade (page 150) that also includes dried cranberries. It's a marvelous combination.

Next time you have that pumpkin-carving party, save those seeds. Not only are they a tasty, straight-from-the-source snack, they also have incredible health benefits.

Toast your own pumpkin seeds by washing off the pulp and leaving them overnight to dry. On a wax paper–lined baking sheet, spread them in a single layer. Sprinkle with some coconut oil and mix to coat. Bake in a preheated 325°F oven for 15 to 30 minutes, checking them throughout so they don't burn. They are done when golden.

If you find pumpkin seeds in the ground form, try adding them to fill out the taste profile of muffins and breads (especially zucchini and banana), or to thicken stocks and soups.

CULTIVATION CENTERS

United States, Mexico, Europe, Africa

AROMA & FLAVOR

When toasted, pumpkin seeds are warm, faintly floral, and nutty. The taste is nutty—like pine nuts and less like walnuts.

MEDICINAL USES

helps, treats, prevents, or aids prostate enlargement, menopause symptoms, cholesterol control and heart disease risk, iron deficiency, arthritis

COMMON FORMS

seeds: dried whole or ground

COMPLEMENTS

baked goods like quick breads, cakes, and muffins; salads and vegetables; use on the crust of yeast breads

PAIRS WELL WITH

cardamom, cinnamon, cloves, cumin, garlic, ginger, nigella, onion, oregano, thyme

Sassafras

cinnamon wood, saxifras (bark), filé powder (dried leaves)

When I was young, my mom would sometimes stop by the video store on her way home from work, and I always hoped she'd bring home a western. All I wanted to drink was what the cowboys drank: sarsaparilla, which was apparently made with birch and sassafras. That it definitely contributed to root beer, was a magical alternative.

Sassafras was traditionally used medicinally in tea and to flavor medicines. It's not unlike nutmeg in that its flavor is a cross between camphor and woodiness.

Sassafras is best in beverages. Steep it in tea with ginger, mint, or honey, or try an old-fashioned root beer recipe. My favorite thing to do with sassafras is to give it to my friend who started a home brew beer club in exchange for the final product. It can pick up a stout or add a base layer to a lager. When cooking with either filé powder or sassafras, add it toward the end of cooking. Allowing it to boil will taint the spices.

CULTIVATION CENTERS

Eastern and southern United States, Asia

AROMA & FLAVOR

Sassafras has an earthy, wooden aroma with a hint of camphor or mint. The taste is similar but more faint.

MEDICINAL USES

Sassafras was used by Louisiana Choctaw Indians for fevers and by early settlers in North America for pain relief, blood pressure problems, and arthritis and kidney issues. In the 1960s, the US FDA banned sassafras oil, used as a diuretic, due to its high safrole content, a weak carcinogenic that is also present in nutmeg, cinnamon, mace, and black pepper.

COMMON FORMS

bark, dried small chunks, powder

COMPLEMENTS

beer, Cajun or Creole dishes (filé powder), chocolate, coconut, confections, meat dishes, salads, sausages, soft drinks

PAIRS WELL WITH

basil, black pepper, chiles, cinnamon, licorice, mace, nutmeg

Vanilla

Vanilla is the edible pod of an orchid native to Mexico. Aztecs and Totonacs harvested it for flavoring chocolate. The cultivation process was a mystery until it was realized that hand pollination could replace the work that Mexico's special variety of bees was responsible for. It has since spread to grow in similar tropical climates. Vanilla has seduced the world with its opulent aroma indicative of an amalgamation of chocolate, tobacco, and lavender honey. Aromatically, few spices can compete with vanilla.

The demand for vanilla is so great that imitation vanilla extract, without vanillin in it, is now common on supermarket shelves. Do yourself a favor and opt for the more expensive real stuff. You'll use less of it so it lasts longer. There's also a nasty aftertaste in false vanilla. Mitigate the expense by ordering it in bulk online. Keep it in a zip-top bag in an airtight jar to maximize freshness. You can make your own extract by infusing pods in high-proof alcohol such as grain alcohol or vodka.

Vanilla enhances any sweets, creams, cakes, and cookies. In savory dishes, try it in cream sauce with mollusks and crustaceans or with succulent meat like veal. Or keep some on hand to use sparingly with coffee and tea. Have some warm bread? Combine some vanilla with butter and spread it on for a euphoric experience.

CULTIVATION CENTERS

Mexico, Madagascar, Caribbean
(Puerto Rico, Guadeloupe), Indian Ocean
(Réunion, Comoro), Tahiti, Indonesia

AROMA & FLAVOR

Vanilla has a rich, velvety sweet aroma
that is simultaneously delicate and
smooth. The taste of the seeds is under-
whelming compared to the fragrance,
but when added to a dish it imparts
those aromatic qualities to the taste
of the food.

MEDICINAL USES

Helps treat cancer metastasis and sickle
cell anemia.

COMMON FORMS AND VARIETIES

whole bean pods, extract, paste,
powder; varieties include Mexican
vanilla, Bourbon (French) vanilla

COMPLEMENTS

chocolate, coffee, and coconut; citrus
and other fruit and fruit-based desserts;
ice creams, custards, and puddings;
lobster and crustaceans; sweets,
pastries and confections; veal

PAIRS WELL WITH

allspice, anise, basil, chiles, cinnamon,
lemon peel, mint, nutmeg

RECIPES

Creole Spice Blend 140

Chesapeake Bay–Style Seasoning Blend 141

Chile-Infused Pickling Spice Blend 142

Taco (Taceaux) Seasoning Blend 143

Pumpkin Seeds Autumn Blend 144

Mulling Over Spice Blend 145

Creole Barbecue Dry Rub 146

Poudre de Colombo Rum Paste 147

Jerk-Style Pineapple Paste 148

Adobo Mezcal Marinade 149

Pumpkin Seeds Fish Marinade 150

Queen's Carnitas Marinade 151

Spicy Peanut Marinade 152

Kickin' Chicken Marinade 153

Grandma Martha's New Mexico
Green Chile Bean Sauce 154

Sweet Baby Gavin's Guava Sauce 155

Smoky "Holey" Mole Sauce 156

Backcountry Chimichurri Sauce 158

Two-Shack "Como el Otro"
Hot Sauce 159

Red "DB" Chile Sauce 160

New Orleans Barbecue Shrimp Sauce 161

Left: Chile-Infused Pickling Spice Blend (page 142)

Creole Spice Blend

crawfish, shrimp, and crab boils, and as a general seasoning for soups, stews, and roasts

Living in South Louisiana makes one hanker for the impending crawfish boil season. Our four seasons are crawfish, crab, shrimp, and oyster. Whether Cajun (Lafayette) or Creole (New Orleans), every family's secret boil spice recipe is closely guarded. Here's a good starting point for Creole spices. **MAKES ABOUT ¾ CUP**

2 ancho chiles

2 guajillo chiles (or
1 tablespoon ground
cayenne pepper)

1 tablespoon ground allspice

1 tablespoon ground
celery seeds

1 tablespoon ground
dill seeds

1 tablespoon paprika

1 tablespoon coarse sea salt

1½ teaspoons freshly
ground black pepper

1½ teaspoons freshly
ground white pepper

1 teaspoon ground cloves

1 teaspoon onion powder

1 teaspoon garlic powder

1 teaspoon dried thyme

1 teaspoon dried oregano

1 teaspoon filé
powder (optional)

Grind the ancho and guajillo chiles in a spice grinder. Transfer them to a small bowl and mix in the allspice, celery seeds, dill seeds, paprika, salt, black pepper, white pepper, cloves, onion powder, garlic powder, thyme, oregano, and filé powder (if using). Store in an airtight jar for 6 months to 1 year.

Chesapeake Bay–Style Seasoning Blend

crab and shrimp marinades, boils, and sauces, and as a dip for boiled seafood

Nearly everyone I've met has a different take on how to use Chesapeake Bay seasoning. A colleague who grew up in Annapolis taught me the locals' secret: they start with a jar of the seasoning, discard a third of it, fill it back up with sea salt, and shake to mix. **MAKES ½ CUP**

3 tablespoons sea salt

2 teaspoons ground
cayenne pepper

2 teaspoons ground allspice

2 teaspoons paprika

2 teaspoons celery seeds

1½ teaspoons
ground bay leaf

1 teaspoon ground
cardamom

1 teaspoon ground
cinnamon

1 teaspoon dry
yellow mustard

1 teaspoon ground cloves

1 teaspoon ground ginger

½ teaspoon freshly
ground black pepper

Mix all the ingredients together. Store in an airtight container in a cool, dry, dark place for 6 months to 1 year.

Chile-Infused Pickling Spice Blend

carrots, green beans, okra, onions, pickled cucumbers

Pickling is a wonderful method to simultaneously preserve vegetables and learn which spice pairings you favor. Allspice is a dynamic spice to pair with peppercorns, lending both taste and aesthetic value. Jars of various pickled vegetables are a grand sight lining the back wall of a kitchen counter. **MAKES 3/4 CUP**

2 tablespoons
coarse sea salt

2 tablespoons sugar

1 tablespoon allspice berries

2 teaspoons mustard seeds

1 teaspoon white
peppercorns

1 teaspoon pink
peppercorns

1 teaspoon black
peppercorns

1 teaspoon green
peppercorns

1 teaspoon dill seeds

1 teaspoon whole cloves

1 teaspoon annatto
(optional, for color)

1 cinnamon stick

Mix all the ingredients together. Store in an airtight jar for up to 3 months. Add 10 garlic cloves and 2 cayenne or serrano chiles to the blend before pickling. This amount of pickling spice can be used for roughly 5 pounds of vegetables.

Recipe Tip: To pickle vegetables, make sure to sterilize the jars first. Make the brine using 3 to 4 cups distilled white vinegar. Various pickling methods are available online, but I'm partial to the process described in Emeril Lagasse's classic book *Louisiana Real and Rustic*.

Taco (Taceaux) Seasoning Blend

meat and vegetarian tacos and burritos

This blend is a notched-up version of traditional taco seasoning with a bit of heat (cayenne) and a twist (lemon peel). Making your own allows you to put in goodies like cocoa powder or coffee. When cooking with the blend, experiment by adding toasted pumpkin seeds or roasted corn. MAKES ABOUT ⅓ CUP

1 tablespoon whole allspice

1 tablespoon cumin seeds

1 teaspoon dried lemon peel

1 teaspoon black peppercorns

1 tablespoon paprika

1 tablespoon coarse sea salt

2 teaspoons ground cayenne pepper

1 teaspoon onion powder

1 teaspoon garlic powder

1 teaspoon dried Mexican oregano

1 teaspoon semisweet cocoa powder

1. Grind the allspice, cumin, lemon peel, and peppercorns in a spice grinder.

2. Mix the ground spices with the paprika, salt, cayenne, onion powder, garlic powder, oregano, and cocoa powder. Store in an airtight jar in your pantry. The blend will keep almost indefinitely.

Recipe Tip: Sauté garlic and ginger with celery, green bell peppers, and onion. Then brown 1½ pounds chicken, beef, pork, or tofu. Drain the fat and add ½ cup chicken or vegetable stock and Taceaux Seasoning, and bring it to a boil. Reduce the heat and simmer until thick, 10 to 20 minutes depending on the protein used.

Pumpkin Seeds Autumn Blend

chicken, fish, poultry, rabbit

Approaching Halloween, it's always a tad deflating to see folks throwing away the "brains" of their newly created jack-o-lanterns. Those tasty seeds are an incredibly robust spice when dried and toasted. **MAKES ABOUT 1½ CUPS**

¼ cup toasted pumpkin seeds (see page 132)

2 tablespoons whole allspice

1 teaspoon ground cayenne pepper

½ tablespoon paprika

½ teaspoon ground cinnamon

½ teaspoon coarse sea salt

1 cup bread crumbs

2 eggs, beaten

½ cup annatto oil (page 118), divided

2 chipotle chiles, stemmed and seeded, finely chopped

1. Combine the pumpkin seeds, allspice, cayenne pepper, paprika, cinnamon, and salt in a food processor and pulverize the pumpkin seeds. Transfer to a small bowl and mix in the bread crumbs.

2. Pour the eggs into a shallow dish and set aside. Heat ¼ cup of annatto oil in a medium skillet over medium heat. Add the chiles and roast them for 3 to 5 minutes or until they start to brown.

3. Combine the chiles with the spiced bread crumbs in a second shallow dish.

4. Add the remaining ¼ cup of annatto oil to the skillet and increase the heat to medium-high. Coat both sides of your chosen protein first in the egg wash and then in the spices. Fry each side in the heated annatto oil.

Recipe Tip: If done with blackened potato wedges, you can very easily make a jack o' lantern on your plate as the annatto oil and chiles will make your protein rich yellow or orange.

Mulling Over Spice Blend

alcohol (apple pie drink), cider, wine

Mulled cider was a treat that kept us warm through long, cold winters. Sitting by the stove drinking warm cider was a highlight for my brother and I when we visited our grandparents. This recipe is a combination of that nostalgia and some tricks I learned later on. **MAKES ABOUT ¾ CUP**

3 green cardamom pods

2 whole nutmegs, cracked

2 tablespoons whole cloves, plus additional as needed

2 tablespoons dried ginger pieces

2 tablespoons allspice berries

1 tablespoon fresh lemon peel

1 tablespoon fresh orange peel

2 (2- to 3-inch) cinnamon sticks

1 star anise

1 vanilla bean

1. Place the cardamom pods and whole nutmeg inside a cloth bag or between two towels, and crack them open using a mallet. Place them in a jar with the cloves, ginger, allspice berries, lemon peel, orange peel, cinnamon sticks, star anise, and vanilla bean. Seal the jar so it's airtight and store for up to 3 months. (If you don't have an airtight container, keep the vanilla bean in a zip-top bag so it doesn't dry out.)

2. When ready to use, slice the vanilla bean lengthwise and scrape out the seeds into the blend. Remove and discard the cardamom pods as well.

Recipe Tip: To make mulled cider or wine, pour 3 cups cider or 1 (750-milliliter) bottle of wine into a saucepan. Loosely tie the mulling spices in cheesecloth and add it to the pan. Slice an orange into wedges and stud each wedge with 2 to 5 cloves and add to the saucepan. Bring to a boil then reduce the heat and simmer for 15 to 20 minutes. If making mulled wine, stir in two shots (about 2 ounces) of tawny port wine. Remove the bag and oranges. Hint: Adding a couple spoonfuls of orange juice concentrate at the onset makes a world of goodness.

Creole Barbecue Dry Rub

all things pork: belly, chops, ribs

Barbecue dry rubs are one of our distinctly North American food traditions. One of the best ones to be had is courtesy of Devin De Wulf, founder of the Red Beans and Rice Mardi Gras Krewe and Parade. Devin cooks for every krewe member during the costuming sessions. **MAKES 1½ TO 2 CUPS**

1 cup dark brown sugar

3 tablespoons dark chili powder

3 tablespoons ground cayenne pepper

5½ teaspoons Creole Spice Blend (page 140)

2½ teaspoons sea salt

Mix all the ingredients together. Store in an airtight jar in a cool, dark place for up to 6 months.

Recipe Tip: To use, add ½ cup onion ½ cup garlic cloves to the blend and rub over a rack of ribs. Seal in a zip-top bag and refrigerate for at least 2 hours or overnight. Preheat a grill to medium heat and grill the ribs for 10 minutes. Turn them over and grill until cooked through, about 5 minutes.

Poudre de Colombo Rum Paste

chicken, goat, pork, veggies

Colombo powder came to the Caribbean by way of Sri Lankan immigrants. I have an affinity for rum but never expected it to make a great curry paste for stew meat, rice, plantains, and fish. It can be used as a rub or turned into a paste.

MAKES ¼ TO ⅔ CUP

1 tablespoon white rice

1 teaspoon allspice berries

½ teaspoon black peppercorns

½ teaspoon fenugreek seeds

½ teaspoon cumin seeds

½ teaspoon coriander seeds

1 teaspoon coconut oil

2 garlic cloves, crushed

2 chiles of your preferred heat level, seeded and stemmed

1 tablespoon dark rum

1 tablespoon chicken stock

½ teaspoon ground turmeric

½ teaspoon dry yellow mustard

1 tablespoon olive oil

1. In a small skillet over medium heat, lightly toast the rice for about 1 minute. Transfer to a dish and let cool. In the same skillet, toast the allspice, peppercorns, fenugreek, cumin, and coriander seeds for 1 to 2 minutes. Add to the dish and let cool. Grind together the toasted rice and spices in a spice grinder.

2. Melt the oil in the skillet over medium heat. Add the garlic and chiles and sauté until fragrant, 2 to 4 minutes.

3. Put the garlic and chiles, toasted spices, rum, chicken stock, turmeric, mustard, and olive oil in a food processor and pulse until combined and a paste is formed. The paste will keep in an airtight container in the refrigerator for up to 2 weeks.

Recipe Tip: Rub the blend or paste over your chosen protein and place in a zip-top bag in the refrigerator for 2 hours.

Jerk-Style Pineapple Paste

chicken, pork, poultry

Jamaican jerk is notorious for its tangy combination of sweetness and heat. I discovered pineapple jerk marinade—called al pastor—while on a scuba diving trip in Mexico with my father. This is my attempt to recreate that spellbinding sauce. **MAKES ABOUT 1½ CUPS**

6 teaspoons coconut oil, divided

1 onion, chopped

1 (1-inch) piece fresh ginger, minced

4 scallions, chopped

3 garlic cloves, minced

1 or 2 Scotch Bonnet or habanero chiles, stemmed and seeded

¼ cup brown sugar

¼ cup apple cider vinegar

2 tablespoons soy sauce

2 teaspoons ground allspice

1 teaspoon salt

½ teaspoon ground cinnamon

½ cup fresh pineapple chunks

Juice of 1 lime

1. In a medium skillet over medium heat, add 2 teaspoons of oil. When hot, add the onion, ginger, scallions, garlic, and chiles and sauté until golden, 4 to 5 minutes.

2. Transfer to a food processor and add the brown sugar, vinegar, soy sauce, allspice, salt, cinnamon, pineapple, lime juice, and the remaining 4 teaspoons of oil. Pulse until combined and a paste is formed. Use immediately.

Recipe Tip: To marinate, cover your protein of choice with the paste and refrigerate for at least 3 hours or overnight. Grill over low heat or bake in a preheated 325°F to 350°F oven for about 1 hour, depending on the protein. Add another ½ cup fresh pineapple chunks to the chicken about 15 minutes before it finishes cooking. If you can, grill over wood coals.

Adobo Mezcal Marinade

chicken

Adobo developed in Spain but is used extensively in Latin America and the Philippines. Canned chipotle chiles in adobo sauce are easily found, but there is no substitute for starting out with your own ingredients. MAKES 1 CUP

1 tablespoon canola oil

2 chipotle chiles, stemmed and seeded

2 guajillo or ancho chiles, stemmed and seeded

4 tablespoons mezcal

1 tablespoon cumin seeds

1 tablespoon black peppercorns

5 garlic cloves, minced

1 tablespoon ground paprika

2 tablespoons peanut oil

1 tablespoon dried Mexican oregano

1 tablespoon kosher salt

1 (1-inch) piece fresh ginger, minced

½ cup white vinegar

¾ cup chicken stock

1. Heat the oil in a small skillet over medium heat. Add the chipotle and guajillo chiles and briefly toast them, about 2 minutes. Transfer the chiles to a bowl of cold water and let them soak for 30 minutes.

2. Put the mezcal in a small saucepan over medium heat and reduce it by half.

3. In the skillet over medium heat, toast the cumin and peppercorns. Transfer to a dish and let cool, then grind them in a spice grinder.

4. Strain the chiles from the water and put them in a food processor with the ground cumin and pepper mixture, mezcal reduction, garlic, paprika, peanut oil, oregano, salt, and ginger. With the processor running, slowly add ½ cup of vinegar until the mixture is combined and smooth. Add the chicken stock and pulse to incorporate.

5. Transfer the marinade to the small saucepan over medium-low heat and let it simmer and reduce by half, about 15 minutes. The finished marinade should be smooth and thick. Refrigerate in an airtight container for up to 2 weeks.

Recipe Tip: Marinate chicken or pork for 2 to 4 hours. For cooking, brown the pork or chicken then add the sauce along with another 1 cup chicken stock and 1 teaspoon sugar. Cook until the sauce has thickened and the protein is cooked through.

Pumpkin Seeds Fish Marinade

seafood like trout, bass, flounder, monkfish, seabass, scallops, and shrimp

This recipe is one I came up with in college. I still crave it because the cranberries pack a punch of flavor wherever they land, creating succulent fish and a bullet of tangy fruit in the same bite. **MAKES ⅔ CUP**

1 tablespoon annatto oil (page 118)

4 tablespoons roasted pumpkin seeds

2 tablespoons dried cranberries

2 garlic cloves, minced

1 teaspoon coarse sea salt

4 tablespoons dry white wine

2 tablespoons extra-virgin olive oil

1 teaspoon cracked allspice

1. In a small skillet over medium heat, heat the annatto oil. Add the pumpkin seeds, cranberries, garlic, and salt and sauté until golden yellow, 4 to 5 minutes.

2. Transfer to a medium bowl and mix in the wine, olive oil, and allspice. Use immediately.

Recipe Tip: Create an aluminum foil "oven" on a baking sheet (take two sheets of foil on top of each other and fold up the sides all around to make a "pool" shape that will hold the liquid marinade). Pour half the marinade in the pool, then add the fish, and pour the remaining marinade over the fish. Drizzle the juice of ½ lemon over the fish and sprinkle with the zest of ½ lemon. Cover with slices from ½ lemon, 2 fresh rosemary sprigs, and 1 bunch fresh mint leaves. Season with salt. Create another foil "oven" and place it over the fish so it's enclosed. Bake in a preheated 350°F oven until the fish is cooked through.

Queen's Carnitas Marinade

brisket, pork belly, pork shoulder

As a world traveler and host for BBC Travel, Aric S. Queen has been around the world and back again and has proudly provided this recipe. The orange juice and cola brilliantly enhance common ingredients. If you're keen on some heat to balance out the sweet, add a couple guajillo or chipotle chiles. MAKES 4 CUPS

2 cups freshly squeezed orange juice

2 cups cola

1 teaspoon ground allspice

1 tablespoon ground cumin

½ teaspoon pure vanilla extract

Mix all the ingredients together. Use immediately.

Recipe Tip: Drizzle the marinade over pork shoulder or brisket as it cooks. Or put a pork shoulder into a slow cooker for 6 hours on low. Shred the meat, drizzle marinade over it, and let it sit for 30 minutes. Then broil until crispy.

Spicy Peanut Marinade

beef, chicken, pork chops, veggies

This recipe is courtesy of Pia and Simon Pearce and is inspired by a vintage copy of Gourmet *magazine. Pre-internet, cutting out recipes and modifying them was the thing to do. I'm overjoyed they provided this recipe because it absolutely needs to be shared.* MAKES ABOUT 1¼ CUPS

½ cup minced onion

¼ cup extra-virgin olive oil

¼ cup freshly squeezed lemon juice

3 tablespoons creamy peanut butter

3 tablespoons soy sauce

2 tablespoons dark rum

1 tablespoon sugar

1 tablespoon minced fresh ginger

1 teaspoon ground cayenne pepper or red pepper flakes

1 teaspoon coarse sea salt

½ teaspoon ground allspice

Place all the ingredients in a food processor and process to mix well. Use immediately.

Recipe Tip: Marinate chicken, pork, or other protein in a zip-top bag in the refrigerator for 2 hours or overnight. Grill or fry. To make a sauce, bring ½ cup marinade to a boil in a stainless steel or enamel saucepan. Whisk in ½ cup heavy (whipping) cream and cook, whisking constantly, until smooth and thickened.

Kickin' Chicken Marinade

all things chicken: legs, wings, thighs, and breasts, though best with dark meat

This marinade was an inspired accident when visiting a friend who had so few spices we had to be spontaneous. The idea is to make the chicken as juicy and sweet as possible, and cut it with a little heat from chiles, pepper, and allspice.

MAKES ABOUT ¾ CUP

4 tablespoons dark rum

½ vanilla bean or
1 teaspoon pure vanilla
extract (optional)

½ cup honey

1 tablespoon ancho
chili powder or ground
cayenne pepper

1 (2-inch) piece fresh
ginger, minced

½ teaspoon coarse sea salt

½ teaspoon ground allspice

½ teaspoon freshly
ground black pepper

1. In a small saucepan over low heat, reduce the rum by half. Remove the pan from the heat and let cool.

2. Split the vanilla bean (if using) lengthwise and scrape the seeds into the rum. Stir in the honey, chili powder, ginger, salt, allspice, and black pepper. Use immediately.

Recipe Tip: I love adding shredded pineapple to the marinade, but try it with apple, papaya, or any tropical fruit for a tangy, sweet addition.

Grandma Martha's New Mexico Green Chile Bean Sauce

barbecue, chicken, chile stews, eggs, fish, potatoes

Visit the American Southwest, and you will cross paths with the amazing green chile. You'll be asked to choose "red, green, or Christmas" with your food in most New Mexico restaurants. With this recipe, green chile has finally made it out of Grandma Martha's kitchen and into mine. MAKES 9 TO 10 CUPS

3 cups dried pinto beans

7 cups water

2 tablespoons canola oil

1 pound ground beef

1 white onion, diced

3 garlic cloves, minced

3 to 4 tablespoons red chili powder, such as cayenne

1 cup green chiles, such as Lemitar or Hatch, chopped

1. Cook the beans and water in a pressure cooker for 1 hour.

2. In a large skillet over medium heat, add the oil. When hot, add the ground beef, onion, and garlic and sauté until browned, 7 to 8 minutes. Stir in the chili powder, then stir in the beans. Finally, add the green chiles to the mix.

3. Transfer the mixture to the pressure cooker and cook for 15 more minutes.

4. Delicious right out of the pressure cooker, the chili is even better the next day. If storing, freeze in an airtight container.

Recipe Tip: If you cannot find Hatch or Lemitar New Mexico chiles, use Anaheim and jalapeños. Alternatively, slow cook the beans (step 1) for 7 hours and the whole mixture (step 3) for 1 hour.

Sweet Baby Gavin's Guava Sauce

chicken, poultry, pork (this sauce is good on everything)

Legend has it that Chef Gavin, a New Orleans character, abhorred the $8 corn syrup–laden barbecue sauce at the local market and set out to make his own. Nine dollars later he claimed to have invented the cheapest barbecue sauce in the land, for half the cost. When challenged about the price, he declared that his was worth $18. I agree. This is his recipe. **MAKES 3 CUPS**

14 ounces guava pulp

½ pound brown sugar

1 (6-ounce) can tomato paste

4 tablespoons apple cider vinegar

4 tablespoons Two Shack "Como el Otro" Hot Sauce (page 159)

3 tablespoons tequila

1 tablespoon ground allspice

1 tablespoon freshly ground black pepper

½ tablespoon salt

1 teaspoon ground cayenne pepper

Juice of 2 limes

Mix all the ingredients together. Refrigerate in an airtight container for up to 1 week.

Recipe Tip: To make guava chicken, combine 1½ cups guava sauce with ¾ cup cheap, light beer, 5 ounces soy sauce, 2 sliced garlic cloves, ½ chopped onion, and 2 chopped tomatoes. Put it all in a slow cooker with a 10-pound chicken at 250°F for 3 to 4 hours or until cooked through. Check occasionally and continue cooking if necessary.

Smoky "Holey" Mole Sauce

eggs, fowl, grilled fruit and vegetables, poultry

Mole is the classic Mexican chocolate sauce signature of the states of Oaxaca—the land of seven moles—and Puebla. This recipe is a spin on Santa Fe's Coyote Café mole rojo with a smoky twist and has me salivating about a mezcal margarita pairing. **MAKES 3 TO 4 CUPS**

6 ancho chiles, seeded and stemmed

6 chipotle chiles, seeded and stemmed

6 guajillo chiles, seeded and stemmed

1½ quarts water

¼ cup raisins

½ teaspoon cumin seeds

½ teaspoon black peppercorns

½ teaspoon whole allspice

3 or 4 whole cloves

1 cinnamon stick or 2 teaspoons ground cinnamon

8 tablespoons peanut oil, divided

2 tablespoons pumpkin seeds

2 tablespoons pine nuts

2 tablespoons whole almonds

4 corn tortillas, 2 of them shredded

4 garlic cloves

½ onion, chopped

1 teaspoon smoked paprika

2 tomatillos, husked

3 Roma tomatoes, chopped

¼ cup Mexican chocolate

1½ cups chicken stock

1 tablespoon mezcal

1 teaspoon smoked salt

1. In a medium skillet over medium-low heat, toast the ancho, chipotle, and guajillo chiles to release their flavor, about 4 minutes. Transfer the chiles to a saucepan and cover with the water. Place the pan over the lowest heat possible and let the chiles reconstitute for 30 minutes. After 15 minutes, add the raisins. Drain the water.

2. While the chiles and raisins soak, in a small skillet over medium heat, lightly toast the cumin, peppercorns, allspice, cloves, and cinnamon (if using a cinnamon stick). Transfer to a dish and let cool, then grind in a spice grinder.

3. Heat 1 tablespoon of oil in a medium skillet over medium heat. Add the pumpkin seeds, pine nuts, almonds, shredded tortillas, garlic, and onion, and sauté until golden, about 5 minutes.

4. Transfer to a food processor and add the toasted ground spices and paprika. Process until combined. Add the chiles and raisins, tomatillos, tomatoes, and remaining 7 tablespoons of oil, and process into a paste.

5. Place the chocolate in a heatproof bowl and set it over a saucepan containing 1 to 2 inches of boiling or steaming water. Melt the chocolate, stirring it frequently.

6. In a large cast-iron skillet over medium heat, combine the chicken stock and mezcal. Once hot, add the paste and chocolate and stir to combine. Reduce the heat to medium-low and simmer for 30 minutes, stirring constantly, adding more stock or water to keep the sauce smooth and not too thick. Season with the salt. Refrigerate in an airtight container for 3 to 4 days or freeze.

Recipe Tip: To serve the sauce warm, allow it to cool for 5 to 10 minutes, stirring it occasionally. Pour it over grilled chicken, turkey, eggs, or add to soups and stews.

Backcountry Chimichurri Sauce

barbecued steak and burgers, chicken, chorizo and sausages, or use as a dip for bread and grilled fruits and veggies

Chimichurri is a classic South American green sauce used for meats, chicken, sausages, chorizo, and cheese. It brightens any salted meat and is great in butternut squash and winter soups. This sauce makes me nostalgic for tents, sleeping bags, and days spent under the stars in the Argentine backcountry. **MAKES 1 TO 1½ CUPS**

3 bunches fresh parsley leaves, stems discarded

1 bunch fresh mint leaves, stems discarded

1 bunch fresh tarragon leaves, stems discarded

1 small pickled onion and its juice

3 garlic cloves, chopped

1 ancho chile or jalapeño, stemmed and seeded

⅓ cup extra-virgin olive oil, plus additional if needed

Freshly squeezed lemon juice

Coarse sea salt

Freshly ground black pepper

Put the parsley, mint, tarragon, onions, garlic, and chile in a food processor. With the machine on, slowly drizzle in the olive oil until it reaches your desired consistency. Squeeze in some lemon juice and season with salt and black pepper. Store in an airtight container for up to 3 days. The flavors are best after 1 day.

Two-Shack "Como el Otro" Hot Sauce

chicken, pork, other meats, vegetables

This recipe is courtesy John "Two-Shack" Nicks. He says, "Many hot sauces are a mixture of vinegar, pepper of one or more varieties, and salt. I like to make a more complex hot sauce. I like the 'Two Dick Billy Goat' sauce at the Marfa, Texas, Thunderbird restaurant. I tried to duplicate it and came up with this. It will not be too hot for most people." **MAKES ABOUT 3 CUPS**

1 cup apple cider vinegar

½ (6-ounce) can tomato paste

1 small tomatillo or green tomato, chopped

4 dried cayenne peppers, chopped

3 Pasilla Bajio dried chiles, seeded (or keep seeds if you want more heat)

2 Anaheim peppers, pith removed, or mild Hatch peppers, if available

1½ teaspoons coarse sea salt

1 small carrot, shredded

1 small red onion, chopped

1½ teaspoons date molasses or black strap molasses

Mix all the ingredients together in a food processor. Refrigerate in an airtight container for up to 1 week.

Recipe Tip: Use the hot sauce for grilling or in a roasting pan with chicken or pork with more served on the side. If more heat is required, add cayenne pepper.

Red "DB" Chile Sauce

beans, burgers, burritos, eggs, tacos

New Mexico is chile HQ in the United States so I'm grateful to Gabriel Monthan, one of its native sons, for bestowing on us a traditional red chile sauce. His "DB" Chile pairs perfectly with Grandma Martha's New Mexico Green Chile Bean Sauce (page 154). This is a pistol whip of a red chile sauce. MAKES ABOUT 2 CUPS

¼ cup all-purpose flour

8 cups dried New Mexico red chiles, about 16 to 20 chilies

2 cups water

4 garlic cloves

1 tablespoon ground cumin

½ tablespoon coarse sea salt

1. Place a small skillet over medium-low heat. Add the flour and brown it, stirring constantly so it doesn't burn. The aroma should be nutty.

2. In a food processor or blender, add the browned flour, chiles, water, garlic, cumin, and salt and process until smooth.

3. Put the sauce in a small saucepan over low heat and cook for 30 minutes, stirring occasionally. Refrigerate in an airtight container for up to 3 weeks or freeze it.

Recipe Tip: If the sauce is thicker than you want after 30 minutes of cooking, add more water to get your desired consistency.

New Orleans Barbecue Shrimp Sauce

shrimp

Beeta Mohajeri's dreams of barbecued prawns led to her creating this outstanding barbecue shrimp recipe, which uses the Creole Spice Blend (page 140). This sauce is so delicious you'll be tempted to eat it with a spoon. You can. MAKES 1 CUP

2 tablespoons
unsalted butter

20–30 medium-size shrimp,
peeled and deveined

2 tablespoons Creole
Spice Blend (page 140)

¾ cup heavy
(whipping) cream

Worcestershire sauce

2 scallions, sliced,
for garnish

1. Heat the butter in a large skillet over medium heat. When hot, add the shrimp and sauté until they start to turn pink and curl, about 3 minutes per side.

2. Stir in the Creole seasoning, coating the shrimp. Then stir in the heavy cream, increase the heat to high, and reduce the liquid by half, stirring frequently, 3 to 5 minutes. Finally, add several dashes of Worcestershire sauce and stir to combine.

3. Transfer the shrimp and sauce to dishes and garnish with the scallions.

Recipe Tip: This is best served with slices of French baguette for dipping in the sauce.

Eastern Mediterranean, Middle East, and Africa

SPICES 165   RECIPES 185

The first route that sent flavors between Europe, India, and East Asia was the Silk Road. Leading the trade were the peoples of the Fertile Crescent and North Africa. Arab traders, who for centuries had traded with India and Asia, profited greatly by opening the markets to Europe. The Turkish Empire infused its own blend of Persian sweetness and spice into already-established Arab food customs, setting the tone for Middle Eastern food. Yet, despite these influences, one of the remarkable traits of Middle Eastern cuisine is that it was little influenced by the cuisines of faraway regions. Perhaps that speaks to the diversity of terrain, or the people's adherence and respect for tradition.

Along the North African coast, the Berbers—inhabitants of what are now Morocco, Algeria, Tunisia, and Libya—traded with the Carthaginians two thousand years ago. Later, the Phoenicians, Arabs, and Ottomans took turns crossing through and rotating control of an exceptional amount of trade goods, including spices. From this supply developed the spice blends *ras el hanout*, *charmoula*, and *harissa*. Similar trade existed by sea along Africa's western coast, especially after Bartolomeu Dias rounded the Cape of Good Hope in 1487, which was the only known sea route to India. When chile peppers from the Americas were introduced, they crawled through the continent and came out the other side as peri peri sauce and berbere, an Ethiopian spice blend.

Much of this part of the world is dry and arid, yet certain pockets are temperate and damp. Agricultural practices had to be safeguarded against drought, rainy seasons, shortages, and opportunistic adversaries. We are the direct beneficiaries of those practices and cultivations. Tamarind you'll recognize as the fundamental taste in Worcestershire sauce. Sesame seeds dot our hamburger buns. My favorite peanut butter substitute is in the form of *tahini*. There are limitless possibilities with the spices in this chapter and they also often combine famously with those from other world regions.

SPICES

Anise 166   Coriander 168

Cumin 170   Grains of Paradise 172

Licorice Root 174   Poppy Seeds 176

Saffron 178   Sesame Seeds 180

Tamarind 182

Anise

aniseed, sweet cumin, common anise

Long before sugar dominated the culinary landscape, a spice 13 times sweeter patrolled the cakes and digestifs of the ancient world: anise. The small, aromatic seeds were cultivated by the Greeks, Romans, and Egyptians, and coveted by Charlemagne and the Edwards of England.

Many cultures, especially European ones, have at least one liqueur devoted to honoring this taste and benefiting from its properties as a digestif. Romans understood its digestive properties in cooking as well, using anise to season *mustaceum*, a licorice-flavored, stomach-soothing cake. Modern day Europeans from Portugal to Scandinavia have their own version of anise pastries and cookies. It's fancied in Asia in salty dishes like meats, fish, and cheese.

Though opinion varies on the best form to cook with, anise's flavor quickly dissipates when ground. Whole seeds are tiny enough that they don't need pulverization. However, if your recipe or instinct calls for it, the seeds are typically easier—and tastier—to crush if they are first toasted. If making a pasta sauce, aniseed is a dynamic and healthy substitute for sugar when balancing the acidity of the tomato paste. Have some on hand to sprinkle on your next cheese plate or charcuterie board. Having trouble with nightmares? There's a legend that suggests stuffing your pillow with aniseeds ensures a good night's sleep. Sweet dreams!

CULTIVATION CENTERS

Greece, Egypt, Turkey, Lebanon, South America, Syria, southern Europe (Italy, Spain, Germany), India, Pakistan, China, Russia, Japan

AROMA & FLAVOR

Anise is sweet and fragrant. Forever associated with licorice, it resonates with camphor and is slightly mellifluous—think a more elegant star anise.

MEDICINAL USES

helps, treats, prevents, or aids asthma; appetite, nausea relief, and cramps; colic and bronchitis in children; halitosis; dehydration; digestion; flatulence; stomach ulcers; anise is an ingredient in some lozenges and cough drops

COMMON FORMS

seeds, whole and ground

COMPLEMENTS

breads, cakes and pastries; cheese; chicken and pork; fruits, fruit salad, applesauce, and jams; pasta with tomato and vegetable sauces; soups and stews with fish and shellfish

PAIRS WELL WITH

allspice, cilantro, cinnamon, clove, coriander, cumin, dill, fennel seeds, juniper, mace, nutmeg, mace, star anise, sumac

Coriander

Coriander seeds draw less ire than the leaf of the plant—cilantro—but have a similar range of flavors, especially when toasted. While cilantro has as many lovers as haters, coriander seeds are usually welcomed by all. It is one of the oldest known spices. Mentioned in Sanskrit texts from 5000 BCE? Check. Seeds found in Egyptian tombs? Yep. An ingredient prescribed for medicinal purposes in ancient Greece by Hippocrates? Of course. It has permeated almost every cuisine since.

That flavor that you taste from hot dogs to sandwich meat is coriander. Nearly 1 million pounds of coriander is consumed in the United States each year. In India, it is used in chutneys, curries, and masalas. The blend trend continues to Morocco and Tunisia where it is common to use in stews and lamb rubs. In Mexico, coriander is used for sweet dishes like bread pudding, as well.

Coriander is a charismatic spice to experiment with because of its forgiving nature. The flavor of whole coriander differs from ground seeds, but either pairs nicely with most other spices. You'll also get different results depending on how and when you incorporate it into your cooking. Most importantly, coriander is one of your best remedies because it can cover accidental overseasoning. Used too much turmeric or cumin? Add an equal amount of coriander as a neutralizer. The only real rule: don't toast the seeds if you're using them in baked goods.

CULTIVATION CENTERS

Middle East, India, Asia, North and South America, Southeast Asia, Argentina, Romania

AROMA & FLAVOR

Coriander is sharp with a flowery, sweet bouquet. It tastes of tangy sweetness with slightly bitter, citrusy, and nutty complements.

MEDICINAL USES

helps, treats, prevents, or aids constipation and diarrhea, bloating, flatulence, stomachaches, indigestion and nausea, yeast infections, insomnia, colic, type 2 diabetes, colon cancer, inflammatory skin diseases such as eczema and psoriasis, cholesterol issues and high blood pressure

COMMON FORMS AND VARIETIES

seeds, whole and ground; varieties include Moroccan coriander (spherical, darker) and Indian coriander (elliptical, sweeter)

COMPLEMENTS

cakes, confections, and sweets; curries, masalas, blends; fish, seafood, and marinades for them; fruits and vegetables meats, poultry, and sausage; mushrooms, lentils, legumes, beans, and potatoes; pickles, chutneys, salsas, and tomato sauces

PAIRS WELL WITH

black pepper, cardamom, clove, coconut, cumin, fennel seeds, garlic, ginger, mint, turmeric

Cumin

white cumin, green cumin, jeera

Despite hearing cumin as "come in" as a kid, I didn't accept the invitation until much later in life when I took to adding cumin when other spices weren't available. It wasn't an original idea.

As opposed to coriander, which in Sanskrit means "bug-smelling," cumin was known as "good smells" in Greek. They used it in a similar manner to black pepper, with a container on the dinner table. However, cumin wasn't limited to flavor. Romans cumin-laced their tea with the thought it would result in a fairer complexion. The students of the Roman scholar, Pliny, found it assisted in faking sickness. In Germany, women flavored breads with cumin to ensure their lovers stayed loyal. Cumin is mentioned in the Christian Bible, was a symbol of love, and was used in Egyptian mummification practices.

You'll rarely encounter cumin-free Mexican food. For quite some time my tacos were always fiery but lacked something. Once I was shown that I had left cumin on the bench, the game changed.

It will also bolster flavor in your pastes and sauces. Once you dry-roast the seeds, grind them right before you add them to your recipe to preserve their oil. They are quite powerful once toasted, so use them judiciously. Remember, it is so much easier to add more than try to take away. Use it in moderation and it will shower that love on your dish.

CULTIVATION CENTERS

Turkey, Egypt, Syria, China, India, Iran, Mexico, Argentina

AROMA & FLAVOR

Cumin certainly has an earthiness, but a light, piney, lemony scent. It tastes equally like bitter wood, and reminds me of throwing dried fir branches on a campfire.

MEDICINAL USES

helps, treats, prevents, or aids type 2 diabetes and associated cataracts, digestion, stress relief, lowers blood pressure, flatulence and cramping, colon cancer and cervical cancer risks, epilepsy, tuberculosis, food poisoning

COMMON FORMS AND VARIETIES

seeds, whole and ground; varieties include cumin and a variety known as black or imperial cumin (often confused with Nigella)

COMPLEMENTS

beans, legumes, and potatoes; breads; casseroles, tacos, burritos, and enchiladas; cheese; chili, sausages, stews, and heavy dishes; couscous; curries, stuffings, pastes, and rubs; kebabs; meat, lamb, and pork

PAIRS WELL WITH

ajowan, allspice, basil, black pepper, caraway, chiles, coriander, fennel seeds, garlic, ginger, mustard, oregano, pumpkin seeds, saffron, scallions, tamarind, turmeric

Grains of Paradise

Guinea pepper, Melegueta pepper, alligator pepper

Toward the end of a film shoot in Ghana, my team of Ghanaian assistant directors took me out to share a meal. Ghanaian food is heavy, rich, and wonderful, and so I dove into the spicy insanity of *fufu* and *kontomire* without reservation. A spice known as Guinea pepper, it's a common Ghanaian ingredient. It was much later that I learned it is known to us as grains of paradise.

Because of this spice, the West African coast was also once known as the Pepper Coast. Its similarity to and replacement for black pepper made grains of paradise hugely popular in Europe until sea routes to India were established. Grains of paradise include all the best parts of black pepper with a more well-rounded and complete taste.

Grains of paradise has perhaps the coolest name in the spice rolodex. Fortunately, its personality matches its name. For the wood-fire grill, adding grains of paradise to the pepper mill before seasoning your meat adds a layer of subtlety. A couple grains dropped into your red wine glass can give it a funky boost. Toasting is not essential, but it will draw out the flavor a bit. If you have a friend who is into home-brewing beer, suggest a grains of paradise lager or porter. Make sure you reserve yourself a six-pack.

CULTIVATION CENTERS

Ghana, West Africa

AROMA & FLAVOR

Grains of paradise evoke an aroma
of smooth, woody pepper, and some
detect lemon (although for me it's
orange, if anything). There is a late-onset
heat that coats the mouth with level,
peppery magic.

MEDICINAL USES

helps, treats, prevents, or aids weight
loss and weight control, blood sugar,
stomachache, diarrhea, inflammation;
it may improve cardiovascular health as
it does in wild gorillas

COMMON FORMS

seeds: ground and whole

COMPLEMENTS

beer, cordials, cocktails, and aquavit;
fish, shellfish, and mollusks; rubs, pastes,
and marinades; nuts and berries; salads;
steaks, pork, and poultry; warm pastries
and sweet cakes

PAIRS WELL WITH

allspice, black pepper, cardamom, chiles,
coriander, ginger, lemon peel, mace,
nutmeg, rosemary, thyme

Licorice Root

licorice, liquorice, sweetwood, sweetroot

The jellybeans I hoarded as a kid were my little jewels, all except the detested dark purple ones—the licorice flavor. This was all I knew of licorice until I chewed on an actual root. I was seduced by its intoxicating flavor.

Licorice flavor is a confectioner's dream. Renowned as an extract, it is in liqueurs, cordials, sweets, and candy. The saccharine compound found in the root, glycyrrhizin, outpunches sugar in sweetness 50 times over. Its flavor has much more to offer. The silkier powder is added to juice, fruit salad, teas, and tinctures. The powder will clump if there's too much moisture, so keep it in an airtight container in a dry spot. The root sticks are wonderful to keep around as they are great to chew on.

Many compare anise and fennel to licorice, but I find the camphor notes in those spices soften the impact of that tangy quality. So when experimenting at home, use licorice sparingly until you're comfortable with the strength of the flavor, as it can be quite overpowering.

One of the more curious and exciting applications of licorice is that of the Basques in northern Spain. They sharpen the long straight root and grill meat with it, imparting the sweetness to the protein. I imagine that could be blissfully extended to grilled fruit, too. Marshmallows on the end as well might be a memory-making experience for a child who loves licorice.

CULTIVATION CENTERS

Middle East, Turkey, Afghanistan, southern Europe, Russia, Asia, western United States

AROMA & FLAVOR

One whiff of licorice and its subdued sweetness is noticed. The taste brings a syrupy thick sweetness that feels heavy and thick, like it wants to stick around for the next thing you eat (and it might).

MEDICINAL USES

helps, treats, prevents, or aids intestinal problems, liver issues, teeth cleansing, inflammation, sore throats and coughs; pregnant women, and folks with kidney issues or high blood pressure should not eat licorice

COMMON FORMS

root, dried: sticks, slices, extract, powder

COMPLEMENTS

almost all fruits; chocolate, coconut, and creams including ice cream; confections, sweets, cookies, and brownies; pastries, breads, and cakes

PAIRS WELL WITH

ajowan, amchur, anardana, anise, fennel seeds, mint, sesame seeds, star anise, tamarind

Poppy Seeds

opium seeds, maw seeds

The urban legend that eating poppy seed bagels—a personal favorite—can trigger a positive drug test for opiates and/or morphine didn't enter my brain until I had to take a test for a job.

Morphine, opium, and codeine are derived from the alkaloids in the sap of poppy seed pods before they ripen. The ripe pods, harvested and dried, are eventually cracked open to reap the hundreds of seeds inside, which have lost the opiate component. They are almost iridescently blue and black and crackly. Their bitterness is not immediately inviting, but they are nutty, warm, and delicious with the complements listed below.

The cultivation of poppy seeds as a spice and for medicinal properties goes back to ancient times. Arab traders brought it with them in the great exchanges with the Far East. There's evidence the Greeks harnessed the poppy's pain-relieving properties. Egyptians and Romans flavored breads and oils with the seeds. Poppy found its way into Indian confections, Turkish breads, and Austrian dumplings. Almost anything strong in lemon can take a dose of poppy assistance.

Follow the simple spice rules of toasting and poppy seeds release more flavor. It's important to store them in a cool, dry place. Poppy seeds are extremely oily and can turn rancid quicker than other dried spices.

CULTIVATION CENTERS

Turkey, Iran, China, Southeast Asia, Tasmania, India, Holland, France, United States, Canada

AROMA & FLAVOR

The aroma of poppy seeds is akin to the warm muskiness of damp firewood. The taste is just slightly bitter, almost astringent, but when roasted has a nutty sweetness.

MEDICINAL USES

Once used for pain relief, sedative assistance, cholera, dysentery, and intestinal issues

COMMON FORMS AND VARIETIES

seeds, whole and ground; varieties include European poppy seeds (black), Turkish poppy seeds (brown), Indian poppy seeds (yellow, smallest)

COMPLEMENTS

breads, cakes, muffins, and bagels; crackers, cookies, and pastries; curries for fish and meat; custards, cream desserts, lemon pies, and sweets; eggs; pasta and tomato and cream sauces; potatoes, vegetables, and salads; salad dressing, honey, and vinegar; sauces, pastes, and dessert fillings

PAIRS WELL WITH

ajowan, cardamom, chiles, coriander, cumin, grains of paradise, juniper, lemon peel, nutmeg, saffron, sesame seeds, tamarind, turmeric

Saffron

Spanish saffron, hay saffron, crocus

We've all had that meal that we dream about forever after. Mine was in Valencia, Spain, and the brilliant marigold-hued seafood paella famous to the city.

It's not without irony that the world's most expensive spice could flutter away with an errant cough. Pound for pound, the threads of saffron are more valuable than gold. The color has sacrosanct connotations across cultures. Buddhist monks used it to color their robes, and Irish royalty tinted their garments with it. Both Greeks and Hindus consecrated their temples with saffron. Cleopatra is said to have used it in her vanity products.

Saffron is insanely difficult to harvest but has been done since time immemorial. Individual flower stigmas are plucked immediately upon blossoming. Though a pound of saffron—about 250,000 dried threads—can sell for $5,000, thankfully you only need a pinch per use.

Saffron has had varied uses throughout the geographic culinary landscape. It's practically blasphemous to make paella without using saffron. Iberians also use it for fish and seafood soups. Popular in dishes featuring rice and risotto, saffron flavors dishes from Mumbai to Milan. It's even used to season coffee in certain Arab cultures.

Beware of imposters. Powdered saffron is often cut with turmeric or sunflower. The only sure way to know you're getting the real McCoy is to buy the threads, toast them, and mash them in a mortar and pestle. Put them in warm milk and they'll immediately bleed silky goldenrod into the liquid.

CULTIVATION CENTERS

Italy, Spain, Eastern Mediterranean (Turkey, Iran, Greece), Spain, France, India, United States, Mexico

AROMA & FLAVOR

The smell and taste of saffron are wine-like. A flowery presence on the nose corresponds with a honeyed taste that can be slightly acerbic.

MEDICINAL USES

helps, treats, prevents, or aids depression, menstrual and uterine pain, male infertility and erectile dysfunction, memory loss, insomnia, multiple sclerosis, Parkinson's disease, indigestion, joint pain

COMMON FORMS AND VARIETIES

stigmas, threads and ground; varieties include Navelli, Abruzzo Italian saffron, La Mancha Spanish saffron, Kashmiri saffron, Tasmanian saffron, Iranian saffron, U.S. saffron, Mexican saffron (lowest grade)

COMPLEMENTS

curries, stews, rice dishes, polenta, and risotto; fish, shellfish, lobster, seafood paellas and soups; meat and poultry; potatoes, vegetables, tomato sauce, cream sauces, and bouillabaisse; puddings, cakes, scones, ice cream, yogurts, and flan

PAIRS WELL WITH

basil, black pepper, cardamom, cinnamon, cloves, coriander, cumin, garlic, mint, nutmeg, parsley, scallions

Sesame Seeds

sesame seeds, simsim, gingelly, benne, til

Every time my father brought home sesame seed buns for our hamburgers, my brother and I felt like we were millionaires. Plain buns were just inferior.

The origins of sesame seeds are not easily pinned down, but most sources agree they were first cultivated in Northern or Western Africa and quite quickly found their way to India. There is a representation of baker's bread and sesame seeds carved into the wall of an Egyptian tomb that dates back four thousand years. China has made expert use of sesame seeds for millennia as well, yet it is a non-native spice. Romans and Greeks were known to take them on their distant war campaigns, perhaps because of the nature of the seed's content.

Sesame seeds are remarkable because they are considered one of the world's oldest oilseeds. The oil makes up about half of the seed itself, and is a valuable commodity because it is nonvolatile and so doesn't easily turn rancid. The seeds are brimming with protein, iron, manganese, zinc, and antioxidants, making them a popular spice in every region where they're found.

Certain Asian traditions ascribe magical powers to sesame seeds, believing they bring good luck. If it's toasted good luck that makes mango stir-fry with black sesame so incredible, so be it.

Toasting sesame seeds is definitely worth the time it takes. Take care to not over-toast as they can become bitter. When golden, their nutty sweetness intensifies. Try substituting black sesame seeds for white. They add aesthetic value and have a richer taste.

CULTIVATION CENTERS

East Africa, Egypt, Middle East, Greece, Mexico

AROMA & FLAVOR

Sesame has a decadent creamy aroma and an oily, almond-like or nutty sweet taste.

MEDICINAL USES

helps, treats, prevents, or aids high blood pressure, cholesterol issues, high blood pressure and heart disease, cancer, Alzheimer's disease, healing of wounds

COMMON FORMS AND VARIETIES

seeds, whole; varieties include white seeds, brown seeds, and black seeds

COMPLEMENTS

bread, pita, rolls, biscuits, crackers, cake, pastries, sweets, and confections; grilled meat, chicken, and fruit; noodles, dumplings, and rice; salad dressings, vinegar, and cooking oil; stir-fried, steamed, and roasted veggies; sweets like dates, licorice, and honey

PAIRS WELL WITH

allspice, cardamom, chiles, cinnamon, cloves, coriander, garlic, ginger, lemon peel, mace, licorice, mustard, nutmeg, oregano, pumpkin seeds, shallots, sumac, thyme, vanilla, wasabi

Tamarind

Indian date, assam

Tamarind comes from the pods of a massive tree thought to be native to the tropical regions of East Africa, although some believe it was first cultivated in India or Southeast Asia. Regardless of its origins, tamarind established itself as a divinely honeyed acidulant used similarly to how lemon and lime are used in the West. Its rounded succulence makes it a souring agent with more layers than its simpler, citrusy counterparts.

Tamarind is neither a seed nor a pod nor a root. Instead, the pulp that surrounds the seeds inside the pods is harvested, during which it turns dark brown or black. From there it's dried into blocks or processed into a concentrate.

In the kitchen, tamarind has a number of intriguing uses. Its tangy freshness moderates chiles in a pleasing and palatable manner. It gives a bold edge to yogurt, fruit juices, and savory drinks. Recently, a friend's Moroccan mother made me a heavenly tamarind-flavored mango lassi yogurt drink, which blew my mind and opened up a world of flavorful possibilities.

It's wonderful when a recipe calls for tamarind concentrate because it is so easy to work with. However, many recipes require tamarind water (or juice). Make a juice from a pulp block or from concentrate. Take ¼ cup of concentrate or a 2-inch piece of block and soak it for 10 to 20 minutes in 1 cup of preboiled water. Strain through cheesecloth and discard any residue. Tailor the amounts to your preferred consistency.

CULTIVATION CENTERS

East Africa, India, Middle East, Southeast Asia, Caribbean, Mexico

AROMA & FLAVOR

Tamarind has a sweet, tangy scent. A matching acidic taste is combined with fruit and honey-like notes. The result is sweet but sharp and sour for a pleasant, refreshing flavor.

MEDICINAL USES

helps, treats, prevents, or aids dysentery and digestive issues (is used as a laxative in Thailand); eye problems such as cataracts, infection, conjunctivitis, and dryness; used in India for asthma relief and for fevers; cholesterol problems; heart disease and high blood pressure; used in Ayurvedic medicine for wounds, sore joints, and sore throats

COMMON FORMS AND VARIETIES

pulp in the form of dried blocks, concentrate, and ground; varieties include Indian tamarind and Thai tamarind

COMPLEMENTS

curries, sambar, chutneys, and satay; desserts, candy, and sweets; fish, meat, poultry, and eggs; fruit drinks, juices, jams, and jellies; legumes, lentils, beans, potatoes, and veggies; nuts and pickled foods; rice dishes, stir-fries, soups, and stews; samosas and dumplings; sauces, marinades, bitters, and seafood pastes

PAIRS WELL WITH

ajowan, amchur, black pepper, chiles, cloves, galangal, garlic, ginger, grains of paradise, scallions, turmeric

RECIPES

Ras el Hanout Blend 186

Advieh Persian Blend 187

Baharat Blend 188

Feh El Omri Blend 189

Dukkah Egyptian Dry Rub 190

La Kama Dry Rub 191

Peri Peri Dry Rub 192

Qâlat Daqqa Tunisian Dry Rub 193

Berbere Rub 194

Tunisian Tabil Paste 195

Black Tahini Paste 196

Chaimen Armenian Spice Paste 197

Charmoula Paste 198

Poppy Paste 200

Harissa Paste 201

Homemade Saffron Mayo Marinade 202

Moroccan Lamb Tajine Marinade 203

Tamarind Yogurt Marinade 204

Saffron Sauce 205

Left: Charmoula Paste (page 198)

Ras el Hanout Blend

fish, marinades and rubs, meat such as lamb, chicken, goat, and beef,
or in soups, stews, rice, or couscous

Ras el hanout is a North African blend that traditionally contained the best spices the seller had to offer, anywhere from 10 to 50 different ones. Ras el hanout is comparable to that of India's garam masala in terms of importance and versatility. Here's a starter blend; adjust the ingredients to your taste. MAKES ABOUT ¾ CUP

3 tablespoons cumin seeds

2 tablespoons coriander seeds

1 teaspoon green cardamom pods

1 teaspoon anise seeds

1 teaspoon black peppercorns

1 teaspoon grains of paradise

1 teaspoon fennel seeds

1 tablespoon dried rosebuds

1 teaspoon dried lavender

1 teaspoon ground nutmeg

2 tablespoons paprika

1 tablespoons ground turmeric

1 teaspoon ground cinnamon

1 teaspoon ground ginger

1 teaspoon ground mace

1 teaspoon ground cayenne pepper or chili powder

1. In a small skillet over medium heat, toast the cumin, coriander, cardamom, anise, peppercorns, grains of paradise, and fennel until fragrant, 1 to 2 minutes. Transfer to a dish and let cool, then loosely grind in a spice grinder. Transfer to a small bowl.

2. Crush the rosebuds, lavender, and nutmeg in a mortar or loosely grind them in a spice grinder. Add to the small bowl and mix in the paprika, turmeric, cinnamon, ginger, mace and cayenne.

3. Store in an airtight jar for up to 1 year.

Recipe Tip: Add or subtract flavors as you see fit. For visual appeal, avoid completely crushing the rosebuds and lavender. Add whole grains of paradise and cinnamon sticks to the jar for use in marinades. For use in stews and soups, make this blend with whole spices, not ground.

Advieh Persian Blend

couscous, lamb, pilafs, rice dishes, roasts

Advieh is a pungent Persian spice blend and one of the main ingredients used in haroset or charoset, a fruit and nut paste made during Passover. Try adding rose petals, rosebuds, or lemon peel and create your own blend. It's also not very hot, so it's great for beginning cooks. **MAKES ½ CUP**

1 tablespoon coriander seeds

5 green cardamom pods

1 teaspoon cumin seeds

1 teaspoon grains of paradise

1 teaspoon black peppercorns

1 cinnamon stick or 2 teaspoons ground cinnamon

1 teaspoon ground ginger

1 teaspoon nutmeg

1 teaspoon ground rose petals (optional)

Coarse sea salt

Dash of paprika

1. In a small skillet over medium heat, toast the coriander, cardamom, cumin, grains of paradise, and peppercorns for 1 to 2 minutes. Transfer to a dish and let cool.

2. Add the toasted spices to a spice grinder and loosely grind. Transfer to a bowl and mix in the cinnamon, ginger, nutmeg, and rose petals (if using). Stir in a pinch each of salt and paprika. Store in an airtight jar for up to 3 months or until the rose petals dry out.

Recipe Tip: Advieh blends are open to interpretation. Add or subtract ingredients such as turmeric, lemon peel, mace, and/or saffron. Mix it with oil, vinegar, yogurt, or sour cream to make a paste.

Baharat Blend

beef, lamb, meat stews, stuffings, tomato sauces

Baharat blends are used from Tangiers to Turkey. It has light notes of spiciness and sweetness. You can season nearly everything with it. Baharat can be used as a condiment, dry rub, marinade, or combined with oil or vinegar for a paste.

MAKES ½ CUP

1 tablespoon cumin seeds

1 tablespoon coriander seeds

1 tablespoon whole cloves

1 tablespoon black peppercorns

2 teaspoons cardamom pods

1 tablespoon ground cinnamon

1 tablespoon Hungarian sweet paprika

1 tablespoon ground nutmeg

Sea salt to taste

In a small skillet over medium heat, toast the cumin, coriander, cloves, peppercorns and cardamom for 1 to 2 minutes. Transfer to a dish and let cool, then grind in a spice grinder. Mix in the cinnamon, paprika, and nutmeg. Store in an airtight jar for 6 months to 1 year.

Recipe Tip: This spice blend can take some heat, so add some cayenne pepper if that's your jam. Don't forget to salt your steak prior to cooking. Make an easy kebab marinade by stirring in ½ cup yogurt or oil.

Feh El Omri Blend

chicken, couscous, fish, rice, vegetable-based sauces

This blend is courtesy of Nisrine Omri's family. Her aunts and grandmother choose and dry their own spices and herbs and then have them ground at a mill. They make enough for the year, so Nisrine and I slashed the quantities for practicality. MAKES ABOUT 1½ CUPS

8 tablespoons caraway seeds

6 tablespoons coriander seeds

1 tablespoon dried rose petals (about 10–15)

1 tablespoon dried ginger

1 tablespoon ground cinnamon

1 tablespoon dried rosemary

1 tablespoon dried thyme

1 tablespoon dried basil

½ teaspoon black pepper

½ teaspoon galangal

½ teaspoon allspice

½ teaspoon ground cloves

Grind all the ingredients together in a spice grinder. Store in an airtight jar for up to 1 year.

Recipe Tip: Add a few garlic cloves to a few tablespoons of Feh with some (Tunisian!) olive oil and mash with a mortar and pestle. It makes a pungent, flavorful paste you can use as a base for delicious sauces.

Dukkah Egyptian Dry Rub

chicken, grilled or fried fish, pork, poultry, steak

Dukkah is a nut-based mix that is an excellent dry rub for proteins. Hazelnuts are traditional, but chickpeas, sesame seeds, and pistachios are in the rotation as well. I can't get enough of pistachios, so I went in that direction. **MAKES ABOUT 1 CUP**

2 tablespoons
sesame seeds

¼ cup hazelnuts

2 tablespoons pistachios

1 tablespoon
coriander seeds

1 tablespoon cumin seeds

2 teaspoons
black peppercorns

1¼ teaspoon dried mint

1 teaspoon dried thyme

Pinch coarse sea salt

1. In a small skillet over medium-low heat, toast the sesame seeds for about 1 minute. Transfer to a dish and let them cool. In the same skillet, toast the hazelnuts then add them to the dish. Finally, toast the pistachios then transfer them to the dish to cool. Place the nut-seed mixture in a food processor and pulse to coarsely grind.

2. In the skillet over medium heat, toast the coriander, cumin, and peppercorns for 1 to 2 minutes. Transfer to a dish and let cool, then grind in a spice grinder. Transfer to a small bowl and mix in the ground nut-seed mixture. Stir in the mint, thyme, and salt. Store in an airtight jar for up to 3 months.

Recipe Tip: Add extra-virgin olive oil to make a dipping sauce for bread or to drizzle over yogurt, sour cream, or feta cheese.

La Kama Dry Rub

chicken, fish, lamb, poultry, and to flavor soups and stews

La kama is from the Moroccan city of Tangiers. It is used to season tagines, slow-cooked dishes prepared in clay pots. It also flavors harira, *a soup eaten to break the Ramadan fast. This blend is not hot though it is a bit peppery.* **MAKES ¼ CUP**

2 teaspoons ground cumin

2 teaspoons ground grains of paradise

2 teaspoons freshly ground black pepper

2 teaspoons ground turmeric

2 teaspoons ground cinnamon

1 teaspoon ground nutmeg

1 teaspoon ground mace

1 teaspoon ground ginger

Mix all the ingredients together. Store in an airtight jar for up to 3 months.

Recipe Tip: La kama can be as simple as black pepper, cinnamon, turmeric, nutmeg, and ginger. I love the slow onset of heat from the grains of paradise, though it is not the norm to use it.

Peri Peri Dry Rub

chicken, seafood, shrimp

Peri peri is a complex, slightly tangy, fiery blend and sauce prevalent in Mozambique, Angola, and Namibia. It is not to be confused with the piri piri pepper, which Portuguese explorers brought home from Mozambique, although it's sometimes labeled as Portuguese Piri Piri seasoning. **MAKES ABOUT ¼ CUP**

2 dried piri piri chiles or other hot chiles, stemmed and seeded

1 dried ancho or chipotle chile, stemmed and seeded

2 tablespoons paprika

1 teaspoon onion powder

1 teaspoon garlic powder

1 teaspoon dried lemon peel

1 teaspoon dried oregano

1 teaspoon dried tarragon

1 teaspoon salt

1 teaspoon ground grains of paradise

2 tablespoons olive oil

1 garlic glove, minced

Zest of ½ lemon

Juice of ½ lemon

1. In a small skillet over medium-low heat, toast the piri piri and ancho chiles for about 2 minutes. Transfer to a dish to cool.

2. Loosely crush or grind the chiles in a mortar and pestle. Transfer to a bowl and mix in the paprika, onion powder, garlic powder, lemon peel, oregano, tarragon, salt, and grains of paradise. Store in an airtight jar for up to 6 months.

3. To make into a marinade, mix 2 tablespoons of the blend with the olive oil, garlic, lemon zest, and lemon juice. Use immediately.

Recipe Tip: Piri piri chiles can be explosive so use them judiciously. The blend has so many flavors, however, that I find the heat more manageable than in other fiery offerings. Start small and work up from there.

Qâlat Daqqa Tunisian Dry Rub

meat stews, tagines, vegetables, lentils, beans, legumes

Qâlat daqqa, or Tunisian five-spice mix, is on the other end of the heat spectrum from harissa and tabil. It has a bite from pepper, a slow-release burn from grains of paradise, and a sweetness from cinnamon. All that is balanced by earthy nutmeg and cloves. **MAKES ¼ CUP**

2 teaspoons grains
of paradise

2 teaspoons whole cloves

2 teaspoons ground nutmeg

1 teaspoon
ground cinnamon

1 teaspoon
black peppercorns

Grind all the ingredients together to a fine powder. Store in an airtight jar for up to 6 months. Add to other marinades in this book or use as a dry rub.

Recipe Tip: Add a squeeze of lemon juice after cooking with qâlat daqqa to give an acidic balance to the spice blend.

Berbere Rub

lamb, steak, use as a starter to soups and stews

My mother introduced me to Ethiopian food. Everything is delicious, especially those thick stews flavored with berbere. Add this blend to your soups and stews and especially your slow-cooking recipes. **MAKES ½ CUP**

1 tablespoon
coriander seeds

1 teaspoon green
cardamom seeds

5 to 7 whole cloves

1 teaspoon allspice berries

1 teaspoon
black peppercorns

1 teaspoon grains
of paradise

½ teaspoon fenugreek

1 (1-inch) cinnamon stick

1 teaspoon nigella seeds

4 tablespoons sharp (hot)
Hungarian paprika

3 dried chiles, heat
level of choice

1 tablespoon ground
cayenne pepper

1 teaspoon dried
ginger powder

1. In a small skillet over medium heat, toast the coriander, cardamom, and cloves, stirring constantly, for 1 to 2 minutes. Transfer to a dish and let the mixture cool. In the same skillet, toast the allspice, peppercorns and grains of paradise for 1 to 2 minutes. Add to the dish to cool. Finally, toast the fenugreek and add to the dish to cool.

2. In a spice grinder, grind the cinnamon and nigella and transfer it to a small bowl. Grind the toasted spices in the spice grinder and add them to the bowl. Add the paprika.

3. In the skillet over medium heat, toast the chiles for 2 to 3 minutes. Transfer to a mortar and pestle and crush them. Add to the bowl with the other spices, cayenne, and ginger, and mix together. Store in an airtight container for up to 3 months.

Recipe Tip: To make a paste, reconstitute the untoasted chiles in warm water for 20 minutes. Drain and roast them in a bit of olive oil with minced ginger, onion, carrot, garlic, and the rest of the ingredients in the list. Add more olive oil and some vinegar in a 3:1 ratio and mix until a paste forms. Marinate proteins for several hours.

Tunisian Tabil Paste

couscous, curries, grilled meat and fish, rice

Tabil, which means coriander, is a Tunisian spice blend featuring—what else?—coriander, plus a supporting cast of regional spices and garlic. It can be used a bit like a spicy curry. It's also similar to, but less aggressive than, Harissa Paste (page 201). **MAKES ABOUT ½ CUP**

5 tablespoons coriander seeds, hulled from pods

2 tablespoons caraway seeds

1 tablespoon ground cumin

1 tablespoon ground anise

1 tablespoon chili powder

2 teaspoons garlic powder

5 tablespoons extra-virgin olive oil, divided

Coarse sea salt

Freshly ground black pepper

Grind the coriander and caraway in a spice grinder. Transfer to a small bowl and mix in the cumin, anise, chili powder, and garlic powder. Mix in the olive oil to form a thick paste. Season with salt and pepper. Refrigerate in an airtight jar for up to 2 weeks.

Recipe Tip: Add a red hot chile pepper, minced onion, cinnamon, and turmeric to the paste to make a bastardized version of Hrous, a super hot Tunisian paste. Both go great over fish and meat cooked on the grill.

Black Tahini Paste

dipping sauce for bread, snacks, and veggies or as a spread for sandwiches and pitas

Black tahini is a delicious way to add some color to your charcuterie plate and see the aghast look on your guests' faces. Black sesame seeds are found in Asian and Indian specialty markets and have a very similar taste to their white counterpart. MAKES ¾ TO 1 CUP

1 cup hulled black sesame seeds

About 5 tablespoons extra-virgin olive oil or grapeseed oil, divided

1 tablespoon ground coriander

Freshly squeezed lemon juice

Coarse sea salt

1. In a small skillet or cast-iron pan, toast the sesame seeds to take the bitter edge off them and enhance their flavor, 5 to 7 minutes, taking care not to burn them.

2. Transfer the seeds to a food processor and add 3 tablespoons of oil and the coriander. Process until well incorporated. With the processor running, slowly add in as much of the remaining 2 tablespoons of oil as needed to get your desired consistency. Add lemon juice to taste and season with salt.

3. Refrigerator in an airtight container for up to 2 weeks, but it's best when freshly made.

Recipe Tip: Tahini makes a healthy snack. Substitute white seeds for black as desired or to make hummus. Unhulled sesame seeds are rougher in texture and untoasted seeds will be slightly more acrid and less nutty.

Chaimen Armenian Spice Paste

beef, soups, stews, vegetables

Chaimen is the principal flavoring spice for Armenian basturma, *salted beef that is dried by hanging in the open air.* Chaimen *means fenugreek in Armenian, which is one of the main components of this blend. The paste is made with yogurt and a quick tomato sauce.* **MAKES ABOUT 1½ CUPS**

2 tablespoons fenugreek

1 tablespoon cumin seeds

1 teaspoon coriander seeds

1 teaspoon allspice berries

2 tablespoons mild Hungarian paprika

1 teaspoon ground cayenne pepper

1 teaspoon garlic powder

1 teaspoon coarse sea salt

½ teaspoon sugar

2 tablespoons water

2 tablespoons tomato paste

1 cup plain, thick yogurt

2 bunches fresh parsley, chopped

1. In a small skillet over medium heat, toast the fenugreek, cumin, coriander, and allspice for 1 to 2 minutes. Transfer to a dish and let cool, then grind to a powder in a spice grinder. Transfer to a small bowl and mix in the paprika, cayenne, garlic powder, and salt. This spice blend will keep in an airtight jar for about 1 month.

2. In a large bowl, dissolve the sugar in the water. Add the tomato paste and mix together. Mix in the yogurt. Stir in the chaimen spice blend and parsley. Refrigerate in an airtight container for up to 1 week.

Recipe Tip: Use as a 1-hour marinade for beef and heavy meats, or as a dipping sauce.

Charmoula Paste

chicken, grilled fish and seafood, veggies

Charmoula, also spelled "chermoula," is a Maghreb (North African) spice paste that, like several ancient spice blends, has divergent variations depending on region. This recipe is Moroccan in nature. In Tunisia, charmoula is sweet and red and made with raisins. For all versions, charmoula works best to marinate grilled seafood and fish. It's delicious as a topping on chicken and vegetables as well. MAKES ½ CUP

1 tablespoon cumin seeds

1 teaspoon coriander seeds

½ teaspoon
black peppercorns

¼ cup extra-virgin olive
oil plus 1 teaspoon,
plus more if needed

1 (1-inch) piece fresh
ginger, minced

2 garlic cloves, minced

2 teaspoons mild paprika

1 teaspoon ground
cayenne pepper

1 teaspoon freshly
grated lemon peel

½ teaspoon coarse sea salt

1 bunch fresh cilantro,
stemmed and chopped

1 bunch fresh parsley,
stemmed and chopped

1 tablespoon freshly
squeezed lemon juice

1. In a small skillet over medium heat, toast the cumin, coriander, and peppercorns for 1 to 2 minutes. Transfer to a dish and let cool.

2. Heat 1 teaspoon of oil in the skillet over medium heat. Add the ginger and garlic and sauté until golden, 1 to 2 minutes.

3. Place the ginger and garlic in a mortar and pestle or a blender with the toasted spices and blend together. Combine the paprika, cayenne, lemon peel, salt, cilantro, and parsley in a food processor and process until it becomes consistent.

4. Slowly incorporate the lemon juice and as much of the remaining ¼ cup of oil as you need to form a paste. Best if used within 1 hour.

Recipe Tip: The spices can be ground into a powder, but often the blend comes as a chunky spice mix. This is a good one to practice your mortar and pestle skills. The marriage of the parsley, cilantro, and oil is a bit of dance, so play with the quantities to suit your taste.

Poppy Paste

breads, dressings, pies

Poppy paste is used for all things sweet and can be generously added to fillings and spreads for cakes, pies, sweets, and bread. A smear on a warm croissant is divine. MAKES 1 CUP

4 tablespoons sugar

3 tablespoons water

5 tablespoons poppy seeds

2 tablespoons honey

1 tablespoon sesame seeds

½ tablespoon pure vanilla extract or vanilla seeds

3 dried apricots, chopped (optional)

In a small saucepan, bring the sugar and water to a simmer for about 3 minutes, stirring frequently. Stir in the poppy seeds, honey, sesame seeds, vanilla, and apricots (if desired). Simmer for 5 minutes. Let rest and use for fillings, toppings, and any sweets or combine in any muffin, cupcake, or sweet bread batter. Refrigerate until it thickens. Store in an airtight container for up to 5 days.

Recipe Tip: Add a bit of lemon zest and/or lavender to give the paste some zest or floral backing. Add vinegar and lemon juice to make a sweet salad dressing.

Harissa Paste

bread, couscous, marinating lamb and fish, tagines

My friend Nisrine raves about Tunisian sauces. "We eat lots of sauces with lamb and veggies. They are eaten with French bread, which costs 5 cents—a holdover from French colonialist subsidies." Harissa is one of the most popular pastes across North Africa and is an essential condiment on any late-night doner kebab. **MAKES ½ CUP**

1 ounce hot chile such as habanero, cayenne, or bird's eye, stemmed and seeded

1 ounce mild chile such as ancho, guajillo, or chipotle, stemmed and seeded

1 teaspoon coriander seeds

1 teaspoon cumin seeds

1 teaspoon caraway seeds

4 tablespoons extra-virgin olive oil, divided

3 garlic cloves, minced

1 teaspoon dried mint

Coarse sea salt

1. Place the chiles in a small bowl and cover with warm water. Soak for 20 to 30 minutes. Drain the chiles.

2. In a small skillet over medium heat, toast the coriander, cumin, and caraway for 1 to 2 minutes. Transfer the seeds to a dish and let them cool, then grind in a spice grinder.

3. In the skillet over medium heat, add 1 tablespoon of oil. When hot, add the chiles and garlic and sauté for 2 to 3 minutes. Transfer to a food processor and add the ground spices and mint. With the processor running, drizzle in the remaining 3 tablespoons of oil to form a thick paste. Season with salt.

4. Refrigerate in an airtight glass jar for up to 2 months.

Recipe Tip: When storing, cover with a thin layer of extra-virgin olive oil on top. Use as a paste, sauce, or marinade.

Homemade Saffron Mayo Marinade

fish, especially fatty fish like salmon, tuna, and mackerel, or on grilled or baked meats

This recipe was inspired by my friend Paul, who uses mayonnaise to marinate fish because it's an emulsion and acts as a time-release to the other flavoring agents. Just about everything goes well with mayo, which is why it's the perfect vehicle for ras el hanout and its symphony of flavors. MAKES ABOUT 1 CUP

½ teaspoon saffron threads

1 egg yolk

2 tablespoons freshly squeezed lemon juice

2 teaspoons Dijon mustard

1 teaspoon white wine vinegar

¾ cup canola oil

2 tablespoons Ras el Hanout Blend (page 186)

½ teaspoon coarse sea salt

½ teaspoon grains of paradise

1. In a small dish, soak the saffron in 1 tablespoon of warm (not scalding) water for 15 minutes.

2. Place the egg yolk, lemon juice, mustard, and vinegar in a food processor and process until thoroughly blended. With the machine running, slowly add the oil and process until the mayonnaise is thick. Blend in the saffron and saffron water. Mix in the ras el hanout, salt, and grains of paradise. Because of the raw egg yolk, use the mayo immediately.

Recipe Tip: Mayonnaise simultaneously traps in moisture and keeps the marinade on the protein for the duration of the cooking process, instead of slipping off like oil and vinegar. Marinate proteins for 1 hour before cooking. Alternatively, use the mayo as a dipping sauce, but be aware than it contains raw egg yolk.

Moroccan Lamb Tajine Marinade

lamb and any hearty meat

Ras el hanout, why are you so good? Its sublime combination of spices enhances nearly any grilled meat. The blend is ubiquitous in Middle Eastern markets, and somehow avoided my gaze until I had life-changing ras el hanout–seasoned lamb made by my friend's Moroccan mom, Fatima. MAKES 2 CUPS

1 tablespoon Ras el
Hanout Blend (page 186)

½ cup olive oil

3 garlic cloves, chopped

1 large onion, chopped

1 tablespoon honey

To make the marinade, mix together the ras el hanout, oil, garlic, onion, and honey. Use immediately with 2 to 3 pounds of lamb stew meat (bone-in, if preferred).

Recipe Tip: Marinate lamb for about 3 hours in the refrigerator. Cook lamb in the marinade in a clay pot (tagine on medium, covered,) or roasting pot for 7 minutes. Add 2 or 3 freshly chopped tomatoes and 2 cups water. Cook for 30 to 45 minutes on medium-low, uncovered. The meat should be tender at this point. Add chopped vegetables of your choice (cabbage, carrots, green apples, butternut squash, for example) and 2 cups cooked chickpeas. Cook for another 15 to 20 minutes. For the last 10 minutes of cooking, add 1 cup raisins and a couple pinches salt. As it roasts, you may need to add water to the pan as the liquid evaporates. Serve with tea and mints.

Tamarind Yogurt Marinade

grilled lamb, goat, beef, seafood, and fish

Tangy tamarind makes an excellent marinade for heavier meats and fatty sea-food. Tamarind imparts a candy-like (read: sweet) effect and I love the way it juxtaposes with salty meats and seafood. Some anise and licorice are added to enhance the effect. **MAKES 1½ CUPS**

1 teaspoon grains
of paradise

½ teaspoon anise seeds

1 tablespoon sesame seeds

1 teaspoon cumin seeds

½ teaspoon coriander seeds

1 cup plain yogurt

3 tablespoons water

1 tablespoon tamarind
pulp concentrate

1 teaspoon freshly
grated lemon zest

½ teaspoon fennel seeds

½ teaspoon garlic powder

Coarse sea salt

Freshly squeezed lemon
juice (optional)

1. In a small skillet over medium-low heat, toast the grains of paradise and anise seeds for 1 to 2 minutes. Transfer to a dish and let cool, then mash loosely in a mortar and pestle.

2. In the same skillet, toast the sesame seeds, cumin, and coriander for 1 to 2 minutes. Transfer to a dish to cool, then grind loosely in a spice grinder.

3. In a medium bowl, mix together the toasted spices, yogurt, water, tamarind, lemon zest, fennel, and garlic powder, and season with salt. Stir in a squeeze of lemon juice (if using). Refrigerate in an airtight container for up to 2 days.

Recipe Tip: This marinade can swing double duty as a sauce so make twice the amount. Marinate your protein for about 4 hours in half the marinade. When it is done cooking, season the protein with salt and top it with the rest of the marinade/sauce just prior to serving.

Saffron Sauce

chicken, duck, rabbit, and light game, or on seafood like fish, shrimp, scallops, clams, or mussels

Saffron is part of Mediterranean life. This sauce is reminiscent of Italian and Spanish cream sauces featuring their high-grade saffron. It is best to use threads, as powdered saffron often contains filler. It's expensive, but you generally end up getting your money's worth since only a little is required. MAKES 1 CUP

½ teaspoon saffron threads

¼ cup vegetable stock, warm

½ cup dry white wine

2 teaspoons peanut oil, divided

2 garlic cloves, minced

¼ cup heavy (whipping) cream

2 tablespoons unsalted butter

½ teaspoon fish or anchovy paste

1 teaspoon cumin seeds, ground

1 teaspoon dried mint leaves

Salt to taste

1. In a small bowl, crush the saffron and soak it in the warm (not hot) stock for about 15 minutes until a golden hue develops.

2. In a medium saucepan over medium heat, combine the wine, 1 teaspoon of oil, and garlic. Once the wine is steaming, reduce the heat to medium-low and stir in the cream. Slowly stir in the butter, fish paste, and remaining 1 teaspoon of oil. Add the saffron and stock. Cook for about 5 minutes, then stir in the cumin and mint. Use immediately.

Recipe Tip: For best results, add 1 pound of your protein of choice, chopped, in the steaming wine in step 2. Cook for about 5 minutes (or until clam or mussel shells have opened) then transfer to a bowl, leaving the liquid in the saucepan. If using mussels or clams, remove the meat from the shells once they are open. Discard any that didn't open. Return the protein to the pan after the cumin and mint has been added. Cook until the fish or chicken pieces are cooked through (5 to 10 minutes) or shrimp, clams, or mussels are mixed thoroughly with the sauce (2 to 4 minutes). Be sure to remove from the heat before the sauce breaks down. Salt to taste and serve.

Europe and the Mediterranean

SPICES 209   RECIPES 231

uropeans sought to conquer the world in search of spices. First by land, then by sea, they scoured the globe for flavors to satisfy their yearning palates. The frequent invasions and conflicts of Southern and Western Europe (the Moors and Ottomans, respectively) facilitated a gastronomic conversation that developed the complexity and robustness of the cuisines of those regions. In Northern Europe, less outside influence confined the insular lessons of food dynamics to similar principles and tastes. Dill, mustard, and fennel are standards in Northern Europe and Scandinavia. Southern Europe is not dissimilar but seamlessly added uses for chiles, paprika, nutmeg, and saffron.

European flavors complement and enhance without overpowering—there's a balance. European food generally isn't associated with spiciness and is instead more focused on herbs. We are, however, quite used to the spices Europe first cultivated. Any gin drinker is familiar with the piney, sweet flavor of juniper berries. Celery seeds are guests in nearly every sausage that enters my skillet. Their soft bitter flavor goes well with the salty pork and spicier chorizo. Mustard is a steadfast companion to the roasts, broils, and stews of Northern Europe, where soul-warming food gets folks through long, cold winters. Dill seeds and fennel seeds provide spices to complement their herbaceous components. Paprika is commonly found in dishes further south. Fenugreek and sumac are quite popular along the Mediterranean and have made their nests in Middle Eastern cooking as well.

Whether you're acquainted with these flavors or discovering them for the first time, the spices in this chapter are astonishingly forgiving tools for your culinary toolbox. If you already cook traditional European food, this chapter is an ideal resource for flavors you are already familiar with, as well as new ones to expand your own recipes. A terrific starting point is adding a jar of juniper berries to your spice cabinet. You can throw them into food—particularly roasted meat—or drinks for an added boost of refreshment.

SPICES

~~~~

Caraway 210   Celery Seeds 212

Dill Seeds 214   Fennel Seeds 216

Fenugreek 218   Horseradish 220

Juniper Berries 222   Mustard Seeds 224

Paprika 226   Sumac 228

Caraway

Roman cumin, German cumin, Persian cumin, karawya, wild cumin

Caraway so closely resembles several other spices it is called various forms of cumin—Roman, foreign, wild—and suggests the aroma and taste of anise, fennel, and dill. Caraway weaves its ways through legends and folklore from *Alice in Wonderland* to the belief that caraway love potions would keep lovers and spouses from adultery.

Caraway is a Stone Age spice whose culinary purposes dates back at least five thousand years. There's evidence that suggests it was cultivated in central Asia as well. Holland was the main producer, however. Nowadays, it is used extensively in Germany, Austria, Scandinavia, and Britain. It is playfully referred to as "foreign" cumin in some Asian customs.

Robust Northern European food is best served by caraway. Soups, stews, potatoes, sausages, sauerkraut, sauerbraten, boiled cabbage, and roasts benefit from caraway's ability to offset their heavy components and reduce post-meal gas. Cheese is caraway's other strong genre. While Alsatians in France find it appealing with Muenster, Hungarians and Dutch use it in Liptauer and Tilsiter, respectively. Caraway excels in breads, cakes, candies, and confections; as a breath sweetener; and in blends such as garam masala, harissa, and tabil in Tunisia, zhug on the Arabian Peninsula, and dahi wada in India. Try caraway on grilled fruit and veggies.

Caraway is packed full of volatile oils, so buy whole seeds as they break down when ground. They can be toasted to bring out the favored flavors, but toasting too long will cause intensified acridity.

CULTIVATION CENTERS

Germany, Holland, Britain, Poland, Mediterranean, India, Canada and North America, Russia

AROMA & FLAVOR

Caraway conjures anise, fennel, and dill in its aroma and taste and is sweet, though somewhat particular. A trace of bitterness with a nutty, sharp quality can linger as an aftertaste.

MEDICINAL USES

helps, treats, prevents, or aids digestion and calms the stomach, intestinal and urinal cramping, type 2 diabetes, tuberculosis

COMMON FORMS

seeds, dried, whole and ground

COMPLEMENTS

bread, cakes, pastries; hearty meats, sausages, pork, fowl, poultry; root vegetables, mushrooms, and cabbage; stews and soups

PAIRS WELL WITH

allspice, celery seeds, chiles, cinnamon, coriander, cumin, fennel seeds, juniper, nutmeg

Celery Seeds

garden celery, wild celery, smallage

Celery seeds come from wild celery that originally grew in European salt marshes. They are one of humanity's oldest hangover cures, having been utilized by the Romans the mornings after their legendary feasts. The miniscule seeds are not from the bulbous celery plant we are so familiar with, but does hail from a very close relative known as smallage, sometimes called wild celery.

While the plant is quite bitter, celery seeds have the mild flavor of the vegetable we're familiar with. It is a renowned pairing with all things tomato, which is perhaps why we love seeds and stalks in our Bloody Marys. It also navigates an elegant cross-section in sausage-loving Louisiana. Alligator sausage, boudin, Andouille, I throw celery seeds on all. A beautiful twist for using celery seeds is to first sauté some hot Italian sausage in a pork-based *arrabiata* sauce. When making an Argentine parrilla, the first thing off the grill is choripan—chorizo bites in sweet bread. I use a dash of celery seeds every time.

Celery seeds loses flavor rapidly when ground. This is more of a concern with commercial celery salt, but luckily you can easily make it yourself by mixing equal amounts of salt of your choice and ground celery seeds with a pinch of a pungent herb like parsley. If you must buy celery salt, keep it refrigerated to prevent flatness.

CULTIVATION CENTERS

France, Britain, Scandinavia, Hungary, Northern India, Northern Africa, China, United States

AROMA & FLAVOR

Celery seeds have an alluring bouquet reminiscent of a freshly cut lawn. Its taste bites with bitterness but also warmth and camphor. The seeds sweeten during the cooking process.

MEDICINAL USES

helps, treats, prevents, or aids arthritis, gout, cholesterol problems, ulcers, strokes, high blood pressure; Greeks and Romans used it to reduce swelling, in tonics, and as an aphrodisiac and sedative

COMMON FORMS

seeds, whole and ground

COMPLEMENTS

breads and crackers; chutneys, relishes, blends, dressings, and pickles; meats, fish, chicken, and eggs; salads and vegetables, especially tomato sauce, juice, and soups; sauces, stews, and soups

PAIRS WELL WITH

black pepper, caraway, chiles, coriander, cumin, fennel seeds, ginger, grains of paradise, sage, tamarind, turmeric

Dill Seeds

dill

Dill cultivation is thought to have started around five thousand years ago, but it was heralded as a medicinal and magical tool as much as a culinary one. For foods typical to the chilly climates of Northern Europe and Russia, its qualities as a spice are undeniable. The name dill is derived from *dilla,* a word that in Old Norse means "soothing." Dill tea was used to soothe stomachs and colic in Nordic babies, which was also the practice of the Assyrians, Greeks, Egyptians, and Romans. Yet the folklore is equally as fascinating. Break a hex placed on you by spreading salt and dill around where you live and work. Or put some in wine to make a love potion. Have some extra? Place it above your door to disarm anyone who seeks to steal or do you harm.

Now that dill seeds are in your cabinet and you're safe from spiritual harm, start experimenting. Play with the levels when you make broths, soups, and stews; use it to season root vegetables, cabbage, and especially carrots, a relative. Dill can mask taste flaws or unwanted flavors in lower quality meats and fish. Or, if desired, you can make your own homemade pickles using dill and garlic.

Seeds differ in size and shape depending on where they are from. European dill, shorter and wider than Indian dill, is more intense but has a smoother taste. Store in a cool, dry place and toast whole seed for a more robust flavor.

CULTIVATION CENTERS

Mediterranean, Russia, Poland, England, Scandinavia, Turkey, United States, northern India, Japan

AROMA & FLAVOR

Dill mimics its cousins caraway and anise. The aroma is sweeter although it can taste harsher and more acerbic.

MEDICINAL USES

helps, treats, prevents, or aids colic, halitosis, appetite; used as a sedative; Egyptians and Greeks used it as for hiccups; in India, it is used for stomach relief and indigestion

COMMON FORMS AND VARIETIES

seeds, whole and ground; varieties include European dill, American dill, Indian dill

COMPLEMENTS

boiled and grilled fish; breads and rice; cheese; hearty winter foods and vegetables of Northern Europe; lentils and beans; meat stews and soups; pickled veggies; sausages, lamb, and processed meats; seafood

PAIRS WELL WITH

anise, caraway, celery seeds, coriander, cumin, dill weed, fennel seeds, fenugreek, juniper, mustard seeds, paprika, sumac, turmeric

Fennel Seeds

common fennel, bitter fennel, sweet fennel

Fennel the spice, the herb, and the vegetable have all made their mark on my life. My favorite mussels in New Orleans are the *moules au fenouil* at Café Degas. The leaves were a staple in the mayo and on the salmon sandwiches my fishermen dad and brother made. The seeds, though, made the earliest appearance in my life: flavoring the pepperoni on my preferred pizza.

Native to Europe, fennel is popular across the globe. The seeds—the spice part of the plant—are similar enough in character to anise and cumin that in many countries they are used interchangeably. In Indonesia, it is sometimes referred to as *jintan manis*—sweet cumin—as it's considered a cumin varietal. In Hindi it is called *moti saunf*, big anise. Fortunately, fennel seeds complement so many other spices the confusion can be forgiven.

Fennel seeds are amazing when mixed into bread dough, or take store-bought bread to another level when baked with the seeds on top. They're great for typical North American breakfast foods like eggs, bacon, and toast but also on muffins and pastries. If you're particular to aperitifs and digestifs, the versatile seed also flavors the liqueurs of Europe: Sambuca, Strega, anisette, pastis, and absinthe.

Fennel is one of the few seeds that does not require toasting, but if you do, they will be easier to grind. Toasted, they become a tad sweeter and emit a final note akin to molasses; however, they quickly burn and become bitter.

CULTIVATION CENTERS

France, Italy, Morocco, India, United States, Russia, Germany, Middle East, Hungary, Argentina

AROMA & FLAVOR

Fennel is often compared with anise for its licorice aroma and taste—both share the same compound, after all.

MEDICINAL USES

helps, treats, prevents, or aids Alzheimer's disease; heart disease, stroke, and high blood pressure; indigestion and colic; menstrual cramps; dementia; inflammation; cancer; glaucoma; hiccups; eyesight; snakebites and scorpion stings in India

COMMON FORMS AND VARIETIES

seeds, whole and ground; varieties include sweet fennel and bitter fennel

COMPLEMENTS

breads, baked goods, and crackers; curries and spice blends; fish soups and stews; grilled fish like tuna, salmon, and mackerel; roast pig and duck; sausages, pepperoni, meatballs, salami, and smoked meats (especially in Italy); to balance the boldness of smoky grilled meat and veggies

PAIRS WELL WITH

allspice, cardamom, chiles, cinnamon (cassia), true cinnamon, cloves, coriander, dill seeds, cumin, fenugreek, galangal, garlic, ginger, mace, mustard seeds, nutmeg, turmeric

Fenugreek

fenugreek seeds, Greek hay, goat's horn, cow's horn, bird's foot, methi

First cultivated in Europe, Egypt, and likely India, fenugreek was considered an aphrodisiac and used in all stages of the reproductive process. It was made into a potion to improve male virility and impotence as well as taken by mothers to improve milk flow and alleviate menstrual cramps. They should not be used for these purposes today. Pregnant women should avoid fenugreek because it could induce a miscarriage. Fenugreek seeds are used in the production of certain contraceptives.

Fenugreek is less common in the Western Hemisphere, probably due to the seeds' bitter taste before they're toasted. In India, Asia, and the Middle East it is considerably more popular and included in all manner of blends, pastes, curries, and chutneys. As with asafoetida, it should be used judicially so as to not overpower a dish. Toasting improves the flavor and dissipates the smell, which strongly resembles maple syrup.

Toasting also helps to brittle the solid, pebble-like seeds. Putting an untoasted seed in your mouth is akin to biting a stone. Pulverizing them in the spice grinder is the preferred method of breaking them down, but they can be crushed as well. Another technique to soften fenugreek seeds is to leave them overnight in water; they'll bulge and perhaps sprout. In this form they're a stimulating addition to salads with lemon or balsamic vinegar.

CULTIVATION CENTERS

Eastern Mediterranean, India, Pakistan, Turkey, France, Germany, Greece, Lebanon, United States, Argentina

AROMA & FLAVOR

Fenugreek seeds are biting and bitter and smell faintly nutty prior to toasting. Their toasted aroma smells like melted butter or maple syrup and the heat mellows their bitterness.

MEDICINAL USES

helps, treats, prevents, or aids type 2 diabetes and insulin resistance; weight control; high cholesterol; kidney stones, gallstones, and cataracts; breast, pancreatic, and prostate cancers; liver disease and bacterial infections; traditionally used to break a fever, as an aphrodisiac, or to promote lactation in nursing mothers and even livestock

COMMON FORMS

seeds, whole, broken (crushed) and ground

COMPLEMENTS

batter of fried foods; breads and flat breads; curries, dals, and chutneys in India and Southeast Asia; icings, fake maple syrup; lentils, beans, and legumes; salads, vegetables, and veggie curries; spice blends and pastes

PAIRS WELL WITH

asafoetida, black pepper, chiles, coriander, garlic, ginger, mustard seeds, star anise, tamarind, turmeric

Horseradish

Horseradish is a root in the same family of plants as wasabi and mustard; it originated in Europe and the Mediterranean and was valued for its medicinal properties. The Egyptians and Greeks used it as early as 1500 BCE both for pain relief and as an aphrodisiac. Once it came to Germany and Britain, it was used as a flavoring agent for meat and oysters and in cordials and tonics. Early settlers brought it to the colonies where it eventually became a popular condiment for steak, sausages, raw fish and seafood, and boiled shrimp.

My new love, horseradish ice, can be traced to a Danish tradition of freezing horseradish. In any form, it's still best when applied to cut fatty and oily foods or to provide a jolt of pungency to otherwise bland starches. In France, it's diluted with vinegar and oil to make mignonette. A quick horseradish sauce is easy to whip up and is a fine supplement to potato salads, meat sandwiches, and seafood plates. A horseradish sauce with dill enlivens an ordinary cheese plate or charcuterie board.

Unlike other spices, horseradish loses its pungency when cooked. Only do so if you want a gentler flavor. Grating it can be an eye-opening (or closing) experience. It may be easier to buy grated horseradish in vinegar at the store. My preference is powdered, found in specialty spice shops. If you do buy fresh, avoid sprouting, damaged, or blemished roots, as they may be too acrid.

CULTIVATION CENTERS

United States, Canada, Europe

AROMA & FLAVOR

Horseradish is faint until cut, at which point it has a pungency that will singe your nostrils. The powder has a pleasant aroma, faintly of sour fruit. Its taste is fierce but full and pleasantly biting. Many describe it as bitter, but I find it on the astringent side.

MEDICINAL USES

helps, treats, prevents, or aids bronchitis, ear infection, flu, strep throat, pneumonia, gastrointestinal illness, low cholesterol, cancer, urinary tract infections; traditionally used for kidney stones, colds, and as a cough medicine

COMMON FORMS

root: whole, grated, dried, flakes, powdered

COMPLEMENTS

baked and cooked fruit; fish, smoked salmon, seafood, and shellfish; potatoes, legumes, lentils, and beans; raw fish, sushi (imitation wasabi), oysters, and clams; roast beef, sausages, ham, processed meat, pork, pickled and fresh eggs and other heavy, fatty proteins; root vegetables

PAIRS WELL WITH

black pepper, caraway, celery seeds, dill seeds, fennel seeds, lemon peel, mustard seeds, parsley, sesame seeds

Juniper Berries

The juniper tree is native to Europe, likely Britain or possibly Norway and Russia. There are over 70 varieties but not all are edible. The berry is actually a form of pinecone from a juniper shrub, an evergreen responsible for the piney quality of juniper. It's a revelation when added to full-bodied meat sauces and stews.

Juniper berries are like a secret weapon due to their delicious complexity. Simultaneously sweet, bitter, and sour, there is nary a steak or fowl that can resist their mouthwatering charm. Cocktails, in particular, benefit from a handful of crushed juniper berries.

Like many, my first introduction to juniper was the refreshing taste of a classic gin and tonic. Gin and its iterations have carried juniper flavor across continents. Crushing the berries prior to use liberates its flavor in your food. It doesn't take much. The berries you use should be soft and pliable. Dried berries are more intense and should also be squashed.

Note: Pregnant women and those with kidney problems should stay away from juniper.

CULTIVATION CENTERS

Britain, Italy, Turkey, United States, India

AROMA & FLAVOR

Juniper is unmistakably piney, but fresh, citrusy, and fruity. The taste is sharp, astringent if not tangy, with a bitter-sweet aftertaste.

MEDICINAL USES

helps, treats, prevents, or aids type 2 diabetes and lowering blood sugar; kidney and liver damage; heart problems and high blood pressure; as a diuretic; cold sores, wounds, and urinary tract infections; colds and bronchitis; traditionally used to clear tapeworms, gastrointestinal issues, and gonorrhea

COMMON FORMS

berries, fresh and dried whole, crushed, ground (rarely)

COMPLEMENTS

berries like blackberries and blueberries; cheeses, pickled meats, and charcuterie; cocktails, cordials, and liqueurs; fowl, poultry, and stuffing for such; meat, pork, and game marinades; plums; roasts, stews, and soups; sauces for duck, quail, squab, boar, venison, and gamey proteins; terrines, pâtés, pickles, sauerkraut

PAIRS WELL WITH

allspice, bay leaf, black pepper, caraway, dill seeds, garlic, ginger, green onion, mustard seeds, nutmeg, parsley, rosemary, sage, scallions, thyme

Mustard Seeds

white, black, brown, and Chinese mustards

Mustard is a popular spice with varieties worldwide. Cultivated since ancient times, it was used as a flavoring agent, condiment, and in traditional medicine. Black and brown mustard are closely related and used more in India and Asia and sometimes Europe. In the West, we're most accustomed to white mustard, which is actually faint yellow and the largest and mildest of the varieties.

The most common use for mustard is still as a condiment. Today's prepared mustards vary in consistency, strength, and color. Mild mustards are processed with part or all of the hull of the seed. These include whole-grain mustard, Bordeaux mustard, and burgundy-hued Beaujolais mustard. Dijon is the fashionable example of strong mustards, which are hulled. American mustard is hulled as well, but differs from Dijon by using only white seeds and tinting with turmeric for a bright yellow hue.

Mustard is easy to make, and innovating and adjusting it to your particular tastes is encouraged. Simply make a paste from dry mustard powder and add your favorite flavors, be they honey, dill, thyme, lemon, or even ancho chiles.

To activate the heat in mustard, let the seeds dry; alternatively, soak the seeds in cold water for no more than 10 minutes then grind into a paste. Using different liquids yields different heat levels. Water and beer will be hot and spicy; milk will be milder and more pungent. Vinegar stops the development of spiciness. Toasting whole seeds before grinding is not essential but will enhance the flavor.

CULTIVATION CENTERS

Europe, Great Britain, United States, Canada, Nepal, South America, India, Asia

AROMA & FLAVOR

Mustard is relatively quiet; pungency develops once its enzymes are activated by liquid. White mustard is the gentlest, with the sharpness and heat increasing in potency with each darker, smaller version. Mustard in general is piquant, with a grainy spiciness.

MEDICINAL USES

helps, treats, prevents, or aids diabetes and insulin control, cholesterol issues, cancer growth, heart disease, prostate issues, brain function; traditionally used for cold relief and congestion, scorpion stings, to promote blood flow and cleanse toxins from the body

COMMON FORMS AND VARIETIES

seeds: dried whole, cracked, ground; varieties include white mustard (European, largest), brown mustard (China, Africa, Asia), black mustard (India and Iran, smallest)

COMPLEMENTS

barbecue rubs and pastes; beans, legumes, and lentils; casseroles; eggs, egg salad; fish and seafood; grilled, roasted, and cold meats; pickled veggies, sauerkrauts, cabbage, Brussels sprouts, and cauliflower; poultry, pork, and sausage; salad dressings and vinegars

PAIRS WELL WITH

anise, asafoetida, black pepper, cardamom, celery seeds, chiles, cloves, coriander, cumin, dill seeds, fennel seeds, fenugreek, galangal, garlic, ginger, grains of paradise, nigella, nutmeg, oregano, paprika, star anise, turmeric

Paprika

tomato pepper, pimiento, sweet paprika, Hungarian paprika,
Spanish paprika

Paprika is a pepper, but also a powder of dried peppers. It originated in the Americas, however it is in this chapter because certain aspects of it are inherently European. The Spanish were the first to manufacture the dried pepper powder after Columbus and his contemporaries returned with it from the New World. It found its way to Turkey and settled in Hungary after the invasion by the Ottomans. Spanish smoked paprika is illustrious because the peppers are slowly dried over smoky fires. It has received a protected origin denomination and label (DOP), to protect it from fraudulent replication or claims of origin.

Paprika is a wonderful spice to have in your arsenal—you likely already do. It bears a tad more dynamism than one-note peppers like cayenne (heat) or ancho (smokiness). Varieties fluctuate greatly from barely perceptible heat levels to quite hot. The label will advise. Paprika can also be the protagonist in a rescue operation of an underseasoned dish. Whereas you can't "save" a dish at the end with spices that need to be heated or cooked, paprika is right at home near the finish line. Paprika's high sugar content means it cannot withstand high heat without losing its flavor and turning bitter. It also changes color from brick red to brownish-orange to burnt sienna. Add it toward the end of your cooking process to mitigate those circumstances.

CULTIVATION CENTERS

Hungary, Spain, Portugal, Morocco, United States, Mexico, Israel

AROMA & FLAVOR

Depending on the type used, paprika can be spicy, smoky, pungent, piquant, aromatic, mild, or sharp. Tastes vary depending on the region, especially Hungarian paprika where the word paprika can include many forms of pepper. In Spain, La Vera paprika is smoky and smoothly hot.

MEDICINAL USES

see Chiles (page 120); traditionally used for colds and flu and to promote circulation

COMMON FORMS AND VARIETIES

dried pepper, ground; varieties include Spanish paprika (smokier, hot, sweet, bittersweet), Hungarian paprika (various array of flavors)

COMPLEMENTS

cheese, yogurt, sour cream, and cream sauces; chicken, turkey, poultry, fowl, goose, and duck; eggs and omelets; fish, shellfish, crawfish, crabs, shrimp, and seafood; olives, onions, beans, potatoes, eggplant, corn, tomato mushrooms, chickpeas, and legumes; rice and pasta; sausages, salamis, chorizo, and pork; soups, stews, goulash, curries, and marinades; veal, game, and rabbit

PAIRS WELL WITH

allspice, amchur, black pepper, other chiles, cilantro, coriander, cumin, fenugreek, galangal, garlic, ginger, lemon peel, nutmeg, oregano, pumpkin seeds, saffron, sumac, turmeric

Sumac

Sumac is an ancient spice indigenous to the Mediterranean. The Romans used it to sour foods prior to the introduction of citrus. Often used for ornamental, aesthetic, dyeing, and tanning purposes, sumac berries are a brilliant red when ripe. The shrub is distantly related to the American shrub poison sumac, poison ivy, and poison oak, though there is no danger in eating sumac the spice. It is so versatile I haven't found an occasion where sumac didn't improve the flavor of the dish. Somehow they are simultaneously fruity, sour, sweet, astringent, and berrylike. I feel they touch every part of my palate.

If you come away with just one new tool from this book, I hope it is sumac. It is generously forgiving and should be within reach of every home cook. Whole sumac, though not the easiest to find, is a powerful ally anytime you need a souring agent that requires a fuller body than lemon. Powdered sumac is more common, but check the date to assure freshness.

Whole berries are soaked in water for about 30 minutes to soften the seeds and release the sumac juice. Use 2½ ounces of berries per 1 cup of water. Strain and use for dressings, flavorings, and marinades. Powder is perfect for sprinkling on food just before eating. In Turkey, it's on the table next to salt and pepper.

CULTIVATION CENTERS

Mediterranean, Italy, Sicily, Middle East, Turkey

AROMA & FLAVOR

Sumac is wondrously tangy and tart. The aroma of the whole berries is faint, but once ground is significantly zestier. The sourness is citrus-like but smoother and less harsh than lemon juice.

MEDICINAL USES

helps, treats, prevents, or aids asthma, diarrhea; used in the Middle East to soothe an upset stomach; high in antioxidants

COMMON FORMS AND VARIETIES

berries: whole and ground; there are many sumac varietals including decorative plants; certain wild sumacs, especially in North America, are poisonous; avoid white and green sumac

COMPLEMENTS

hummus, chickpeas, walnuts, almonds; fish stews, fish, seafood; meat balls, lamb, and barbecued meats; rice, legumes, pilaf, and baba ghanoush; salad, vegetables, eggplant, onions and dates; as a lemon substitute or souring agent in drinks and spicy flatbread dips

PAIRS WELL WITH

anardana, black pepper, chiles, cilantro, coriander, cumin, garlic, ginger, grains of paradise, mint, parsley, paprika, scallions, sesame seeds, thyme

RECIPES

Herbes et Épices de Provence Blend 232

Quatre Épices Blend 233

Sumac Eggplant Paste 234

Sumac Blackberry Agrodolce Marinade 235

Honey Mustard Whiskey Marinade 236

Apple Caraway Marinade 237

Lemon Mustard Marinade 238

Balsamic Horseradish Marinade 239

Juniper White Wine Marinade 240

Dill, Mint, and Sumac Seafood Marinade 241

Limoncello-Fennel Poultry Marinade 242

Red Wine Paprika Goulash Sauce 243

Horseradish Sauce 244

Tarragon Sauce 245

Port Juniper Sauce 246

Chive Blossom Mignonette 247

Red Mojo Sauce 248

Paprika Mustard Sauce 249

Wayward Orange Sauce 250

Sicilian Saffron Pasta Sauce 251

Left: Sumac Blackberry Agrodolce Marinade (page 235)

Herbes et Êpices de Provence Blend

chicken and poultry, duck, soups and broths, vegetables

Celery seeds, dill seeds, and fennel seeds make this blend the herb and spice crossover for herb-loving Europe. I have a jar of this next to the salt and use it on pretty much everything. MAKES ABOUT ½ CUP

3 tablespoons dried thyme

2 tablespoons dried parsley

1 tablespoon dried marjoram

2 teaspoons celery seeds

1 teaspoon dried tarragon

1 teaspoon fennel seeds

1 teaspoon dried rosemary

½ teaspoon dried lavender

½ teaspoon dried dill seeds

2 bay leaves, ground

Mix all the ingredients together. Store in an airtight jar in a cool, dark place for up to 6 months.

Recipe Tip: Want something a little less potent? Subtract the dill and lavender. Consider adding 1 teaspoon savory or basil if you have some.

Quatre Épices Blend

meat, poultry, slow-cooked roasts

Quatre épices, French for four spices, is used for terrines and charcuterie, pâtés, stews, braises, and dishes that require long simmering. There's some discretion allowed on which four spices are used, but peppercorns and nutmeg are definitely included. Cloves, ginger, and cinnamon play musical chairs for the final two spots. **MAKES ABOUT ¼ CUP**

1½ tablespoons black or white peppercorns

1 tablespoon whole cloves

1 tablespoon ground nutmeg

1 teaspoon ground ginger

Grind the peppercorns and cloves in a spice grinder. Mix with the nutmeg and ginger and store in an airtight jar in a cool, dark place for 6 months to 1 year.

Recipe Tip: If substituting, replace cinnamon with ginger. Or pepper for allspice.

Sumac Eggplant Paste

eggplant, salad dressing, yogurt

This paste balances lemony sumac and smoky charred eggplant. The mix plays as dressing, marinade for veggies, and a dip for pita and carrots. I like it as an appetizer with toasted croutons and garnished with feta cheese and a dot of olive tapenade. Thanks to Gustavo Turcios Rivera for providing this recipe. MAKES 1 CUP

1 large eggplant

8 tablespoons extra-virgin olive oil, divided

½ onion, minced

1 garlic clove, minced

1 tomato, finely chopped

½ bunch fresh basil, minced

½ bunch fresh mint leaves, minced

1 teaspoon ground sumac

½ teaspoon ground cumin

Freshly squeezed lime juice

Coarse sea salt

Freshly ground black pepper

1. Holding the eggplant with tongs, toast it over the burner flame. Turn it continually until the skin is evenly toasted and the skin has a papery consistency. Wrap the eggplant in a paper towel and let it cool.

2. Heat 1 tablespoon of olive oil in a medium skillet over medium heat. Add the onion and garlic and sauté until golden, 4 to 5 minutes. Transfer to a large bowl.

3. To that bowl, add the remaining 7 tablespoons of olive oil, tomato, basil, mint, sumac, and cumin and stir to mix well. This dressing can be refrigerated in an air-tight jar for 1 to 2 weeks.

4. Once cool, the skin of the eggplant should come off easily and can be discarded. Add the eggplant flesh to the bowl. Mash it up with a fork, or pulse it in a food processor, and mix evenly with the dressing. Squeeze in a bit of lime juice and season with salt and pepper. Use immediately.

Recipe Tip: Toasting the eggplant softens the flesh inside. The hardest part of this recipe is keeping an eye on the egg-plant as it is being roasted.

Sumac Blackberry Agrodolce Marinade

duck, fatty cuts of beef, red meat, steak

This technique I learned as a gastrique from my friend Beeta Mohajeri. It is a reduction of equal parts sweet and sour and is a base sauce that can be turned into just about anything. Beeta uses corn syrup instead of honey or sugar because it refines the texture. MAKES ABOUT 2 CUPS

1 cup light corn syrup

1 cup white vinegar

½ cup water

1 cup fresh blackberries

5 or 6 pitted dates

1 teaspoon ground sumac

1 teaspoon sesame seeds

1 teaspoon dried thyme

1. Mix together the corn syrup, vinegar, and water in a medium saucepan over medium heat for 45 minutes to 1 hour until the sauce has reduced by half. Add the blackberries and dates and simmer until the mixture becomes a slightly thickened tart syrup, 4 to 5 minutes. Remove the pan from the heat and let it cool.

2. Stir in the sumac, sesame seeds, and thyme.

3. Pulse in a food processor to mix loosely. Let cool and refrigerate, covered, until it congeals.

Recipe Tip: Use as a marinade by making double, and marinate steak or duck in half the amount for 30 minutes. Use the rest as a sauce. Substitute 1 tablespoon za'atar blend for the sumac, sesame seeds, and thyme.

Honey Mustard Whiskey Marinade

hearty fish and chicken

There's nothing better on a cold day than a bit of whiskey to warm your stomach, but mine goes first in the pan to play with the flavors. Economical Irish whiskey always does the trick here. Throw a couple whole grains of paradise in there for "hidden" surprises. MAKES 1 CUP

2 teaspoons dry
Dijon mustard

¼ cup cold water

1 teaspoon fennel seeds

3 tablespoons honey

2 tablespoons apple
cider vinegar

2 tablespoons Irish whiskey

½ cup distilled white vinegar

Zest of 1 lemon

Juice of 1 lemon

Coarse sea salt

Freshly ground black pepper

1. Mix the mustard into the cold water and let it stand for 15 minutes.

2. In a small skillet over medium heat, toast the fennel seeds until aromatic, about 1 minute. Transfer to a dish and let cool.

3. In a small saucepan, boil down the honey, apple cider vinegar, and whiskey by half. Slowly stir in the distilled white vinegar. Remove the pan from the heat. Stir in the lemon zest, lemon juice, fennel, and mustard sauce. Season with salt and pepper.

4. Refrigerate in an airtight container for up to 1 week.

Recipe Tip: Best for fatty fish or chicken. Marinate fish for 1 hour and chicken for at least 4 hours or overnight. Fry in clarified butter or ghee.

Apple Caraway Marinade

poultry, pork chops, sausages, tenderloin

Another gastrique—sugar deglazed with vinegar—this one highlights the romance between apples and caraway. This is best used to flavor pork, as a marinade or a sauce, but is equally delicious on rabbit, chicken, turkey, or with stuffing. It's a nice addition alongside sauerkraut and horseradish sauce. MAKES 2 ½ CUPS

2 sweet apples, cored and chopped

1 teaspoon juniper berries

½ teaspoon fennel seeds

1 cup honey

1 cup apple cider vinegar

½ cup water

2 teaspoons caraway seeds

1 teaspoon paprika

½ teaspoon ground cinnamon

1. Put the apples in a saucepan and cover with water by at least 1 inch. Bring to a boil, then reduce the heat to low and simmer until the apples are soft, 20 to 30 minutes. Drain.

2. With a mortar and pestle, loosely crush the fennel seeds and juniper berries.

3. In a medium saucepan, bring the honey, apple cider vinegar, and ½ cup of water to a boil, reduce the heat to medium, and simmer until it thickens slightly, 10 to 15 minutes. Add the apples and cook on a slightly higher heat for 4 to 5 minutes. Reduce the heat to low and stir in the caraway, juniper-fennel mix, paprika, and cinnamon. Simmer for 2 to 3 minutes then remove the pan from the heat and let cool for 10 minutes.

4. Pulse in a food processor until the apples are puréed and combined with the sauce.

5. Refrigerate in an airtight container for up to 5 days.

Recipe tip: Though this marinade is designed for salty meats and fish, it pairs divinely as a sauce with cold charcuterie, cheese plates, and the roasted meats listed above. Let it cool and thicken in the refrigerator and serve cold.

Lemon Mustard Marinade

chicken, salmon, tuna

This sauce is a stage for herbes de Provence. Leave some to the side to garnish the protein along with a squeeze of lemon or dash of vinegar for an herbaceous boost. This recipe is fantastic because it can be made quickly, so it's a great go-to for an impromptu meal. MAKES ¼ CUP

2 tablespoons whole-grain Dijon mustard

2 teaspoons honey

1 teaspoon fennel seeds

1 teaspoon Herbes et Êpices de Provence Blend (page 232)

Zest of ½ lemon

Juice of 1 lemon

Pinch coarse sea salt

Pinch paprika

Pinch freshly ground black pepper

Mix all the ingredients together in a small bowl. Use immediately.

Recipe Tip: This is best with salmon. Make an aluminum foil tray to catch juices from the fish, and put it on a baking sheet. Put a salmon fillet on the tray and slather it with the marinade, then cover the fish with thin slices from ½ a lemon. Bake in a preheated 350°F oven for 35 minutes or until cooked through.

Balsamic Horseradish Marinade

beef, fatty fish, lamb, meats

This recipe came into being when I packed for a move and discovered I had four bottles of balsamic vinegar of various shapes and sizes. Luckily, balsamic vinegar makes a wonderful marinade. Try it on its own with your favorite herbs and spices, or supplement it with horseradish sauce. MAKES ABOUT 1 CUP

½ cup Horseradish
Sauce (page 244)

1 cup balsamic vinegar

1 teaspoon fennel seeds

1 teaspoon dill seeds

1 teaspoon freshly
ground black pepper

1 teaspoon dried parsley

In a small bowl, combine all the ingredients. Mix well. Use immediately.

Recipe Tip: Marinate your protein in a zip-top bag in the refrigerator. Fish should be marinated for only 30 minutes. Steaks can be marinated for up to 4 hours. Then drain, pat the protein dry with a paper towel, and grill. I recommend drizzling a little extra horseradish sauce on the finished product.

Juniper White Wine Marinade

chicken, game, poultry, rabbit

This recipe allows juniper and its rich color a chance to shine. In deep red and dark marinades and sauces, it can be lost, as can some of its flavor, if appropriated by syrupy wines and heavy flavors. This white wine marinade doesn't let those luscious berries hide. MAKES ABOUT 2 CUPS

8 tablespoons extra-virgin olive oil, divided

3 shallots, sliced

2 garlic cloves, minced

1½ cups pinot grigio or dry white wine

1 teaspoon fennel seeds

1 tablespoon grains of paradise, cracked

1 tablespoon dried juniper berries, crushed

1 teaspoon dried parsley

3 fresh rosemary sprigs or 1 teaspoon dried

6 fresh sage leaves, chopped

Heat 1 tablespoon of olive oil in a medium skillet over medium heat. Add the shallots and garlic and sauté for 2 to 3 minutes. Add the wine, fennel seeds, grains of paradise, juniper, parsley, rosemary, sage, and remaining 7 tablespoons of oil. Stir to combine, reduce the heat to low, and heat for 5 minutes. Use immediately.

Recipe Tip: To marinate, rub down the protein with 3 minced garlic cloves and place in a zip-top bag. Pour in the marinade and shake well. Refrigerate for 2 to 4 hours.

Dill, Mint, and Sumac Seafood Marinade

fish, scallops, shrimp

Many Middle Eastern spices found their way to Sicily and up the "Boot" of Italy well over a thousand years ago. This composition is so tasty and tangy my mom actually wrote it down, something she rarely does. **MAKES ABOUT 1½ CUPS**

1 teaspoon dill seeds

½ cup extra-virgin olive oil

½ cup white wine

¼ cup finely chopped fresh mint leaves

1 teaspoon sumac

1 tablespoon honey

Sea salt

Freshly ground black pepper

Juice of 2 lemons

1. In a medium skillet over low heat, lightly toast the dill seeds, gently shaking the pan, for about 1 minute. Remove the pan from the heat and mix in the olive oil, wine, mint, sumac, and honey, and season with salt and pepper. Whisk in enough lemon juice to make the marinade tangy but not sour.

2. Let the marinade sit for at least 1 hour before using.

Recipe Tip: Use as a marinade or to baste when grilling fish, scallops, or shrimp. Pair with rice.

Limoncello-Fennel Poultry Marinade

chicken, poultry

My mother and I conceptualized this recipe over a phone call and we've been try-ing to outdo each other since. This is my version with fennel, sumac, and thyme. To make a marinade, grind the sumac, add it to 1 cup of wine with the herbs, fennel, and oil. **MAKES ABOUT 1½ CUPS**

1 teaspoon whole sumac berries

1 cup dry white wine, such as Soave

4 tablespoons extra-virgin olive oil

2 tablespoons Herbes et Épices de Provence Blend (page 232)

2 tablespoons limoncello

1 teaspoon fennel seeds

Grind the sumac berries in a spice grinder. Transfer to a small bowl and add the wine, olive oil, herbes, limoncello, and fennel. Use immediately.

Recipe Tip: Use as a basting sauce when roasting a whole chicken and alternate basting with the sauce and additional limoncello.

Red Wine Paprika Goulash Sauce

ground beef, stew game or pork, stew meat

My mother's resolute love of paprika inspired this recipe. She usually has a selection of dry red wines hiding in all pockets of her kitchen. The goulash highlights caraway, black pepper, celery seeds, and the French spice mix quatre épices. Also, it should be stated that it makes the best leftovers known to humankind. MAKES 1½ CUPS

1½ cups dry red wine

1 tablespoon Hungarian paprika

2 teaspoons ground caraway seeds

1 teaspoon black peppercorns

1 teaspoon celery seeds

1 garlic clove, sliced

Combine the wine, paprika, caraway, peppercorns, celery seed, and garlic in a large bowl. The marinade is best used immediately, but it can be refrigerated for up to 3 days.

Recipe Tip: To make goulash, marinate 2 pounds meat, covered, in the refrigerator for 2 to 4 hours. Strain the marinade and set it aside. Pat the meat dry and cover it with a mixture of 1 tablespoon paprika and 2 tablespoons flour.

In a food processor, combine 1 chopped carrot, ½ chopped onion, 1 chopped celery stalk, 1 bunch chopped fresh parsley leaves, and 2 sliced garlic cloves.

Heat 2 tablespoons of oil or lard in a large skillet over medium heat. Add the vegetable mash, leaves of 1 rosemary sprig, and 2 chopped bay leaves, and sauté until golden brown.

Add the meat, 2 tablespoons tomato paste mixed with 1 tablespoon of water and a pinch of sugar, 1 teaspoon quatre épices, and 2 teaspoons salt, and cook until browned. Add the marinade to the skillet, 1 bouillon cube, and another 6 tablespoons of oil.

Bring to a boil—adding water if necessary—then reduce the heat to low and simmer for 1½ to 2 hours, uncovered. If more liquid is required during simmering, add up to a ½ cup of beef broth. Stir in the juice of ½ medium lemon.

The goulash may need to cook longer until a thick sauce develops. You be the judge. This is a great topping for plain potatoes, rice, and noodles, but try it with polenta.

Horseradish Sauce

fish, pot roasts, pork chops, as a spread on sandwiches, potatoes, or eggs

I met Jayne Kennedy through Martha Foose, and we were immediately smitten by our mutual love of food, adventure, and strange travel experiences. She was wonderful and shared this recipe. This sauce mellows out the sharp edges of horseradish. It will keep for several days, getting smoother by the day. It makes an appearance in Jayne's annual St. Patrick's Day slow-cooker corned beef and cabbage meal. MAKES ABOUT 2 CUPS

¾ cup sour cream

¾ cup mayonnaise

6 tablespoons prepared horseradish with its liquid (if making with powder use 1 tablespoon powder to 3 tablespoons water)

½ teaspoon grated lemon zest

2 teaspoons coarse sea salt

Freshly ground pepper

In a small bowl, combine all the ingredients. Cover and refrigerate for at least 30 minutes to allow the flavors to blend. Use immediately or refrigerate in an airtight jar for up to 4 days.

Recipe Tip: This is a great sauce to have on hand to add a dollop to marinades and pastes, especially if you are as obsessed with horseradish as I am. It's marvelous on salmon or slathered on a roast beef sandwich on a crusty roll.

Tarragon Sauce

chicken, fish, poultry

This recipe is courtesy of Miranda "Wink" Thomas. It's a wonderful recipe not only because it tastes otherworldly—it does—but because it highlights tarragon and mustard. It's a sublime dish popular with both kids and guests. **MAKES 2½ CUPS**

2 tablespoons unsalted butter

2 tablespoons all-purpose flour

1½ cups chicken stock

2 tablespoons tarragon vinegar

2 tablespoons Dijon mustard or mustard of choice

¼ cup heavy (whipping) cream

½ cup grated Cheddar cheese

1 teaspoon fresh tarragon or ½ teaspoon dried

Coarse sea salt

1. Melt the butter in a medium skillet over low heat. Stir in the flour. Cook, stirring constantly to make a roux, for 1 minute. Remove the pan from the heat.

2. Whisk in the chicken stock and vinegar until combined and smooth. Whisk in the mustard. Next mix in the heavy cream, cheese, and tarragon. Season with the salt.

3. The marinade is best used immediately but can be refrigerated in an airtight container for up to 2 days.

Recipe Tip: Make tarragon vinegar by steeping French tarragon in vinegar for 2 to 3 weeks. Use a 1:2 ratio of tarragon to vinegar. Strain.

Port Juniper Sauce

duck, pork, root vegetables, venison

Fortified wines like port and madeira pair so delightfully with game that it's almost criminal not to include juniper berries and caraway with them. These three musketeers form the backbone to this reduction that also features cloves and black pepper. Add a bay leaf or two if you're feeling fresh. MAKES 1 CUP

2 tablespoons vegetable oil

½ onion, chopped

3 garlic cloves, minced

1 fresh rosemary sprig

3 tablespoons unsalted butter

1 teaspoon chopped fresh sage

½ cup tawny dry port

3 teaspoons juniper berries, slightly crushed

½ cup distilled white vinegar

½ cup vegetable stock

2 teaspoons caraway seeds, ground

1 teaspoon freshly ground black pepper

1 teaspoon Herbes et Épices de Provence Blend (page 232)

1. In a medium saucepan over medium heat, add the oil. Add the onion, garlic, and rosemary and sauté until golden brown, about 3 minutes.

2. Reduce the heat to low and add the butter and sage. Once the butter has melted, mix in the port and juniper. Simmer until the liquid has reduced by half.

3. Stir in the vinegar and vegetable stock, and continue cooking until the base is very aromatic, 5 to 10 minutes. Remove the pan from the heat and stir in the caraway, black pepper, and Provence blend. Use immediately.

Recipe Tip: To use as a marinade, let the sauce cool. Place the protein or vegetable and marinade in a zip-top bag and refrigerate for 1 hour. Alternatively, add your main protein to the pan of sauce and cook it, turning it over halfway through.

Chive Blossom Mignonette

raw oysters, ceviche, crudo, or in raw vegetable dishes such as coleslaw

This mignonette, courtesy of Angela Zingale, is an essential companion to any oyster plate, whether broiled, grilled, or raw. When spring blooms, chives blossom and must be taken advantage of. They lend a strong, spicy onion kick. The sumac, as always, adds a wonderful tang. MAKES ⅔ CUP

6 purple chive flowers

5 tablespoons extra-virgin olive oil

3 tablespoons red wine vinegar

2 teaspoons ground sumac

2 pinches salt

2 pinches coarsely ground long pepper or black pepper

3 pinches sugar or a drizzle of honey

Juice of ½ lemon or lime

¼ cup boiling water

Pull the blossoms from the chive stems and pluck the purple petals. Add them to a blender along with the olive oil, vinegar, sumac, salt, pepper, sugar, lemon juice, and finally the boiling water. Blend for 20 seconds, no longer. Check the flavor, and add additional lemon juice to your liking. Refrigerate in an airtight container for up to 3 days. Served chilled.

Recipe Tip: Pour over raw fish or oysters right before serving. Use minced chives as a garnish.

Red Mojo Sauce

bread, fish, potatoes

This sauce, courtesy of Paul Rahfield, is the base for his paella, which has legendary status among his friends. This mojo is inspired by those from the Canary Islands, where they soak the chiles in water to dissipate their potency but keep their flavor. MAKES ¾ TO 1 CUP

2 or 3 dried chiles,
such as ñora or pasilla,
seeded and stemmed

1 large garlic clove

⅓ to ½ roasted red pepper

1 tablespoon sherry vinegar

½ teaspoon ground cumin

½ teaspoon smoked paprika

Coarse sea salt

6 tablespoons extra-
virgin olive oil

Stale bread slice (optional)

1. Place the chiles in a medium bowl and cover with water. Soak for 30 minutes, then drain the water and rinse the chiles.

2. Place the chiles in a food processor along with the garlic, bell pepper, vinegar, cumin, paprika, and some salt. With the machine running, drizzle in the olive oil and blend until the mojo is emulsified. For a thicker sauce, add pieces of bread and blend in. Use immediately.

Recipe Tip: Cut back on the chile peppers for red mojo or add more for a style similar to mojo picon. This sauce is an excellent marinade, but also works as a drizzle on roasted potatoes, as a bread dip, and to baste fish and seafood.

Paprika Mustard Sauce

cauliflower, mixed root vegetables

This recipe is one of my mother's favorites. Her husband Rick makes this treasure and they gorge on it to their hearts' content. My brother and I are the eaters in the family, however she's admitted, "I have actually eaten three-quarters of a cauliflower head." Now I know where we get it. **MAKES ABOUT ½ CUP**

4 tablespoons extra-virgin olive oil

3 tablespoons Dijon mustard

1 tablespoon smoked paprika

1 teaspoon ground grains of paradise

Coarse sea salt

In a small bowl, mix together the olive oil, mustard, paprika, and grains of paradise. Season with salt. Use immediately.

Recipe Tip: Put a head of cauliflower in a baking dish and evenly coat it with 4 minced garlic cloves. Pour the sauce over the cauliflower. Bake for in a preheated 450°F oven for 45 minutes, or until the outside is scorched. In a small bowl, combine ¼ cup balsamic vinegar, ¼ cup feta cheese, and 3 tablespoons shaved almonds. Pour this over the cauliflower and serve.

Wayward Orange Sauce

charcuterie, cheese plates, cold meat, or game

This recipe came out of an old, barely legible Irish cookbook. Luckily, Wink Shackleton translated it for me. I love the combination of potent horseradish and tart currant and citrus. This sauce could likely withstand a small spoon of Dijon as well. **MAKES ABOUT 2 CUPS**

Zest of 4 oranges

Juice of 4 oranges

Zest of 2 lemons

Juice of 2 lemons

4 tablespoons currant jelly

1 (1-inch) piece fresh horseradish, finely grated or ½ tablespoon finely ground

1 teaspoon dry or Dijon mustard

2 tablespoons cornstarch mixed with 2 tablespoons water

Mix all the ingredients together in a small bowl. Cover and let stand on the countertop for at least 12 hours. Strain and discard any solids. Bring to a simmer in a small saucepan and gently mix in the cornstarch syrup. Let simmer for 5 minutes until thickened. Let cool and refrigerate in an airtight container for up to 3 days.

Recipe Tip: Cranberry jelly would work in place of currant.

Sicilian Saffron Pasta Sauce

swordfish and pasta (corkscrew suggested)

Italian saffron is more intense than Spanish saffron because of its higher levels of safranal and crocin. Its production is very small; it thrives in a small valley near L'Aquila, Abruzzo, under the majestic Gran Sasso mountain range. If you can afford saffron threads, they're worth the splurge. **MAKES 1½ TO 2 CUPS**

15 to 20 Italian saffron threads or ¼ teaspoon powdered saffron

¼ cup warm water

¼ cup extra-virgin olive oil

Juice of 1 blood orange

Juice of ½ small lemon

¼ cup finely chopped fresh parsley leaves

½ cup puréed tomatoes

6 to 8 small capers or 3 or 4 larger ones, crushed

¼ cup white wine

Coarse sea salt

Freshly ground white pepper

1. In a small bowl, add the saffron threads to the warm (not boiling) water. Set aside and soak for at least 30 minutes. If using powdered saffron, skip this step.

2. In a medium saucepan over medium heat, combine the olive oil, blood orange juice, lemon juice, parsley, and puréed tomatoes. Mix well and bring to a simmer. Stir in the capers. Reduce the heat to low and stir in the wine. Let it simmer for a few minutes and season with salt and white pepper. Stir in the saffron and liquid (or powdered saffron) and remove the pan from the heat.

3. The sauce can be made ahead of time and refrigerated in an airtight container for 1 or 2 days. The flavors improve if made the day before.

Recipe Tip: Place 2 swordfish steaks in the sauce and cook them about 5 minutes per side. Use a fork to break up the fish into small chunks. Toss in a handful of Gaeta olives. Serve over ½ pound cooked corkscrew pasta. Alternatively, the fish can be kept whole and served with the sauce.

REFERENCES

Abdennour, Samia. *Egyptian Cooking and other Middle Eastern Recipes*. Cairo, Egypt, and New York: American University in Cairo Press, 1984.

Aggarwal, Bharat with Debora Yost. *Healing Spices: How to Use 50 Everyday and Exotic Spices to Boost Health and Beat Disease*. New York: Sterling, 2011.

Bayless, Rick, and Deann Groen Bayless. *Authentic Mexican: Regional Cooking from the Heart of Mexico*. New York: HarperCollins, 1987.

Breverton, Terry. *Breverton's Complete Herbal: A Book of Remarkable Plants and Their Uses*. Guilford, CT: Lyons Press, 2011.

Cheng-Huei, Yeh. *Chinese Cuisine (II): Wei Chuan's Cook Book*. Huang Su Huei, 1980.

Christensen, Shanti. *Family Style Chinese Cookbook: Authentic Recipes from My Culinary Journey Through China*. Berkeley: Rockridge Press, 2016.

DeWitt, David. *The Chile Pepper Encyclopedia: Everything You'll Ever Need to Know about Hot Peppers, with More Than 100 Recipes*. New York: William Morrow Cookbooks, 1999.

DeWitt, David, and Nancy Gerlach. *The Barbeque Inferno: Cooking with Chile Peppers on the Grill*. Berkeley: Ten Speed Press, 2001.

D'silva Sankhé, Denise. *Beyond Curry Indian Cookbook: A Culinary Journey Through India*. Berkeley: Rockridge Press, 2016.

Illes, Judika. *The Element Encyclopedia of 5000 Spells: The Ultimate Reference Book for the Magical Arts*. London: Element Books Ltd., 2004

Kiros, Tessa. *Tessa Kiros: The Recipe Collection*. Sydney: Murdoch Books, 2014.

Kowalchik, Claire, and William H. Hylton. *Rodale's Illustrated Encyclopedia of Herbs*. Emmaus, PA: Rodale Press, 1998.

Lagasse, Emeril. *Louisiana Real and Rustic*. New York: William Morrow Cookbooks, 1996.

Lakshmi, Padma, with Judith Sutton and Kalustyan's. *The Encyclopedia of Spices & Herbs: An Essential Guide to the Flavors of the World*. New York: Ecco, 2016.

Miller, Mark, *Coyote Cafe: Foods from the Great Southwest*. Berkeley: Ten Speed Press, 1989.

Nichol, Christina. *Essential Spices and Herbs: Discover Them, Understand Them, Enjoy Them*. Berkeley: Rockridge Press, 2015.

Nickerson, Brittany Wood, *Recipes from the Herbalist's Kitchen: Delicious, Nourishing Food For Lifelong Health and Well-Being*. North Adams, MA: Storey Publishing, 2017.

Nicks, Denver. *Hot Sauce Nation: America's Burning Obsession*. Chicago: Chicago Review Press, 2016.

NIIR Board of Consultants and Engineers. *The Complete Book on Spices & Condiments with Cultivations, Processing & Uses*. Delhi: Asia Pacific Business Partners, 2006.

Ortiz, Elisabeth Lambert, *The Encyclopedia of Herbs, Spices, and Flavorings: A Cook's Compendium*. New York: Dorling Kindersley, 1992.

Ozan, Ozcan. *Sultan's Kitchen: A Turkish Cookbook*. Hong Kong: Periplus Editions, 1998.

Parisi, Grace. *Get Saucy: Make Dinner a New Way Every Day with Simple Sauces, Marinades, Dressings, Glazes, Pestos, Pasta Sauces, Salsas, and More*. Cambridge, MA: Harvard Common Press, 2005.

Peter, K. V. *Handbook of Herbs and Spices, Volume 1*. Cambridge, UK: Woodhead Publishing, 2001.

Prudhomme, Paul. *Chef Paul Prudomme's Louisiana Kitchen*. New York: William Morrow Cookbooks, 1984.

Smith, Art. *Back to the Table: The Reunion of Food and Family*. New York: Hyperion, 2001.

Spicer, Susan. *Crescent City Cooking: Unforgettable Recipes from Susan Spicer's New Orleans*. New York: Alfred A. Knopf, 2007.

Vaughn, J. G., and C. A. Geissler. *New Oxford Book of Food Plants*. New York: Oxford University Press, 1997.

Wolfert, Paula. *The Food of Morocco*. New York: Ecco, 2009.

RESOURCES

For medicinal properties of herbs and spices, I found no better resource than *Healing Spices* by Bharat Aggarwal and Debora Yost. Where possible, this book informed the medical uses sections of *Cooking with Spices*.

Spice shops from where I bought the spices for testing and sampling include Christina's Spice and Specialty Foods in Cambridge, Massachusetts, El Gato Negro and La Simbólica in Buenos Aires, Argentina, and Rosalie Apothecary in New Orleans, Louisiana.

Online retailers Penzeys (www.penzeys.com) and Pendery's (www.penderys.com) are my go-to online retailers.

For recipes, food tips, and information Serious Eats (www.seriouseats.com) is hard to match. An elegant display, well-informed articles, and conscientious contributors set them apart.

Restaurants mentioned in this book are Café Degas in New Orleans, Louisiana, and Coyote Café in Santa Fe, New Mexico.

RECIPE INDEX

A

Adobo Mezcal Marinade, 149
Advieh Persian Blend, 187
Apple Caraway Marinade, 237
Asian Cold Noodle
    Dressing, 104
Asthma Tea, 5

B

Backcountry Chimichurri
    Sauce, 158
Baharat Blend, 188
Balsamic Horseradish
    Marinade, 239
Berbere Rub, 194
Black Tahini Paste, 196

C

Chaat Masala Blend, 48
Chaimen Armenian
    Spice Paste, 197
Charmoula Paste, 198–199
Chesapeake Bay-Style
    Seasoning Blend, 141
Chile-Infused Pickling
    Spice Blend, 142
Chinese Five-Spice Blend, 94
Chinese Sweet Bean Paste, 99
Chive Blossom
    Mignonette, 247
Cinnamon-Turmeric Rub, 53
Creole Barbecue Dry Rub, 146
Creole Spice Blend, 140
Crystalized Ginger, 6
Curry Seafood Sauce, 67

D

Dhana Jeera Vegetable
    Paste, 57
Dill, Mint, and Sumac
    Seafood Marinade, 241

Dragon Fyre Cider, 4
Dukkah Egyptian Dry Rub, 190

F

Feh El Omri Blend, 189

G

Garam Masala Blend, 49
Garam Masala Yogurt
    Marinade, 61
Gomasio Lemon Dressing
    Marinade, 101
Grandma Martha's New
    Mexico Green Chile
    Bean Sauce, 154

H

Harissa Paste, 201
Herbes et Épices de
    Provence Blend, 232
Homemade Saffron Mayo
    Marinade, 202
Honey Mustard Whiskey
    Marinade, 236
Horseradish Sauce, 244

I

Indian Carrot Sauce, 65

J

Jerk-Style Pineapple
    Paste, 148
Juniper White Wine
    Marinade, 240

K

Kalba Korean Marinade, 102
Kashmiri Masala Paste, 58
Kickin' Chicken Marinade, 153

L

La Kama Dry Rub, 191
Lemon Mustard Marinade, 238
Limoncello-Fennel Poultry
    Marinade, 242

M

Madras Curry Rub, 55
Malaysian Coconut
    Curry Paste, 98
Mango Chutney Marinade, 60
Miso Doko Marinade, 105
Moroccan Lamb Tajine
    Marinade, 203
Mulling Over Spice Blend, 145
Mustard Miso Sauce, 109
Mustard Seeds Curry
    Sauce, 66

N

New Orleans Barbecue
    Shrimp Sauce, 161
Nigella Seeds Meat
    Marinade, 64

O

Omam Water, 5

P

Panch Phoron Blend, 50
Paprika Mustard Sauce, 249
Peach-Plum Sauce, 106
Peppercorn Paste, 56
Peri Peri Dry Rub, 192
Poppy Paste, 200
Port Juniper Sauce, 246
Poudre de Colombo
    Rum Paste, 147
Pumpkin Seeds Autumn
    Blend, 144
Pumpkin Seeds Fish
    Marinade, 150

Q

Qâlat Daqqa Tunisian
  Dry Rub, 193
Quarte Épices Blend, 233
Queen's Carnitas Marinade, 151

R

Ras el Hanout Blend, 186
Red "DB" Chile Sauce, 160
Red Mojo Sauce, 248
Red Wine Paprika Goulash
  Sauce, 243

S

Saffron Sauce, 205
Sambaar Masala Blend, 51
Shichimi Togarashi Blend, 95
Sicilian Saffron Pasta
  Sauce, 251

Smoky "Holey" Mole
  Sauce, 156–157
South Pacific Honey
  Paste, 100
Spicy Peanut Marinade, 152
Sri Lankan Curry Rub, 54
Sumac Blackberry Agrodolce
  Marinade, 235
Sumac Eggplant Paste, 234
Sweet Baby Gavin's
  Guava Sauce, 155
Sweet Orange Chili Sauce, 107

T

Taco (Taceaux) Seasoning
  Blend, 143
Tamarind Yogurt
  Marinade, 204
Tandoori Chicken Blend, 52
Tarragon Sauce, 245
Teriyaki Wasabi Sauce, 111
Thai Red Curry Rub, 97

Thai Satay Marinade, 103
Throat Tea, 6
Tunisian Tabil Paste, 195
Two-Shack "Como el Otro"
  Hot Sauce, 159

V

Vadouvan-Lassi Poultry
  Marinade, 63
Vietnamese Lemongrass
  Dry Rub, 96
Vindaloo Curry Paste, 59

W

Wasabi Mayonnaise Sauce, 108
Wasabi Steak Sauce, 110
Wayward Orange Sauce, 250

Y

Yogurt Marinade, 62

INDEX

A

African cuisine, 164
Ajowan
  about, 24–25
  Asthma Tea, 5
  Chaat Masala Blend, 48
  Dhana Jeera Vegetable
    Paste, 57
  Kashmiri Masala Paste, 58
  Omam Water, 5
Allspice
  about, 116–117
  Berbere Rub, 194
  Chaimen Armenian
    Spice Paste, 197
  Chesapeake Bay-Style
    Seasoning Blend, 141
  Chile-Infused Pickling
    Spice Blend, 142
  Creole Spice Blend, 140
  Feh El Omri Blend, 189
  Jerk-Style Pineapple
    Paste, 148
  Kickin' Chicken
    Marinade, 153
  Mulling Over Spice
    Blend, 145
  Poudre de Colombo
    Rum Paste, 147
  Pumpkin Seeds Autumn
    Blend, 144
  Pumpkin Seeds Fish
    Marinade, 150
  Queen's Carnitas
    Marinade, 151
  Smoky "Holey" Mole
    Sauce, 156–157
  Spicy Peanut Marinade, 152
  Sweet Baby Gavin's
    Guava Sauce, 155
  Taco (Taceaux) Seasoning
    Blend, 143

Almonds
  Smoky "Holey" Mole
    Sauce, 156–157
Amchur
  about, 26–27
  Chaat Masala Blend, 48
American cuisine, 114
Anaheim peppers
  Two-Shack "Como el
    Otro" Hot Sauce, 159
Anardana
  about, 28–29
  Chaat Masala Blend, 48
  Mango Chutney
    Marinade, 60
Ancho (poblano) chiles
  about, 122–123
  Adobo Mezcal
    Marinade, 149
  Backcountry Chimichurri
    Sauce, 158
  Creole Spice Blend, 140
  Kickin' Chicken
    Marinade, 153
  Peri Peri Dry Rub, 192
  Smoky "Holey" Mole
    Sauce, 156–157
Anise
  about, 166–167
  Ras el Hanout Blend, 186
  Tamarind Yogurt
    Marinade, 204
  Tunisian Tabil Paste, 195
Annatto
  about, 118–119
  Chile-Infused Pickling
    Spice Blend, 142
  Pumpkin Seeds Autumn
    Blend, 144
  Pumpkin Seeds Fish
    Marinade, 150
Apples
  Apple Caraway
    Marinade, 237

Dhana Jeera Vegetable
  Paste, 57
Peach-Plum Sauce, 106
Apricots
  Poppy Paste, 200
Asafoetida
  about, 30–31
  Chaat Masala Blend, 48
  health benefits of, 4
Asian cuisine, 70
Ayurvedic (holistic) medicine, 4

B

Basil
  Feh El Omri Blend, 189
  Sumac Eggplant Paste, 234
Basques, 174
Bay leaves
  Chesapeake Bay-Style
    Seasoning Blend, 141
  Garam Masala Blend, 49
  Herbes et Épices de
    Provence Blend, 232
  Mustard Seeds Curry
    Sauce, 66
  Yogurt Marinade, 62
Beef
  Grandma Martha's New
    Mexico Green Chile
    Bean Sauce, 154
Bell peppers
  Dhana Jeera Vegetable
    Paste, 57
  Red Mojo Sauce, 248
Bird's eye chiles
  Malaysian Coconut
    Curry Paste, 98
Blackberries
  Sumac Blackberry
    Agrodolce Marinade, 235
Black limes
  Shichimi Togarashi Blend, 95
Black onion seeds
  Yogurt Marinade, 62

Black pepper
  about, 32–33
  Adobo Mezcal
    Marinade, 149
  Advieh Persian Blend, 187
  Backcountry Chimichurri
    Sauce, 158
  Baharat Blend, 188
  Balsamic Horseradish
    Marinade, 239
  Berbere Rub, 194
  Chaat Masala Blend, 48
  Charmoula Paste, 198–199
  Chesapeake Bay-Style
    Seasoning Blend, 141
  Chile-Infused Pickling
    Spice Blend, 142
  Chinese Sweet Bean
    Paste, 99
  Chive Blossom
    Mignonette, 247
  Cinnamon-Turmeric Rub, 53
  Creole Spice Blend, 140
  Dill, Mint, and Sumac
    Seafood Marinade, 241
  Dukkah Egyptian
    Dry Rub, 190
  Feh El Omri Blend, 189
  Garam Masala Blend, 49
  Honey Mustard Whiskey
    Marinade, 236
  Horseradish Sauce, 244
  Indian Carrot Sauce, 65
  Kickin' Chicken
    Marinade, 153
  La Kama Dry Rub, 191
  Lemon Mustard
    Marinade, 238
  Malaysian Coconut
    Curry Paste, 98
  Mango Chutney
    Marinade, 60
  Mustard Seeds Curry
    Sauce, 66
  Nigella Seeds Meat
    Marinade, 64
  Peppercorn Paste, 56
  Port Juniper Sauce, 246
  Poudre de Colombo
    Rum Paste, 147

Qâlat Daqqa Tunisian
    Dry Rub, 193
  Quarte Épices Blend, 233
  Ras el Hanout Blend, 186
  Red Wine Paprika
    Goulash Sauce, 243
  Sambaar Masala Blend, 51
  Smoky "Holey" Mole
    Sauce, 156–157
  South Pacific Honey
    Paste, 100
  Sri Lankan Curry Rub, 54
  Sumac Eggplant Paste, 234
  Sweet Baby Gavin's
    Guava Sauce, 155
  Taco (Taceaux) Seasoning
    Blend, 143
  Thai Red Curry Rub, 97
  Tunisian Tabil Paste, 195
  Vadouvan-Lassi Poultry
    Marinade, 63
  Vindaloo Curry Paste, 59
  Yogurt Marinade, 62
Blade grinders, 12
Blends
  Advieh Persian Blend, 187
  Baharat Blend, 188
  Chaat Masala Blend, 48
  Chesapeake Bay-Style
    Seasoning Blend, 141
  Chile-Infused Pickling
    Spice Blend, 142
  Chinese Five-Spice
    Blend, 94
  Creole Spice Blend, 140
  Feh El Omri Blend, 189
  Garam Masala Blend, 49
  Herbes et Épices de
    Provence Blend, 232
  Mulling Over Spice
    Blend, 145
  Panch Phoron Blend, 50
  Pumpkin Seeds Autumn
    Blend, 144
  Quarte Épices Blend, 233
  Ras el Hanout Blend, 186
  Sambaar Masala Blend, 51
  Shichimi Togarashi Blend, 95
  Taco (Taceaux) Seasoning
    Blend, 143
  Tandoori Chicken Blend, 52

Burdock root
    Dragon Fyre Cider, 4
Burr grinders, 12

C

Capers
    Sicilian Saffron Pasta
      Sauce, 251
Caraway
    about, 210–211
    Apple Caraway
      Marinade, 237
    Feh El Omri Blend, 189
    Harissa Paste, 201
    Port Juniper Sauce, 246
    Red Wine Paprika
      Goulash Sauce, 243
    Tunisian Tabil Paste, 195
Cardamom
    about, 34–35
    Advieh Persian Blend, 187
    Asthma Tea, 5
    Baharat Blend, 188
    Berbere Rub, 194
    Chesapeake Bay-Style
      Seasoning Blend, 141
    Curry Seafood Sauce, 67
    Garam Masala Blend, 49
    Indian Carrot Sauce, 65
    Kashmiri Masala Paste, 58
    Madras Curry Rub, 55
    Mulling Over Spice
      Blend, 145
    Ras el Hanout Blend, 186
    Sri Lankan Curry Rub, 54
    Vadouvan-Lassi Poultry
      Marinade, 63
    Yogurt Marinade, 62
Carrots
    Dhana Jeera Vegetable
      Paste, 57
    Indian Carrot Sauce, 65
    Mango Chutney
      Marinade, 60
    Two-Shack "Como el
      Otro" Hot Sauce, 159
Cashews
    Malaysian Coconut
      Curry Paste, 98

Cassia cinnamon
  about, 72–73
  Chinese Five-Spice
    Blend, 94
  Malaysian Coconut
    Curry Paste, 98
  Peach-Plum Sauce, 106
Cayenne pepper
  about, 124–125
  Berbere Rub, 194
  Chaimen Armenian
    Spice Paste, 197
  Charmoula Paste, 198–199
  Chesapeake Bay-Style
    Seasoning Blend, 141
  Chile-Infused Pickling
    Spice Blend, 142
  Creole Barbecue
    Dry Rub, 146
  Garam Masala Yogurt
    Marinade, 61
  Grandma Martha's New
    Mexico Green Chile
    Bean Sauce, 154
  Kickin' Chicken
    Marinade, 153
  Madras Curry Rub, 55
  Malaysian Coconut
    Curry Paste, 98
  Mustard Seeds Curry
    Sauce, 66
  Pumpkin Seeds Autumn
    Blend, 144
  Ras el Hanout Blend, 186
  Sambaar Masala Blend, 51
  Spicy Peanut Marinade, 152
  Sweet Baby Gavin's
    Guava Sauce, 155
  Taco (Taceaux) Seasoning
    Blend, 143
  Tandoori Chicken Blend, 52
  Two-Shack "Como el
    Otro" Hot Sauce, 159
  Vadouvan-Lassi Poultry
    Marinade, 63
  Yogurt Marinade, 62
Celery salt, 212
  Cinnamon-Turmeric Rub, 53

Celery seeds
  about, 212–213
  Chesapeake Bay-Style
    Seasoning Blend, 141
  Creole Spice Blend, 140
  Herbes et Épices de
    Provence Blend, 232
  Red Wine Paprika
    Goulash Sauce, 243
Ceylon cinnamon
  about, 36–37
  Indian Carrot Sauce, 65
  Sri Lankan Curry Rub, 54
Cheddar cheese
  Tarragon Sauce, 245
Chiles. See also specific
  about, 120–121
  Berbere Rub, 194
  Harissa Paste, 201
  Peri Peri Dry Rub, 192
  Poudre de Colombo
    Rum Paste, 147
  Red "DB" Chile Sauce, 160
  Red Mojo Sauce, 248
  Vindaloo Curry Paste, 59
Chinese cuisine, 70
Chipotle (jalapeño) chiles
  about, 126–127
  Adobo Mezcal
    Marinade, 149
  Peri Peri Dry Rub, 192
  Pumpkin Seeds Autumn
    Blend, 144
  Smoky "Holey" Mole
    Sauce, 156–157
Chive flowers
  Chive Blossom
    Mignonette, 247
Chives
  Vietnamese Lemongrass
    Dry Rub, 96
Chocolate. See also
    Cocoa powder
  Smoky "Holey" Mole
    Sauce, 156–157
Cilantro, 2, 168
  Charmoula Paste, 198–199
  Thai Red Curry Rub, 97
  Vietnamese Lemongrass
    Dry Rub, 96

Cinnamon. See also
    Cassia cinnamon;
    Ceylon cinnamon
  Advieh Persian Blend, 187
  Apple Caraway
    Marinade, 237
  Baharat Blend, 188
  Berbere Rub, 194
  Chesapeake Bay-Style
    Seasoning Blend, 141
  Chile-Infused Pickling
    Spice Blend, 142
  Cinnamon-Turmeric Rub, 53
  Dhana Jeera Vegetable
    Paste, 57
  Feh El Omri Blend, 189
  Garam Masala Blend, 49
  Jerk-Style Pineapple
    Paste, 148
  Kashmiri Masala Paste, 58
  La Kama Dry Rub, 191
  Madras Curry Rub, 55
  Mulling Over Spice
    Blend, 145
  Pumpkin Seeds Autumn
    Blend, 144
  Qâlat Daqqa Tunisian
    Dry Rub, 193
  Ras el Hanout Blend, 186
  Sambaar Masala Blend, 51
  Smoky "Holey" Mole
    Sauce, 156–157
  Vindaloo Curry Paste, 59
  Yogurt Marinade, 62
Cloves
  about, 74–75
  Baharat Blend, 188
  Berbere Rub, 194
  Chesapeake Bay-Style
    Seasoning Blend, 141
  Chile-Infused Pickling
    Spice Blend, 142
  Chinese Five-Spice
    Blend, 94
  Creole Spice Blend, 140
  Feh El Omri Blend, 189
  Garam Masala Blend, 49
  Indian Carrot Sauce, 65
  Madras Curry Rub, 55
  Mulling Over Spice
    Blend, 145

Peach-Plum Sauce, 106
Qâlat Daqqa Tunisian
Dry Rub, 193
Quarte Êpices Blend, 233
Smoky "Holey" Mole
Sauce, 156–157
South Pacific Honey
Paste, 100
Vindaloo Curry Paste, 59
Cocoa powder
Taco (Taceaux) Seasoning
Blend, 143
Coconut milk
Curry Seafood Sauce, 67
Malaysian Coconut
Curry Paste, 98
Thai Satay Marinade, 103
Columbus, Christopher, 3
Coriander
about, 168–169
Advieh Persian Blend, 187
Baharat Blend, 188
Berbere Rub, 194
Black Tahini Paste, 196
Chaat Masala Blend, 48
Chaimen Armenian
Spice Paste, 197
Charmoula Paste, 198–199
Curry Seafood Sauce, 67
Dhana Jeera Vegetable
Paste, 57
Dukkah Egyptian
Dry Rub, 190
Feh El Omri Blend, 189
Garam Masala Blend, 49
Harissa Paste, 201
Kashmiri Masala Paste, 58
Madras Curry Rub, 55
Malaysian Coconut
Curry Paste, 98
Mustard Seeds Curry
Sauce, 66
Peppercorn Paste, 56
Poudre de Colombo
Rum Paste, 147
Ras el Hanout Blend, 186
Sambaar Masala Blend, 51
Sri Lankan Curry Rub, 54
Tamarind Yogurt
Marinade, 204
Thai Red Curry Rub, 97

Tunisian Tabil Paste, 195
Vadouvan-Lassi Poultry
Marinade, 63
Vindaloo Curry Paste, 59
Yogurt Marinade, 62
Cranberries
Pumpkin Seeds Fish
Marinade, 150
Cream
New Orleans Barbecue
Shrimp Sauce, 161
Saffron Sauce, 205
Tarragon Sauce, 245
Crushing, 11–12
Cubeb peppers
about, 88–89
Peppercorn Paste, 56
Cuisines
African, 164
American, 114
Asian, 70
Chinese, 70
European, 208
Indian, 22
Japanese, 70
Latin American, 114
Mediterranean, 208
Middle Eastern, 164
South Pacific, 70
Thai, 70
Cumin
about, 170–171
Adobo Mezcal
Marinade, 149
Advieh Persian Blend, 187
Baharat Blend, 188
Chaat Masala Blend, 48
Chaimen Armenian
Spice Paste, 197
Charmoula Paste, 198–199
Cinnamon-Turmeric Rub, 53
Curry Seafood Sauce, 67
Dhana Jeera Vegetable
Paste, 57
Dukkah Egyptian
Dry Rub, 190
Garam Masala Blend, 49
Harissa Paste, 201
Kashmiri Masala Paste, 58
La Kama Dry Rub, 191
Madras Curry Rub, 55

Malaysian Coconut
Curry Paste, 98
Mustard Seeds Curry
Sauce, 66
Panch Phoron Blend, 50
Poudre de Colombo
Rum Paste, 147
Queen's Carnitas
Marinade, 151
Ras el Hanout Blend, 186
Red "DB" Chile Sauce, 160
Red Mojo Sauce, 248
Saffron Sauce, 205
Sambaar Masala Blend, 51
Smoky "Holey" Mole
Sauce, 156–157
Sri Lankan Curry Rub, 54
Sumac Eggplant Paste, 234
Taco (Taceaux) Seasoning
Blend, 143
Tamarind Yogurt
Marinade, 204
Thai Red Curry Rub, 97
Thai Satay Marinade, 103
Tunisian Tabil Paste, 195
Vadouvan-Lassi Poultry
Marinade, 63
Vindaloo Curry Paste, 59
Yogurt Marinade, 62
Curry leaves
Mustard Seeds Curry
Sauce, 66
Sri Lankan Curry Rub, 54
Vadouvan-Lassi Poultry
Marinade, 63
Curry powder, 42

D

Dates
Sumac Blackberry
Agrodolce Marinade, 235
De Wulf, Devin, 146
Dias, Bartolomeu, 164
Dijon mustard, 224
Homemade Saffron
Mayo Marinade, 202
Honey Mustard Whiskey
Marinade, 236
Lemon Mustard
Marinade, 238

Dijon mustard (*continued*)
  Nigella Seeds Meat
    Marinade, 64
  Paprika Mustard Sauce, 249
  Tarragon Sauce, 245
  Wayward Orange
    Sauce, 250
Dill seeds
  about, 214–215
  Balsamic Horseradish
    Marinade, 239
  Chile-Infused Pickling
    Spice Blend, 142
  Creole Spice Blend, 140
  Dill, Mint, and Sumac
    Seafood Marinade, 241
  Herbes et Épices de
    Provence Blend, 232
Dill weed
  Vietnamese Lemongrass
    Dry Rub, 96
Dressings
  Asian Cold Noodle
    Dressing, 104
Dry rubs
  about, 14
  Creole Barbecue
    Dry Rub, 146
  Dukkah Egyptian
    Dry Rub, 190
  La Kama Dry Rub, 191
  Peri Peri Dry Rub, 192
  Qâlat Daqqa Tunisian
    Dry Rub, 193
  Vietnamese Lemongrass
    Dry Rub, 96

E

Eggplant
  Sumac Eggplant Paste, 234
European cuisine, 208

F

Fennel seeds
  about, 216–217
  Apple Caraway
    Marinade, 237
  Balsamic Horseradish
    Marinade, 239

Chaat Masala Blend, 48
Chinese Five-Spice
  Blend, 94
Herbes et Épices de
  Provence Blend, 232
Honey Mustard Whiskey
  Marinade, 236
Juniper White Wine
  Marinade, 240
Kashmiri Masala Paste, 58
Lemon Mustard
  Marinade, 238
Limoncello-Fennel Poultry
  Marinade, 242
Malaysian Coconut
  Curry Paste, 98
Panch Phoron Blend, 50
Ras el Hanout Blend, 186
Sri Lankan Curry Rub, 54
Fenugreek
  about, 218–219
  Berbere Rub, 194
  Chaimen Armenian
    Spice Paste, 197
  Mustard Seeds Curry
    Sauce, 66
  Panch Phoron Blend, 50
  Poudre de Colombo
    Rum Paste, 147
  Sri Lankan Curry Rub, 54
  Vadouvan-Lassi Poultry
    Marinade, 63
Fermented black soybeans
  Chinese Sweet Bean
    Paste, 99
Foose, Martha, 244
Fruits. *See also specific*
  and spice parings, 16

G

Galangal
  about, 76–77
  Feh El Omri Blend, 189
  South Pacific Honey
    Paste, 100
  Sweet Orange Chili
    Sauce, 107
  Thai Red Curry Rub, 97
  Thai Satay Marinade, 103
Gama, Vasco de, 3

Garlic
  Adobo Mezcal
    Marinade, 149
  Asian Cold Noodle
    Dressing, 104
  Backcountry Chimichurri
    Sauce, 158
  Charmoula Paste, 198–199
  Chile-Infused Pickling
    Spice Blend, 142
  Chinese Sweet Bean
    Paste, 99
  Creole Barbecue
    Dry Rub, 146
  Curry Seafood Sauce, 67
  Grandma Martha's New
    Mexico Green Chile
    Bean Sauce, 154
  Harissa Paste, 201
  Jerk-Style Pineapple
    Paste, 148
  Juniper White Wine
    Marinade, 240
  Kalba Korean Marinade, 102
  Miso Doko Marinade, 105
  Moroccan Lamb Tajine
    Marinade, 203
  Mustard Seeds Curry
    Sauce, 66
  Peri Peri Dry Rub, 192
  Port Juniper Sauce, 246
  Poudre de Colombo
    Rum Paste, 147
  Pumpkin Seeds Fish
    Marinade, 150
  Red "DB" Chile Sauce, 160
  Red Mojo Sauce, 248
  Red Wine Paprika
    Goulash Sauce, 243
  Saffron Sauce, 205
  Smoky "Holey" Mole
    Sauce, 156–157
  Sumac Eggplant Paste, 234
  Sweet Orange Chili
    Sauce, 107
  Thai Red Curry Rub, 97
  Thai Satay Marinade, 103
  Vadouvan-Lassi Poultry
    Marinade, 63
  Vindaloo Curry Paste, 59
  Yogurt Marinade, 62

Gavin, Chef, 155
Genghis Khan, 70
Ghana, 172
Ginger
    about, 78–79
    Adobo Mezcal
        Marinade, 149
    Advieh Persian Blend, 187
    Asian Cold Noodle
        Dressing, 104
    Asthma Tea, 5
    Berbere Rub, 194
    Chaat Masala Blend, 48
    Charmoula Paste, 198–199
    Chesapeake Bay-Style
        Seasoning Blend, 141
    Chinese Sweet Bean
        Paste, 99
    Crystalized Ginger, 6
    Curry Seafood Sauce, 67
    Dragon Fyre Cider, 4
    Feh El Omri Blend, 189
    Gomasio Lemon Dressing
        Marinade, 101
    Jerk-Style Pineapple
        Paste, 148
    Kalba Korean Marinade, 102
    Kashmiri Masala Paste, 58
    Kickin' Chicken
        Marinade, 153
    La Kama Dry Rub, 191
    Malaysian Coconut
        Curry Paste, 98
    Mango Chutney
        Marinade, 60
    Miso Doko Marinade, 105
    Mulling Over Spice
        Blend, 145
    Mustard Seeds Curry
        Sauce, 66
    Nigella Seeds Meat
        Marinade, 64
    Peach-Plum Sauce, 106
    Quarte Épices Blend, 233
    Ras el Hanout Blend, 186
    Shichimi Togarashi
        Blend, 95
    South Pacific Honey
        Paste, 100
    Spicy Peanut Marinade, 152

    Sweet Orange Chili
        Sauce, 107
    Tandoori Chicken Blend, 52
    Vietnamese Lemongrass
        Dry Rub, 96
    Vindaloo Curry Paste, 59
    Yogurt Marinade, 62
Grains of paradise
    about, 172–173
    Advieh Persian Blend, 187
    Berbere Rub, 194
    Homemade Saffron
        Mayo Marinade, 202
    Juniper White Wine
        Marinade, 240
    La Kama Dry Rub, 191
    Paprika Mustard Sauce, 249
    Peri Peri Dry Rub, 192
    Qâlat Daqqa Tunisian
        Dry Rub, 193
    Ras el Hanout Blend, 186
    Tamarind Yogurt
        Marinade, 204
Grating, 13
Greek yogurt
    Garam Masala Yogurt
        Marinade, 61
Green chiles
    Grandma Martha's New
        Mexico Green Chile
        Bean Sauce, 154
Green pepper
    about, 38–39
    Chile-Infused Pickling
        Spice Blend, 142
    Mango Chutney
        Marinade, 60
Grinding, 12
Guajillo (mirasol) chiles
    about, 128–129
    Adobo Mezcal
        Marinade, 149
    Creole Spice Blend, 140
    Smoky "Holey" Mole
        Sauce, 156–157
Guava
    Sweet Baby Gavin's
        Guava Sauce, 155

H

Habanero chiles
    about, 130–131
    Jerk-Style Pineapple
        Paste, 148
Hazelnuts
    Dukkah Egyptian
        Dry Rub, 190
Health, 4–6
Hemp seeds
    Shichimi Togarashi
        Blend, 95
Herbs. See also specific
    defined, 2
    and spice parings, 15
Hibiscus
    Dragon Fyre Cider, 4
Himalayan pink salt
    Tandoori Chicken Blend, 52
Honey
    Apple Caraway
        Marinade, 237
    Asthma Tea, 5
    Chive Blossom
        Mignonette, 247
    Dill, Mint, and Sumac
        Seafood Marinade, 241
    Honey Mustard Whiskey
        Marinade, 236
    Kickin' Chicken
        Marinade, 153
    Lemon Mustard
        Marinade, 238
    Moroccan Lamb Tajine
        Marinade, 203
    Omam Water, 5
    Poppy Paste, 200
    South Pacific Honey
        Paste, 100
    Throat Tea, 6
Horseradish. See also Wasabi
    about, 220–221
    Balsamic Horseradish
        Marinade, 239
    Dragon Fyre Cider, 4
    Horseradish Sauce, 244
    Throat Tea, 6
    Wayward Orange
        Sauce, 250

I

Indian black salt
  Chaat Masala Blend, 48
  Tandoori Chicken Blend, 52
Indian cuisine, 22
Ishikawa, Kaz, 105, 109

J

Japanese cuisine, 70
Japonés chiles
  Shichimi Togarashi Blend, 95
Juniper berries
  about, 222–223
  Apple Caraway
    Marinade, 237
  Juniper White Wine
    Marinade, 240
  Port Juniper Sauce, 246
  Throat Tea, 6

K

Kaffir lime leaves
  Kalba Korean Marinade, 102
  South Pacific Honey
    Paste, 100
  Thai Red Curry Rub, 97
Kashmiri chiles
  Kashmiri Masala Paste, 58
  Sambaar Masala Blend, 51
  Tandoori Chicken Blend, 52
Kennedy, Jayne, 244

L

Lamb
  Sweet Orange Chili
    Sauce, 107
Lassi yogurt
  Vadouvan-Lassi Poultry
    Marinade, 63
Latin American cuisine, 114
Lavender
  Herbes et Épices de
    Provence Blend, 232
  Ras el Hanout Blend, 186
Lemongrass
  Malaysian Coconut
    Curry Paste, 98

South Pacific Honey
    Paste, 100
  Thai Red Curry Rub, 97
  Thai Satay Marinade, 103
  Vietnamese Lemongrass
    Dry Rub, 96
Lemon peel and zest
  about, 80–81
  Charmoula Paste, 198–199
  Gomasio Lemon Dressing
    Marinade, 101
  Honey Mustard Whiskey
    Marinade, 236
  Horseradish Sauce, 244
  Lemon Mustard
    Marinade, 238
  Malaysian Coconut
    Curry Paste, 98
  Mulling Over Spice
    Blend, 145
  Peri Peri Dry Rub, 192
  Taco (Taceaux) Seasoning
    Blend, 143
  Tamarind Yogurt
    Marinade, 204
  Thai Red Curry Rub, 97
  Thai Satay Marinade, 103
  Wasabi Mayonnaise
    Sauce, 108
  Wayward Orange
    Sauce, 250
Lemons and lemon juice
  Asthma Tea, 5
  Backcountry Chimichurri
    Sauce, 158
  Black Tahini Paste, 196
  Charmoula Paste, 198–199
  Chive Blossom
    Mignonette, 247
  Curry Seafood Sauce, 67
  Dill, Mint, and Sumac
    Seafood Marinade, 241
  Garam Masala Yogurt
    Marinade, 61
  Gomasio Lemon Dressing
    Marinade, 101
  Homemade Saffron
    Mayo Marinade, 202
  Honey Mustard Whiskey
    Marinade, 236
  Lemon Mustard
    Marinade, 238

Peri Peri Dry Rub, 192
  Sicilian Saffron Pasta
    Sauce, 251
  Spicy Peanut Marinade, 152
  Thai Satay Marinade, 103
  Throat Tea, 6
  Wasabi Mayonnaise
    Sauce, 108
  Wayward Orange
    Sauce, 250
Lentils (urad dal)
  Sambaar Masala Blend, 51
Licorice root
  about, 174–175
  Tamarind Yogurt
    Marinade, 204
Limes and lime juice
  Chive Blossom
    Mignonette, 247
  Jerk-Style Pineapple
    Paste, 148
  Sumac Eggplant Paste, 234
  Sweet Baby Gavin's
    Guava Sauce, 155
Long peppers
  about, 88–89
  Peppercorn Paste, 56

M

Mace
  about, 82–83
  Garam Masala Blend, 49
  Kashmiri Masala Paste, 58
  La Kama Dry Rub, 191
  Malaysian Coconut
    Curry Paste, 98
  Ras el Hanout Blend, 186
  Thai Satay Marinade, 103
  Vietnamese Lemongrass
    Dry Rub, 96
Mangos
  Mango Chutney
    Marinade, 60
  powder, 26
Marinades
  about, 14
  Adobo Mezcal
    Marinade, 149
  Apple Caraway
    Marinade, 237

Balsamic Horseradish
Marinade, 239
Dill, Mint, and Sumac
Seafood Marinade, 241
Garam Masala Yogurt
Marinade, 61
Gomasio Lemon Dressing
Marinade, 101
Homemade Saffron
Mayo Marinade, 202
Honey Mustard Whiskey
Marinade, 236
Juniper White Wine
Marinade, 240
Kalba Korean Marinade, 102
Kickin' Chicken
Marinade, 153
Lemon Mustard
Marinade, 238
Limoncello-Fennel Poultry
Marinade, 242
Mango Chutney
Marinade, 60
Miso Doko Marinade, 105
Moroccan Lamb Tajine
Marinade, 203
Nigella Seeds Meat
Marinade, 64
Pumpkin Seeds Fish
Marinade, 150
Queen's Carnitas
Marinade, 151
Spicy Peanut Marinade, 152
Sumac Blackberry
Agrodolce Marinade, 235
Tamarind Yogurt
Marinade, 204
Thai Satay Marinade, 103
Vadouvan-Lassi Poultry
Marinade, 63
Yogurt Marinade, 62
Marjoram
Herbes et Épices de
Provence Blend, 232
Mayonnaise
Homemade Saffron
Mayo Marinade, 202
Horseradish Sauce, 244
Mustard Miso Sauce, 109
Wasabi Mayonnaise
Sauce, 108

Mediterranean cuisine, 208
Middle Eastern cuisine, 164
Mint
Asthma Tea, 5
Backcountry Chimichurri
Sauce, 158
Chaat Masala Blend, 48
Dill, Mint, and Sumac
Seafood Marinade, 241
Dukkah Egyptian
Dry Rub, 190
Harissa Paste, 201
Saffron Sauce, 205
South Pacific Honey
Paste, 100
Sumac Eggplant Paste, 234
Mirin
Chinese Sweet Bean
Paste, 99
Kalba Korean Marinade, 102
Miso Doko Marinade, 105
Mustard Miso Sauce, 109
Teriyaki Wasabi Sauce, 111
Wasabi Steak Sauce, 110
Mirza, Salmaan, 62, 66
Miso
Miso Doko Marinade, 105
Mustard Miso Sauce, 109
Mohajeri, Beeta, 65,
102, 161, 235
Molasses
Two-Shack "Como el
Otro" Hot Sauce, 159
Monosodium glutamate
(MSG), 10
Monthan, Gabriel, 160
Mortars and pestles, 11–12
Mustard, 224. See also
Dijon mustard
Chesapeake Bay-Style
Seasoning Blend, 141
Mustard Miso Sauce, 109
Poudre de Colombo
Rum Paste, 147
Mustard seeds
about, 224–225
Chile-Infused Pickling
Spice Blend, 142
Mustard Seeds Curry
Sauce, 66
Panch Phoron Blend, 50
Sri Lankan Curry Rub, 54

Vadouvan-Lassi Poultry
Marinade, 63

N

Nicks, Denver, 120
Nicks, John "Two-Shack," 159
Nigella
about, 40–41
Asian Cold Noodle
Dressing, 104
Berbere Rub, 194
Nigella Seeds Meat
Marinade, 64
Panch Phoron Blend, 50
Sweet Orange Chili
Sauce, 107
Nori seaweed
Shichimi Togarashi Blend, 95
Nutmeg
about, 84–85
Advieh Persian Blend, 187
Baharat Blend, 188
Garam Masala Blend, 49
La Kama Dry Rub, 191
Malaysian Coconut
Curry Paste, 98
Mulling Over Spice
Blend, 145
Qâlat Daqqa Tunisian
Dry Rub, 193
Quarte Épices Blend, 233
Ras el Hanout Blend, 186
Vindaloo Curry Paste, 59
Nuts. See also specific
and spice parings, 18

O

Omri, Nisrine, 189, 201
Onions. See also Scallions
Backcountry Chimichurri
Sauce, 158
Creole Barbecue
Dry Rub, 146
Curry Seafood Sauce, 67
Dhana Jeera Vegetable
Paste, 57
Dragon Fyre Cider, 4
Grandma Martha's New
Mexico Green Chile
Bean Sauce, 154

Onions (*continued*)
  Indian Carrot Sauce, 65
  Jerk-Style Pineapple
    Paste, 148
  Kalba Korean Marinade, 102
  Mango Chutney
    Marinade, 60
  Moroccan Lamb Tajine
    Marinade, 203
  Port Juniper Sauce, 246
  Smoky "Holey" Mole
    Sauce, 156–157
  Spicy Peanut Marinade, 152
  Sumac Eggplant Paste, 234
  Sweet Orange Chili
    Sauce, 107
  Thai Satay Marinade, 103
  Two-Shack "Como el
    Otro" Hot Sauce, 159
  Vadouvan-Lassi Poultry
    Marinade, 63
Open markets, 9
Orange peel
  Mulling Over Spice
    Blend, 145
  Shichimi Togarashi Blend, 95
  Wayward Orange
    Sauce, 250
Oranges and orange juice
  Queen's Carnitas
    Marinade, 151
  Sicilian Saffron Pasta
    Sauce, 251
  Wayward Orange
    Sauce, 250
Oregano
  Adobo Mezcal
    Marinade, 149
  Creole Spice Blend, 140
  Nigella Seeds Meat
    Marinade, 64
  Peri Peri Dry Rub, 192
  Taco (Taceaux) Seasoning
    Blend, 143
Oroshigane, 13

P

Pairings
  fruit and spice, 16
  nut and spice, 18
  protein and spice, 19

spice and herb, 15
  vegetable and spice, 17
Pandan leaves
  Sri Lankan Curry Rub, 54
Paprika
  about, 226–227
  Adobo Mezcal
    Marinade, 149
  Advieh Persian Blend, 187
  Apple Caraway
    Marinade, 237
  Baharat Blend, 188
  Berbere Rub, 194
  Chaimen Armenian
    Spice Paste, 197
  Charmoula Paste, 198–199
  Chesapeake Bay-Style
    Seasoning Blend, 141
  Creole Spice Blend, 140
  Kashmiri Masala Paste, 58
  Lemon Mustard
    Marinade, 238
  Paprika Mustard Sauce, 249
  Peri Peri Dry Rub, 192
  Pumpkin Seeds Autumn
    Blend, 144
  Ras el Hanout Blend, 186
  Red Mojo Sauce, 248
  Red Wine Paprika
    Goulash Sauce, 243
  Smoky "Holey" Mole
    Sauce, 156–157
  Taco (Taceaux) Seasoning
    Blend, 143
  Tandoori Chicken Blend, 52
Parsley
  Backcountry Chimichurri
    Sauce, 158
  Balsamic Horseradish
    Marinade, 239
  Chaimen Armenian
    Spice Paste, 197
  Charmoula Paste, 198–199
  Herbes et Épices de
    Provence Blend, 232
  Juniper White Wine
    Marinade, 240
  Sicilian Saffron Pasta
    Sauce, 251
Pasilla Bajio chiles
  Two-Shack "Como el
    Otro" Hot Sauce, 159

Pastes
  about, 13–14
  Black Tahini Paste, 196
  Chaimen Armenian
    Spice Paste, 197
  Charmoula Paste, 198–199
  Chinese Sweet Bean
    Paste, 99
  Dhana Jeera Vegetable
    Paste, 57
  Harissa Paste, 201
  Jerk-Style Pineapple
    Paste, 148
  Kashmiri Masala Paste, 58
  Malaysian Coconut
    Curry Paste, 98
  Peppercorn Paste, 56
  Poppy Paste, 200
  Poudre de Colombo
    Rum Paste, 147
  South Pacific Honey
    Paste, 100
  Sumac Eggplant Paste, 234
  Tunisian Tabil Paste, 195
  Vindaloo Curry Paste, 59
Peaches
  Peach-Plum Sauce, 106
Peanut butter
  Spicy Peanut Marinade, 152
Peanuts
  Malaysian Coconut
    Curry Paste, 98
  Thai Satay Marinade, 103
Pears
  Kalba Korean Marinade, 102
Pepitas. *See* Pumpkin seeds
Pepper. *See* Black pepper;
    Green pepper; Pink
    pepper; White pepper
Pineapple
  Jerk-Style Pineapple
    Paste, 148
Pine nuts
  Smoky "Holey" Mole
    Sauce, 156–157
Pink pepper
  about, 38–39
  Chile-Infused Pickling
    Spice Blend, 142
  Peppercorn Paste, 56

Pinto beans
    Grandma Martha's New
        Mexico Green Chile
        Bean Sauce, 154
Pistachios
    Dukkah Egyptian
        Dry Rub, 190
Plums
    Peach-Plum Sauce, 106
Poivre, Pierre, 74
Pomegranate seeds, 28
Poppy seeds
    about, 176–177
    Poppy Paste, 200
    Shichimi Togarashi Blend, 95
Proteins, and spice parings, 19
Pulverizing, 12
Pumpkin seeds
    about, 132–133
    Pumpkin Seeds Autumn
        Blend, 144
    Pumpkin Seeds Fish
        Marinade, 150
    Smoky "Holey" Mole
        Sauce, 156–157

Q

Queen, Aric S., 151

R

Rahfield, Paul, 248
Raisins
    Smoky "Holey" Mole
        Sauce, 156–157
Rhizomes, 42, 78, 90
Rice
    Poudre de Colombo
        Rum Paste, 147
    Sri Lankan Curry Rub, 54
Rivera, Gustavo Turcios, 234
Roasting, 13
Rosebuds and rose petals
    Advieh Persian Blend, 187
    Feh El Omri Blend, 189
    Ras el Hanout Blend, 186
Rosemary
    Feh El Omri Blend, 189
    Herbes et Épices de
        Provence Blend, 232

Juniper White Wine
        Marinade, 240
    Port Juniper Sauce, 246
    Vadouvan-Lassi Poultry
        Marinade, 63
Rubs. See also Dry rubs
    about, 14
    Berbere Rub, 194
    Cinnamon-Turmeric Rub, 53
    Madras Curry Rub, 55
    Sri Lankan Curry Rub, 54
    Thai Red Curry Rub, 97

S

Saffron
    about, 178–179
    health benefits of, 4
    Homemade Saffron
        Mayo Marinade, 202
    Saffron Sauce, 205
    Sicilian Saffron Pasta
        Sauce, 251
    Tandoori Chicken Blend, 52
Sage
    Juniper White Wine
        Marinade, 240
    Port Juniper Sauce, 246
    Throat Tea, 6
Salt. See also Himalayan
        pink salt; Indian
        black salt; Sea salt
    about, 2, 10
    Adobo Mezcal
        Marinade, 149
    Chinese Sweet Bean
        Paste, 99
    Chive Blossom
        Mignonette, 247
    Curry Seafood Sauce, 67
    Jerk-Style Pineapple
        Paste, 148
    Peppercorn Paste, 56
    Peri Peri Dry Rub, 192
    Sambaar Masala Blend, 51
    South Pacific Honey
        Paste, 100
    Sweet Baby Gavin's
        Guava Sauce, 155
    Thai Satay Marinade, 103
    Vindaloo Curry Paste, 59
    Yogurt Marinade, 62

Sansho peppers
    about, 88–89
    Shichimi Togarashi Blend, 95
Sassafras
    about, 134–135
Sauces
    Backcountry Chimichurri
        Sauce, 158
    Chive Blossom
        Mignonette, 247
    Curry Seafood Sauce, 67
    Grandma Martha's New
        Mexico Green Chile
        Bean Sauce, 154
    Horseradish Sauce, 244
    Indian Carrot Sauce, 65
    Mustard Miso Sauce, 109
    Mustard Seeds Curry
        Sauce, 66
    New Orleans Barbecue
        Shrimp Sauce, 161
    Paprika Mustard Sauce, 249
    Peach-Plum Sauce, 106
    Port Juniper Sauce, 246
    Red "DB" Chile Sauce, 160
    Red Mojo Sauce, 248
    Red Wine Paprika
        Goulash Sauce, 243
    Saffron Sauce, 205
    Sicilian Saffron Pasta
        Sauce, 251
    Smoky "Holey" Mole
        Sauce, 156–157
    Sweet Baby Gavin's
        Guava Sauce, 155
    Sweet Orange Chili
        Sauce, 107
    Tarragon Sauce, 245
    Teriyaki Wasabi Sauce, 111
    Two-Shack "Como el
        Otro" Hot Sauce, 159
    Wasabi Mayonnaise
        Sauce, 108
    Wasabi Steak Sauce, 110
    Wayward Orange
        Sauce, 250
Scallions
    Jerk-Style Pineapple
        Paste, 148
    Kalba Korean Marinade, 102
    New Orleans Barbecue
        Shrimp Sauce, 161

Scallions (*continued*)
 Nigella Seeds Meat
  Marinade, 64
Scotch Bonnet chiles
 about, 130–131
 Jerk-Style Pineapple
  Paste, 148
Scoville scale, 30, 120,
  122, 124, 126, 128
Sea salt
 Advieh Persian Blend, 187
 Backcountry Chimichurri
  Sauce, 158
 Black Tahini Paste, 196
 Chaat Masala Blend, 48
 Chaimen Armenian
  Spice Paste, 197
 Charmoula Paste, 198–199
 Chesapeake Bay-Style
  Seasoning Blend, 141
 Chile-Infused Pickling
  Spice Blend, 142
 Creole Barbecue
  Dry Rub, 146
 Creole Spice Blend, 140
 Dhana Jeera Vegetable
  Paste, 57
 Dill, Mint, and Sumac
  Seafood Marinade, 241
 Dukkah Egyptian
  Dry Rub, 190
 Garam Masala Yogurt
  Marinade, 61
 Gomasio Lemon Dressing
  Marinade, 101
 Harissa Paste, 201
 Homemade Saffron
  Mayo Marinade, 202
 Honey Mustard Whiskey
  Marinade, 236
 Horseradish Sauce, 244
 Indian Carrot Sauce, 65
 Kickin' Chicken
  Marinade, 153
 Lemon Mustard
  Marinade, 238
 Nigella Seeds Meat
  Marinade, 64
 Paprika Mustard Sauce, 249
 Pumpkin Seeds Autumn
  Blend, 144

Pumpkin Seeds Fish
 Marinade, 150
Red "DB" Chile Sauce, 160
Red Mojo Sauce, 248
Sicilian Saffron Pasta
 Sauce, 251
Spicy Peanut Marinade, 152
Sumac Eggplant Paste, 234
Taco (Taceaux) Seasoning
 Blend, 143
Tamarind Yogurt
 Marinade, 204
Tarragon Sauce, 245
Tunisian Tabil Paste, 195
Two-Shack "Como el
 Otro" Hot Sauce, 159
Serrano chiles
 Chile-Infused Pickling
  Spice Blend, 142
Sesame seeds
 about, 180–181
 Asian Cold Noodle
  Dressing, 104
 Black Tahini Paste, 196
 Dukkah Egyptian
  Dry Rub, 190
 Gomasio Lemon Dressing
  Marinade, 101
 Poppy Paste, 200
 Shichimi Togarashi Blend, 95
 Sumac Blackberry
  Agrodolce Marinade, 235
 Tamarind Yogurt
  Marinade, 204
Shackleton, Charles and
 Miranda (Wink), 104, 250
Shallots
 Juniper White Wine
  Marinade, 240
 Thai Red Curry Rub, 97
Shrimp
 New Orleans Barbecue
  Shrimp Sauce, 161
Silk Road, 164
Sodium chloride, 10
Sour cream
 Curry Seafood Sauce, 67
 Horseradish Sauce, 244
South Pacific cuisine, 70

Soy sauce
 Asian Cold Noodle
  Dressing, 104
 Chinese Sweet Bean
  Paste, 99
 Jerk-Style Pineapple
  Paste, 148
 Kalba Korean Marinade, 102
 Miso Doko Marinade, 105
 Mustard Miso Sauce, 109
 Peach-Plum Sauce, 106
 Spicy Peanut Marinade, 152
 Sweet Orange Chili
  Sauce, 107
 Teriyaki Wasabi Sauce, 111
 Wasabi Mayonnaise
  Sauce, 108
 Wasabi Steak Sauce, 110
Spice Islands, 3, 74, 82, 84
Spices. *See also specific*
 buying, 3, 7, 9
 creating pastes, 13–14
 crushing, 11–12
 defined, 2
 dry rubs, 14
 and fruit pairings, 16
 grating, 13
 grinding, 12
 health benefits of, 4–6
 and herb pairings, 15
 history of, 3
 marinating, 14
 and nut pairings, 18
 and protein pairings, 19
 pulverizing, 12
 roasting, 13
 storing, 7–8
 toasting, 13
 and vegetable pairings, 17
 working with, 8–14
Spice Wars, 32
Star anise
 about, 86–87
 Chinese Five-Spice
  Blend, 94
 Chinese Sweet Bean
  Paste, 99
 Kalba Korean Marinade, 102
 Mulling Over Spice
  Blend, 145
 Peach-Plum Sauce, 106

Sweet Orange Chili
    Sauce, 107
Sumac
    about, 228–229
    Chive Blossom
        Mignonette, 247
    Dill, Mint, and Sumac
        Seafood Marinade, 241
    Limoncello-Fennel Poultry
        Marinade, 242
    Sumac Blackberry
        Agrodolce Marinade, 235
    Sumac Eggplant Paste, 234
Szechuan peppers
    about, 88–89
    Chinese Five-Spice
        Blend, 94

T

Tamari
    Asian Cold Noodle
        Dressing, 104
    Mustard Miso Sauce, 109
Tamarind
    about, 182–183
    Tamarind Yogurt
        Marinade, 204
Tarragon
    Backcountry Chimichurri
        Sauce, 158
    Herbes et Épices de
        Provence Blend, 232
    Peri Peri Dry Rub, 192
    Tarragon Sauce, 245
Thai chiles
    Chinese Sweet Bean
        Paste, 99
    Mustard Seeds Curry
        Sauce, 66
    South Pacific Honey
        Paste, 100
    Thai Red Curry Rub, 97
    Thai Satay Marinade, 103
    Yogurt Marinade, 62
Thai cuisine, 70
Thomas, Miranda "Wink," 245
Thyme
    Creole Spice Blend, 140
    Dukkah Egyptian
        Dry Rub, 190
    Feh El Omri Blend, 189

Herbes et Épices de
    Provence Blend, 232
Sumac Blackberry
    Agrodolce Marinade, 235
Throat Tea, 6
Toasting, 13
Tomatillos
    Smoky "Holey" Mole
        Sauce, 156–157
    Two-Shack "Como el
        Otro" Hot Sauce, 159
Tomatoes
    Dhana Jeera Vegetable
        Paste, 57
    Sicilian Saffron Pasta
        Sauce, 251
    Smoky "Holey" Mole
        Sauce, 156–157
    Sumac Eggplant Paste, 234
Trade, 3, 32, 164
Turmeric
    about, 42–43
    Cinnamon-Turmeric Rub, 53
    Curry Seafood Sauce, 67
    Dragon Fyre Cider, 4
    Garam Masala Yogurt
        Marinade, 61
    Indian Carrot Sauce, 65
    Kashmiri Masala Paste, 58
    La Kama Dry Rub, 191
    Malaysian Coconut
        Curry Paste, 98
    Mustard Seeds Curry
        Sauce, 66
    Poudre de Colombo
        Rum Paste, 147
    Ras el Hanout Blend, 186
    Sambaar Masala Blend, 51
    Tandoori Chicken Blend, 52
    Thai Satay Marinade, 103
    Vadouvan-Lassi Poultry
        Marinade, 63
    Vindaloo Curry Paste, 59
    Yogurt Marinade, 62

U

Umami, 10

V

Vanilla
    about, 136–137
    Kickin' Chicken
        Marinade, 153
    Mulling Over Spice
        Blend, 145
    Poppy Paste, 200
    Queen's Carnitas
        Marinade, 151
Vegetables. See also specific
    and spice parings, 17

W

Wasabi
    about, 90–91
    Teriyaki Wasabi Sauce, 111
    Wasabi Mayonnaise
        Sauce, 108
    Wasabi Steak Sauce, 110
White pepper
    about, 44–45
    Chile-Infused Pickling
        Spice Blend, 142
    Cinnamon-Turmeric Rub, 53
    Creole Spice Blend, 140
    Kashmiri Masala Paste, 58
    Madras Curry Rub, 55
    Quarte Épices Blend, 233
    Sicilian Saffron Pasta
        Sauce, 251

Y

Yellow peas (chana dal)
    Sambaar Masala Blend, 51
Yogurt. See also Greek
        yogurt; Lassi yogurt
    Chaimen Armenian
        Spice Paste, 197
    Curry Seafood Sauce, 67
    Tamarind Yogurt
        Marinade, 204
    Yogurt Marinade, 62

Z

Zingale, Angela, 56, 64

ACKNOWLEDGEMENTS

Thank you to my mom, Cristina, for taking me on your hip across the oceans before I could walk. In doing so, nurturing in me an insatiable curiosity about the world and the ability to be comfortable in uncomfortable situations.

Thank you to my pops, David, for teaching me the art of facilitation through hard work and self-mandated accountability—though I'm sure there are other methods besides splitting and stacking wood for three months straight.

Thank you to my brother, Simon, one of the true maniacs in a kitchen. And Corie, Samantha, and Amelia who have to put up with it!

Grazie, Nonna e Zia Elda, rimarrete sempre nel mio cuore e nei miei ricordi. I vostri mangiarini sono stati le mie prime experienze di gioia pura. Questo libro e' anche per Renzo.

Tom and Carla and the girls, thank you for opening up the world to a curious young man and showing him what it means to be an engaged, respectful world citizen.

Thank you Jon Mallard for bringing and meeting me halfway around the world, stealing boats and pulling me out of a ditch in Appalachia.

Thank you to Team Integrity. Spices don't matter when your steak is possessed by the devil.

Dutch Deckaj and Robyn, the many, many years of work and friendship have allowed me the opportunity to pursue grand adventures such as this.

Thank you especially to my New Orleans family, FC Tesla, and Finn McCool's Irish Pub. With y'all I'm always at home.

To the Dream Brothers, dream on.

To those who have contributed recipes or knowledge to this book, I am in your debt.

Beeta Mohajeri, your food is legendary and I'm honored to have it in print.

I am blessed to feature one of my favorites and mom to the cutest kid alive, Angela Zingale.

Thank you to the founder himself, Devin de Wulf, and the Red and Dead Beans Parade. Come join us every Lundi Gras in New Orleans.

Alfre Woodard, you are a master of your craft and a professional of the highest order. I shared some of your tricks, but some I kept for myself.

I cannot wait, Kazuyuki Ishikawa, to witness your journey as you open your new space.

Thank you to the most scholarly vagabond I know. Denver Nicks, ha ginger amigo.

Thank you to Aric S. Queen, from whom I learned that you shouldn't change a thing once you change everything.

Go visit Gustavo Turcios Rivera at Café Degas on Esplanade Ave in New Orleans. Just let him order for you. Thank you, my friend.

Charles, Miranda, Sophie, and Hugh Shackleton, your generosity knows no bounds. This book would not be complete without those quarantined days in the barn.

Thank you to Pia Pearce and Lady Janet Wilson for the generous contribution of their family recipes.

Thank you to modern-day adventurer Salmaan Mirza. Cheers to jumping blind into outlandish projects with complete strangers.

Jayne Kennedy, I love how you can be best friends with someone after speaking to them once. That happened with you and I am so glad.

Adrien Martin, my food accomplice and sister in spirit, thank you for seeing who I am and always encouraging that.

Paul Rahfield, thank you for allowing me to siphon your knowledge.

Tara Tomasiewicz, for evaluating my creations without judgment.

Thank you Nisrine Omri for your excitement about this project and your invaluable perspective regarding Tunisia.

Thank you Joe MacReynolds and Leroy Miranda for the use of your kitchen while testing recipes. And for the encouragement to always write more.

To my parrilla partner in crime, Scott August, may this book sit in your well-stocked kitchen with all your amazingly obscure salts and peppers.

Caroline O'Brien, thank you for sharing your amazing Dragon Fyre potion and for letting me hang around the farm, picking your figs.

Thank you to my editor Meg Ilasco for being patient, kind, and forthcoming during this process. Thank you to Amy Dickerson for having the intuition to include me in your endeavors.

Finally, thank you to Martha Foose, my culinary hero and one of the kindest people on this planet. Thank you for keeping my nose always pointed in the right direction and my culinary compass pointed due North (from New Orleans to Pluto).

ABOUT THE AUTHOR

Mark C. Stevens is an Italian American dual citizen who was born in Bangor, Maine and grew up in nearby Orono, and Chiavari, Italy. His Italian grandmother is responsible for his love of food, his mother for his love of flavor, and his aunt for his love of travel. When not pursuing culinary delights, Mark works in film and television. He is a Director's Guild of America 1st Assistant Director, and has worked on award-winning and critically acclaimed films and television shows. When he is not filming, you can find him traveling internationally, cooking for friends, or cruising around the South on Bianca, his Moto Guzzi v7 Classic motorcycle. Armed with insatiable curiosity, Mark plans his trips around restaurants, family dinners, and trading recipes with locals.

CPSIA information can be obtained
at www.ICGtesting.com
Printed in the USA
LVHW07s2135300818
587908LV00019B/12/P